BEHAVIOR
and SEQUENTIAL
ANALYSES

BEHAVIOR
and SEQUENTIAL ANALYSES

ANALYSES

For information:

 Sage Publications, Inc.
2455 Teller Road
Thousand Oaks, California 91320
E-mail: order@sagepub.com

Sage Publications Ltd.
6 Bonhill Street
London EC2A 4PU
United Kingdom

Sage Publications India Pvt. Ltd.
B-42, Panchsheel Enclave
Post Box 4109
New Delhi 110 017 India

Printed in the United States of America

Library of Congress Cataloging-in-Publication Data

Sharpe, Tom, 1956-
Behavior and sequential analyses : principles and practice / Tom Sharpe,
John Koperwas.
        p. cm.
Includes bibliographical references and index.
ISBN 0-7619-2560-0 (pbk.)
        1. Behavioral assessment. I. Koperwas, John. II. Title.
BF176.5 .S53 2003
300'.7' 2—dc21
                                        2002153690

03   04   05   06   10   9   8   7   6   5   4   3   2   1

Acquiring Editor:	Jim Brace-Thompson
Editorial Assistant:	Karen Ehrmann
Production Editor:	Sanford Robinson
Indexer:	Molly Hall
Cover Designer:	Janet Foulger

First and foremost I would like to thank my wonderful family, who have always supported my professional efforts in academe and who have always been the main source of joy in my life. I dedicate this text to them. I would also like to dedicate this text to my professional family of graduate students and faculty colleagues who have contributed over the years to my tinkering with and packaging of the methods contained in this text, particularly those who have either been so gracious as to have allowed examples and illustrations of their efforts to be contained in this book, or who have endured my interminable cajoling interactions over a variety of thesis, dissertation, and research projects.

—Tom Sharpe

I would like to dedicate my contribution to this text to my wife, Natalie, whose patience and continuous support offered me the opportunity to spend countless hours working on software development and design and some of the related information contained in this book.

—John Koperwas

Contents

Foreword by Tom Sharpe

Few truly original ideas come to pass in contemporary academe.
Most of what passes for invention is merely existing ideas repack-
aged in appealing ways. But it is the repackaging which often
moves science forward in important and insightful ways.

— Delprato (1999, personal communication)

Applied behavior analysis methods have provided a foundation for my professional efforts from the time I entered the education profession as a teacher and a coach. Before being introduced to the academic discipline in graduate school, I intuitively held the view that the most important variables to the improvement (or, in contrast, deterioration) of most educational situations were the daily practices that teachers and students, or coaches and athletes, were engaged in and how their verbal and nonverbal behaviors affected one another's actions. By chance, and based on my decision to return to graduate school at West Virginia University to supposedly enhance my professional marketability, I fell into what was considered one of the more prominent graduate programs in education and behavior analysis. I was directed to take most of my coursework in the psychology and educational psychology departments that included at that time a veritable hotbed of behavior analytic scholars. In agreement with the methodological proclivities of my physical education faculty mentor (Hawkins, 1992), I became completely at home with defining educational and social science phenomena behaviorally, with the construction of observational category systems for conducting data collection and analysis efforts, and with the methods of data presentation promoted by traditional behavioral methods. What began to plague me, however, were the challenges of describing and analyzing in comprehensive and inclusive ways what I saw as a highly complex and multi-event configuration of behavior interactions in educational settings. As I observed and analyzed many highly interactive settings, I found myself missing out on the documentation of potentially important behavioral events when using the traditionally accepted paper-and-pencil plus stopwatch recording methods coupled with partial interval or momentary time sampling recording techniques. In addition, I found the traditional method of observing only a few behaviors in isolation and using only a single measure of those behaviors extremely limiting to an accurate characterization of the educational settings I was interested in studying.

If I analyze my past experiences with the proper level of scrutiny and reflection, I can look back on a series of seemingly chaotic and randomly ordered professional activities and find a few events that can be seen as definitive in my movement toward what has become my present situation—that is, enthusiastically attempting to organize and package the data collection and analysis methods contained in this book. During the struggle and questioning stage of my dissertation activities, I was cajoled by a variety of faculty to go to the Association for Behavior Analysis (ABA) National Convention for the usual reasons of gaining some professional insight, interacting with other like-minded faculty and graduate students, and seeing what there was to see on the research and development horizon in my areas of supposed interest. At the conference, I happened into a meeting for the Interbehaviorists in ABA special interest group. Completely naïve as to the conceptual, epistemological, and methodological interests and related political stature of the group, I sat in on a discussion of the work of J. R. Kantor by Ed Morris, Paul Mountjoy, Roger Ray, Dennis Delprato, and a variety of other Kantorian scholars. I have gone over this initial experience in my mind as I have written this text, for while I did not realize it at the time, that discussion provided a rich encapsulation of just the challenges I was beginning to articulate and attempt to navigate as a neophyte methodologist, and what I heard that day sent me on the professional road I have been traveling ever since.

These gentlemen were conceptualizing an evolutionary pathway for behavior analysis to meet the description and analysis challenges of multiple organisms engaging in multiple behaviors in the context of multiple ecological event changes. Although most of the terminology and much of the methodological points made at that time simply washed over me, the idea of adding to the primarily linear Stimulus→Response→Consequence (S→R→C) model of B. F. Skinner to look at applied situations as a more complex system of events that oftentimes occur concurrently and affect one another in various degree turned a lightbulb on inside me. While gentlemen such as Ed Morris and Paul Mountjoy waxed long about the philosophical issues inherent to a more systems- and temporally oriented approach to studying behavior in complex and highly interactive settings, what intrigued me most were the contributions to the discussion by Roger Ray. Ray provided a technologically supported methodological position for inclusively describing and documenting behavior occurrences in all their complexity, including both more traditional measures of the characteristics of individual behavioral events (e.g., number, duration, rate, percentage, etc.) and time-based measures designed to explicitly characterize the interactions among those events (e.g., use of multilevel structural and functional categories, kinematic analyses, conditional probability relationships among multi-event occurrences, etc.).

To this day, I come back to the enthusiasm Roger displayed for his work and the explanation and direction Roger provided me with at the end of that meeting. He explained just what he was working toward methodologically. He provided me with a host of materials to read designed to enhance my understanding. Through intermittent interactions, he has helped me to understand complex interactive behavior "in its complexity," as my original mentor articulated (Hawkins, 1992, p. 1) and to express that understanding in my work. And from then to now I have been involved in just that, articulating ways in which behavioral data may be more inclusively and completely documented, described, and analyzed in applied settings in which multiple individuals exhibit multiple behaviors concurrently and in which the interactions among these behaviors have multiple potential functional relationships. What has equally stimulated my activities in this area over the years, and added in substantial ways to the stimulation of the culminating efforts that this book represents, has been my ongoing relationship with John Koperwas. John may be considered one of those few genuinely inquisitive and inventive minds in the contemporary field of software development who has provided a wealth of insight into what is methodologically possible through ever-advancing software programming capabilities. It is in this latter regard that his contributions to this text, and to the software applications referenced in the back of this text that are designed to support thoroughgoing implementation of the methodologies we recommend, have been invaluable.

We have tried to remain true to the important foundations that those coming before us have provided in terms of a rigorous and thoroughgoing scientific method for the study of behavior in applied settings. Some of the most important influences on these text materials are those of Alan Kazdin (Kazdin, 1982), for his clear and concise representation of introductory behavior analytic and single case principles, and John Gottman (Bakeman & Gottman, 1986), who stipulated in a text referred to me by Roger Ray, and whose stipulation I find even more true today in the mainstream of education and social sciences, that

> A small percentage of current research employs observational measurement of any sort. This is true despite the recent increased availability of new technologies such as electronic notepads and videotape recording. It may always be the case because it is more costly to observe than to use other methods such as questionnaires. (p. xiv).

What continues to surprise me is the limited impact of and support for behavior analysis activity in the education, social, and psychological sciences. In addition, many important methodology texts are not updated nor do they go into a new edition; nor do experienced behavior analysts tend to provide either new text materials or packaged data collection and analysis tools for the research and evaluation community that continues to be involved in this type of work.

In relation to the opening quotation by Dennis Delprato, this book is our effort to compile and package in large part the work of others who have either come before us professionally, or who have made important individual methodological contributions to the applied analysis of behavior as an important research methodology. Although not all information related to behavior analysis is included here, and the finer points of some of the information contained in this text may be debated, this text does include all the information that we feel is important to students and faculty with an interest in behavior analysis methods. This text is also an outgrowth of discussions with many colleagues who have wished for such a text as they put together a series of isolated papers and reprints year after year when teaching courses in applied behavior analysis methods. Finally, this is a text designed to be compatible with the software tools described in the back of this book, which have been designed to collect, analyze, and visually represent data and to perform the many reliability, procedural fidelity, and other methodological functions that this book recommends.

OVERVIEW

To accomplish the purposes of this text, four general sections are provided. The first, Behavior Analysis: A History and Introduction, provides an important summary of the historical evolution of applied behavior analysis and related single-subject research methods in the context of how the method may be compatible with others and helpful to the knowledge generation process in the education, social, and psychological sciences. The methods under the applied behavior analysis umbrella are summarized and a compatibility approach is postulated with respect to the many different methodological perspectives that currently exist in the mainstream scientific literature.

Part II of this text, Constructing Observational Systems, provides a detailed procedural primer for constructing a coding or category system for particular research or assessment purposes, including the many assumptions and limitations that should be taken into consideration when conducting behavior analysis research. Reliability and treatment fidelity issues and procedures are discussed in detail, with close attention paid to the steps of criterion standard development, staff training, interobserver reliability, and treatment implementation accuracy. A series of category system illustrations are also provided and taken from a variety of education, social science, and psychology disciplines to provide the reader with hands-on familiarity with how behavior analysis efforts in these respective areas have been implemented with success.

Part III of this text, Recording Tactics, Design Types, and Data Analyses, presents a variety of generally accepted techniques in the areas of collecting, analyzing, and visually representing data. Application procedure detail and potential advantages are provided regarding recording in real time, overcoming validity challenges through more sophisticated research design types, and issues related to graph preparation and the use of statistical analysis support for behavior data.

The last part of this text, Application Illustrations and a Window to the Future, provides recommendations as to how applied behavior analysis methods may be used to enhance a variety of research and development, professional or clinical assessment, and instructional applications across a variety of education, social science, and psychological activities. Included are detailed illustrations of field-based professional evaluation activities, research and development opportunities designed to uncover information not previously available to other research methodologies, and laboratory simulation activities heretofore unavailable through other methods and without the aid of computer technology-supported behavior analysis.

EXERCISES AND PRESENTATION STRUCTURE

In order to achieve the objective of helping students and faculty understand and apply the principles set forth in this text, we have ordered the materials in the 10 chapters according to the logical steps one would undertake in actually conducting a research project. Each chapter includes a set of terms and definitions and a study guide to help the readers summarize and apply their understanding of the main points. These materials lead readers through the step-by-step procedures for designing and implementing behavioral research projects. For those readers interested in greater detail on a topic contained in a particular chapter, references are cited in the chapters and a list of references is provided at the end of the text. We also encourage readers who are already quite familiar with behavior analytic research practice and sophisticated behavior analysts to consult the reference materials provided for a more detailed treatment of the material herein. In addition, as this book was designed to be used as an introductory to intermediate text on behavior analysis research principles, readers will find information in select publications that provides important theoretical and applied complements to the materials here.

CORE FEATURE

A core feature of this text is the importance of a return to the quantitative counting of behavior and event occurrences in a single-subject orientation as an accepted methodological practice. The creation of this text stems from our personal methodological interest and the current lack of a readily accessible text to articulate many points of information at an introductory to intermediate level. In addition, this book is intended as a response to mainstream researchers in the education, social, and psychological sciences who are outspoken in their recommendations to simply do away with behavior analysis as a legitimate method of inquiry due to its emphasis on mechanistic causal assumptions or its inability to more completely and accurately describe and analyze multiple occurrences of interactive behavior in inclusive and meaningful ways. In our view, these researchers have incorrectly perceived behavior analysis, its nature, and what it can and cannot do, to the point of requiring response. This text is also a response to cognitive methodologists who espouse internal explanatory mechanisms to account for behavioral complexity and contextual dependency and who eschew other methodological procedures outside of mainstream cognitive research as somehow inferior. Finally, it is a response to those scientists who have abandoned traditional views of scientific practice for a more existential approach in which investigation revolves around responses to questionnaires that investigate the subjective meanings ascribed to certain events as described by the participants operating within those events.

Through the many professional influences of my early faculty mentors when I was in graduate school, and of the experienced and savvy faculty colleagues I have met in behavior research circles along my professional travels, as well as my own work, I have, with my coauthor, created this text. Through this text, I hope we have packaged in appealing ways a means for doing what Hawkins (1992) has described as not "abandoning behavior analysis but [succeeding in] taking it to another level" (p. 1). Therefore, this text provides what we hope is a compatible summary of traditional and contemporary applied behavior analysis methods that does justice to the principles and practice of applied behavior analysis and serves as an effective introduction to the many systems and sequential methodologies that have begun to frequent the contemporary behavior analysis literature.

Part I

Behavior Analysis: A History and Introduction

1

History and Evolution

All things prepare the event. Watch.

— Eliot (1971, p. 183)

After reading this chapter, you should be able to define the following terms and provide the information requested in the study guide below.

TERMS

Human behavior
Science
Determinism
Conditioned response
Unconditioned response
Respondent conditioning

Operant conditioning
Behavior modification
Applied behavior analysis
Explanation (cause versus probability)

STUDY GUIDE

1. Provide a historical summary of the scientific activity that led to what we now know as the applied analysis of behavior.
2. Summarize the philosophical perspectives that provide foundations for scientific activity.
3. List and describe some of the main features of qualitative and quantitative research methods.
4. List some of the arguments for multiple research method compatibility.

5. Describe some of the myths about behavior analysis that have been popularized.
6. List and describe some of the reasons for the nonuse of behavior analysis data by applied professionals.
7. Explain what is meant by the fallacy of affirming the consequent when using large-group, statistically based research comparisons.

The experimental, and in particular the applied, analysis of behavior has a long and productive history. This is the case even though the method has suffered criticisms and related nonuse by many mainstream professionals in the education, psychological, and social sciences. Many experimental methods now appear in the applied literature, ranging from large group comparisons using a variety of statistical analyses to qualitative methods that focus on the use of existential explanations and subjective analyses. The main purpose of this text is to present a variety of behavior analysis and direct observational methods in the hope of arming faculty and students with important contributors to research activity. To give the reader a better understanding of behavior analysis as a research methodology, this chapter provides a brief history of behavior analysis as a research method, argues for its compatibility with other research methodologies, and debunks some prevalent myths that are detrimental to behavior analysis use.

In the education, social, and psychological sciences, behavior analysis has proved an important methodological contribution when research focus is on one or only a few study participants, and when generality is sought through careful and systematic replication of treatment implementation over time. The method has appeal over traditional large-group designs when another method to control for internal and external validity concerns is warranted. In relation to qualitative research methods in which a small group of individuals or a single setting is studied, behavior analysis methods have a thoroughgoing quantitative component to measure and evaluate treatment effects, and they include a rigorous set of data inspection procedures that are elegant in their simplicity and consistent in their application. Behavior analysis designs are also methodologically compatible with other research perspectives, lending themselves to enhancing the types of information gathered in a particular study. In many respects, then, behavior analysis designs provide an important complement to other methods for conducting research and evaluation.

A BRIEF HISTORY OF BEHAVIOR ANALYSIS

Behavior analysis research designs have long been used in a wide variety of applied education, social science, and psychological disciplines and have produced a substantial scientific literature in many areas. The method was not formally recognized by name until the appearance of work by B. F. Skinner (1938, 1953, 1956) and the related creation of the Association for Behavior Analysis (ABA), and it has been characterized by terms such as *single-subject research, single-case methods, intrasubject replication designs,* and others (Kazdin, 1982). The method in various forms has been used in the applied sciences for over a century. Before we proceed to a more cookbook approach to implementing a behavior analytic study, we discuss where this methodology came from and what it is based on. In providing this sort of information, we hope that readers will develop a greater understanding of the scientific enterprise in general and be receptive to the use of behavior analysis when appropriate to their research questions of interest. Many contemporary mainstream scholars argue that behavior analysis is a radical departure from other research methods, but we hope to demonstrate that it is far more similar to other methods than it is different from them.

The brief history provided here is based largely on two sources (Kazdin, 1982, Chapter 1; Michael, 1991) that have encapsulated in summary form a chronology of the scientific methods contributions on which behavior analysis is founded. We have reorganized the information from these sources, placed our unique emphasis on various parts, and added historical and contemporary innovations by some often neglected contributors who should be included within a chronology.

The period from the late 19th century to the turn of the 20th century saw the beginning of single-subject and small-group research, and of what we now call the *applied analysis of behavior.* The work of Charles Darwin, specifically his foundational text *Origin of Species* (1859), is considered the first important origin of the methodology. Darwin's influence established the idea of the continuity of species. In other words, through a theory of human evolution by natural selection Darwin demonstrated that the study of nonhuman and human behavior is relevant to a greater understanding of a variety of cognitive, perceptual, and evolutionary processes. The following quotation from Skinner (1984, cited in Michael, 1991) provides a summary of what Darwin posited:

> Human behavior is the joint product of (i) contingencies of survival responsible for natural selection, and (ii) contingencies of reinforcement responsibilities for the repertoires of individuals, including (iii) the special contingencies maintained by an evolved social environment. Selection by consequences is a causal mode found only in living things, or in machines made by living things. It was first recognized in natural selection: Reproduction, a first consequence, led to the evolution of cells, organs, and organisms reproducing themselves under increasingly diverse conditions. The behavior functioned well, however, only under conditions similar to those under which it was selected.
>
> Reproduction under a wider range of consequences became possible with the evolution of processes through which organisms acquired behavior appropriate to novel environments. One of these, operant conditioning, is the second kind of selection by consequences: New responses could be strengthened by events which followed them. When the selecting consequences are the same, operant conditioning and natural selection work together redundantly. But because a species which quickly acquires behavior appropriate to an environment has less need for an innate repertoire, operant conditioning could replace as well as supplement the natural selection of behavior.
>
> Social behavior is within easy range of natural selection, because other members are one of the most stable features of the environment of a species. The human species presumably became more social when its vocal musculature came under operant control. Verbal behavior greatly increased the importance of a third kind of selection by consequences, the evolution of social environments or cultures. The effect on the group, and not the reinforcing consequences for individual members, is responsible for the evolution of culture. (p. 477)

Essentially, Darwin subscribed to *logical positivism*, which is closely related to *scientific empiricism*. This school of thought limits propositions either to those that are empirically verifiable through systematic experimentation or to those that are analyses of definitions and relations among terms. Empirically verifiable propositions became the concern of the scientific method, and analysis of definitions and relations between terms the specific task of philosophy. In addition, and promoted by 19th-century philosophers such as Auguste Comte, conceptual and theoretical focus is on the objective examination of all phenomena, a clear antimetaphysical and anticognitive approach to the explanation of events, and the belief in universal and primarily static laws that govern all events (Titus, Smith, & Nolan, 1986).

The foundations for a formal empiricism, or mechanical and experimental science, were also laid through Darwin's contributions. Within this foundation, the following defining elements were added over the course of the early 20th century by a variety of contributors. The following definitions are from Malott and Whaley (1983):

> *Science.* The systematic study of how events or occurrences are related to the production of other events or occurrences (p. 4)
>
> *Determinism.* The notion that an event is produced or results from the active presence of a precise set of conditions (p. 4)
>
> *Analysis.* The task of finding out and describing the precise set of conditions that give rise to specific events (p. 4)
>
> *Application.* The bringing together of the needed conditions in order to produce certain desired events or outcomes (p. 4)
>
> *Unconditioned response.* Response evoked by a stimulus even without prior experience (p. 109)
>
> *Conditioned response.* Response evoked by a stimulus only after pairing that stimulus with one that already causes the response (p. 109)
>
> *Respondent conditioning.* The procedure of pairing two stimuli with the result that one stimulus (conditioned stimulus) acquires the power to cause the response already caused by the other stimulus (unconditioned stimulus) (p. 109)
>
> *Operant conditioning.* A change in the likelihood of a response due to the results of that response (p. 93)
>
> *Learning.* A change in behavior that occurs as a result of experience (p. 93)

Behavior modification. The application of principles of behavioral psychology, and operant psychology in particular, to change actions in a desired manner or direction (pp. 629-630)

Some of the important historical contributors to behavior analysis methods are highlighted in Figure 1.1. Although historical accounts are presented with variable emphasis and inclusion, we hope our account is useful (with potential instructor modifications).

A variety of scholars prominent in the psychological sciences at the turn of the 20th century were engaged primarily in research involving single subjects or small groups and provided important illustrations of the concepts included in the list of definitions above. Wilhelm Wundt, for example, engaged primarily in the study of sensory perception by reporting in qualitative and thoughtful ways the reactions of individual subjects to specific stimulus conditions presented to them. Hermann Ebbinghaus, a contemporary of Wundt, studied memory through analyses of individuals' learning and recall of nonsense syllables by altering stimulus conditions with individual subjects. Sigmund Freud, often considered the father of clinical psychotherapy by the popular culture, promoted early versions of in-depth study of individual cases designed to better understand and conceptualize basic psychological processes, developmental stages, functional relations among symptoms and historical characteristics of the patient, and a variety of cognitive processes he considered to be related to personality and behavior. A primary disadvantage of this type of early scientific activity, however, lay in its lack of experimental control, including unclear descriptions of independent variables or treatments given to subjects, oftentimes vague and poorly defined behavior or cognitive measurement systems, and limited documentation of particular subject characteristics. These types of problems often led to the limited or inappropriate generalization of findings to other subjects and population groups.

An important early behavioral contribution was that of Ivan Sechenov in his text *Reflexes of the Brain.* During a time period when most medical and physiological literature focused on the mental aspects of human thought and consciousness, Sechenov proposed that all aspects of cognition in humans were based on behavioral reflexes. He worked out a carefully designed explanation of complex human behavior through derivations of simple reflexes, their consequences, and their potential combinations that was very similar to more contemporary definitions of respondent conditioning. Through the theoretical model that Sechenov provided, a foundation was offered for a completely behavioral approach to the explanation of phenomena. This foundation

Figure 1.1   History of the Current Field of Behavior Analysis

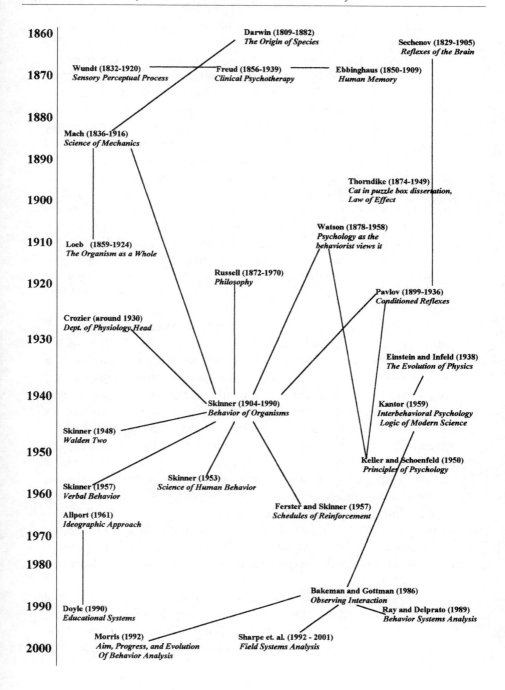

was heavily relied on by the scientists who followed Sechenov, most notably Pavlov and a group of Russian physiologists.

Ernst Mach, a contemporary of Sechenov, provided through his work, *The Science of Mechanics*, a foundation for what we speak of today as a lineal mechanic approach to empirical research and the scientific enterprise. Mach first proposed that the nature and origins of scientific inquiry should be a natural outgrowth of the important practical concerns of daily life and that behavior is one important part of epistemological (i.e., how we know what we know) development. He essentially defined *science* as primarily behavioral, in that it is the objective and systematic pursuit of helping humans become more effective and productive. Mach next defined *cause* as a functional relationship among independent variables (treatments) and dependent variables (measures), and he saw scientific explanation as nothing more than the description of documented functional relationships. Last, Mach proposed that the only effective epistemology must be empirical, with the careful manipulation of events in controlled settings undertaken to discover more of the relationships among those events. In this last regard, Mach perceived the term *events* to be synonymous with the term *behaviors*.

With the advent of a well-defined empirical science, or research method, a flurry of early 20th century experimentation in the psychological sciences took place to further the analysis of behavior as a research method. Edward Thorndike, for example, in his single-subject work with animal intelligence, demonstrated through his famous cats in puzzle boxes experiments that animals could escape from complex mazes in shorter and shorter periods of time, documenting what we now term *trial-and-error* learning. Thorndike's puzzle box experiments were meant to demonstrate that the complex behavior of higher organisms previously thought of as largely a consciousness or mental process could be explained in terms of the inevitable result of a simple principle like the law of effect. Thorndike's work also provided a foundation for what the behavior analysis literature views as operant conditioning. *Operant conditioning* refers to the principle that future responses are changed and conditioned by the form and character of a past response.

A contemporary of Thorndike, Ivan Pavlov, through his animal research, discovered most of the facts and principles of what we know today about respondent functional relations. His empirical investigations provided the first illustrations of convincing experimental analyses of behavior. Two main features of Pavlov's work were careful specification of independent variables (which allowed technological replication of his experiments) and attention to operational detail with measurement systems. In addition, he contributed these important scientific terms to behavior analysis: *conditioning, extinction, discrimination, generalization, unconditioned stimuli,* and *conditioned stimuli.* Pavlov documented that an unconditioned reflex could not function as the basis for more complex behavior because there would be no new functional relations and therefore no learning. Through his famous classical conditioning experiments, in which the unconditioned response of dogs salivating in the presence of food was linked with the conditioned stimulus of a bell until the dogs salivated at the sound of the bell even in the absence of food, he proved that new functional relationships between stimuli and responses could be developed and eliminated in the laboratory and therefore potentially in applied settings with humans. His contribution was, therefore, a pivotal step toward the completely mechanistic accounting for behavior that Mach proposed.

In 1913, John Watson, in his *Psychological Review* article "Psychology as the Behaviorist Views It," provided what could arguably be the most effective scientific call for a focused behavioral position in the psychological and social sciences. Watson took an extremist position that consciousness and mental processes do not have any explanatory value with regard to how humans and animals behave and interact. This position provided the conceptual foundation for a behaviorist movement in the experimental and applied sciences. Based also in large part on the logical positivism of Auguste Comte and the behaviorist views of Bertrand Russell, a formal behaviorist movement in the empirical sciences began. Out of this movement, Loeb and Crozier provided important empirical work that laid the foundation for Skinner's *The Behavior of Organisms* (1938). It is in this text that a detailed and referenced account of the brief historical summary provided above, and select referenced examples of the individuals highlighted, may be accessed for those interested in a more detailed account than that given here. Skinner's pioneering work resulted in the establishment of the Association for Behavior Analysis that thrives internationally to this day.

The contributions of Jacques Loeb are important to explain in relation to his study of the behavior of the entire organism using invertebrate animals. Loeb attempted to explain all behavior occurrences in strictly mechanistic terms. Although this attempt was not completely successful, Loeb contributed much to a more thorough documentation of organismic function without the use of any inferences to mental functions. W. J. Crozier followed a similar quest to avoid all inferences to the mental cause of behavior, and through his work he provided the initial impetus for developing mathematical functional relations between environmental variables and behaviors of organisms. Crozier, who was a faculty mentor of Skinner's when Skinner entered graduate school at Harvard, was the primary influence on Skinner's proposed three-term contingency of Stimulus→Response→Consequence (S→R→C→), and, indirectly, the initial influence on Kantor's conceptualization of the importance of transactional relationships among behavioral events and environmental stimuli. It is primarily to Skinner, and to some extent to Kantor, that the current methodological state of behavior analysis can be attributed. Although Skinner and Kantor diverged in their emphasis of some methodological points, they both provided a fairly complete conceptual language and laid out a rigorously defined set of procedures for conducting behavioral research. In Skinner's pioneering text, *The Behavior of Organisms* (1938), he laid out almost all of the basic concepts that we rely on today, including respondent and operant procedures, rate of response as a main operant dependent variable, the cumulative record as a way of studying rate of response, many methods and results of operant conditioning and operant extinction, complete definitions of conditioned and unconditioned reinforcement, a theory of operant stimulus control as separate from conditioned elicitors of respondent functional relations, stimulus generalization theory, the idea of schedules of reinforcement, the role of motivative and emotional variables that can be defined behaviorally, and the idea that mental processes and private events operate according to the same general scientific laws that govern overt behavior. Later texts in the education and psychological sciences have provided detailed accounting of these principles in relation to applied behavior analysis as a research method and can be relied on for reference (e.g., Cooper, Heron, & Heward, 1987; Sulzer-Azaroff & Mayer, 1991).

Alone, and in collaboration with a number of colleagues—Keller, Ferster and others, to name a few—Skinner (1953, 1956, 1968, 1983, 1984, 1989) also provided a variety of methodological works related to the study of verbal behavior, schedules of reinforcement, pedagogical practices, and the science of behavior in relation to cultural change. His most notable cultural work was a utopian novel written in 1948,

Walden Two. This work was written largely in response to the more metaphysical writings of Henry David Thoreau (1962), in which explanation of the human condition was primarily couched in metaphysical and cognitive terms.

As counterpoint to Skinner's work, J. R. Kantor (1953, 1959, 1969) provided a detailed theoretical model of behavior that (a) minimized the causal emphasis of the lineal mechanics of Mach and (b) endeavored to broaden the view of behavioral interactions to a systems view founded largely on Einstein and Infeld's pioneering contributions to physics in their text *The Evolution of Physics* (1938). Kantor provided a descriptive-analytic alternative to the more narrowly focused causal determinism of Skinner. Kantor's major contribution was the recommendation to measure behavior occurrences according to the time-based sequence in which they occurred in addition to the characteristics of each behavior occurrence itself. This emphasis on the analysis of time-based sequence is most often referred to as the *probability* of a certain behavior or event following after a primary event of interest. In other words, Kantor was primarily interested in which behaviors tended to follow or precede others in time, and not simply how often or how long a particular behavior occurred. He termed his views *interbehaviorism* to communicate that a behavior must always be defined with regard to the larger time-based field of events in which it has occurred. Kantor attempted to direct methodological thinking away from lineal mechanism and the search for ultimate causes, but he was criticized for proffering a philosophy without a method for collecting and analyzing behavioral data in the ways he recommended.

With significant advances in computer technology, many contemporary behavioral methodologists have returned to a Kantorian view to provide a foundation for the development of tools capable of collecting and analyzing the types of time-based measures that Kantor originally recommended. Bakeman and Gottman (1986), for example, provide a detailed illustration of what they term *sequential behavior analysis* methods and provide a reasonably complete accounting of empirical studies using these methods in a range of social science areas, including family therapy, marital interactions, work with disabled children and youth, and educational concerns. Ray (Ray & Delprato, 1989), a contemporary of Bakeman and Gottman, provides a detailed methodological illustration of what he terms *behavioral systems analysis* in an effort to provide a thoroughgoing methodology to Kantor's theoretical position. Sharpe and colleagues (Hawkins & Sharpe, 1992; Sharpe, 1997a; Sharpe, 2001; Sharpe, Hawkins, & Lounsbery, 1998; Sharpe & Koperwas, 2000) provide illustrations of efforts by methodologists in education to develop a thoroughgoing systems-oriented behavioral methodology and design the computer hardware and software tools to adequately support that methodology. Evidence of methodological movement toward a systemic view of the applied analysis of behavior also includes a presidential address given to the Association for Behavior Analysis by Ed Morris and printed in *The Behavior Analyst* in 1992.

In the past few decades, behavior analysis methods have frequently been used in the social and educational sciences, though they have not always been labeled as behavioral. For example, Allport (1961) pioneered what many current qualitative and ethnographic researchers currently term an *idiographic* approach (i.e., the study of the single case) as an important means of discovering information not readily available through the use of more traditional between-group designs. Doyle (1990), in recommending a direction for educational research, argued for increased effort and focus on the quantitative determinants of education practices in specific situations to more accurately discriminate the multiple event relationships among educational participants. He also recommended a behavioral approach to defining particular educational practices in order to increase the accuracy (i.e., treatment fidelity) with which these practices are implemented by others.

Currently, a variety of journals are devoted to the publication of behavior analytic studies across a variety of disciplines. The *Journal of the Experimental Analysis of Behavior*, for example, was started in 1958 to fill the need for a journal outlet for publishing laboratory-based behavior analysis activities and because of the lack of receptivity for this type of work by more visible outlets such as the *Journal of Experimental Psychology* and the *Journal of Comparative and Physiological Psychology*. The *Journal of Applied Behavior Analysis* was founded in 1968 to serve behavior analysis research in applied settings. Other journals were developed in the past decade, such as *Behavior Modification* and *Behavioral Assessment*, to provide additional reporting outlets for behavior analysis research. In addition, journals such as *Behaviour Research and Therapy* were founded in Great Britain as behavior therapy periodicals, providing articles related to respondent-based work and some operant-derived work as well. Though not originally developed for articles devoted to behavior analysis methods, journals such as *Behavioral Science*, initiated by James Greer Miller, are now receptive to publishing behavior analysis studies and articles devoted to forwarding innovative behaviorally based methodological innovations.

In the past few decades, other discipline-specific journals either have been founded for the purpose of publishing behavior analysis research or have become receptive to behavior analysis as a legitimate methodology in the context of publishing empirical efforts. Some examples include the *Journal of Behavioral Education, Education and Treatment of Children, School Psychology Quarterly, Child Development*, and *Teacher Education and Special Education*. In addition, the Association for Behavior Analysis (ABA) was formed in 1974 to serve an interdisciplinary audience of researchers, university faculty, and a variety of professional practitioners with an interest in the experimental and applied analysis of behavior and in behavioral treatment applications. The association has steadily grown to include hosting international conferences throughout the world, financial backing to provide scholarships and grants for those performing important behavior analysis activities, and a formalized certification process for graduate-level applied behavior analysts. The ABA is *the* resource for all conference information and related professional opportunities.[1]

Thus there has been progressive interest in and a plethora of activity involving applied behavior analysis. At this point, it seems important for us to offer the following clear, concise definition of *applied behavior analysis* (Cooper et al., 1987):

Applied behavior analysis is the science in which procedures derived from the principles of behavior are systematically applied to improve socially significant behavior to a meaningful degree and to demonstrate experimentally that the procedures employed were responsible for the improvement in behavior. (p. 14)

The remainder of this chapter presents a case for direct behavioral observation methods, summarizes a compatibility theory with respect to other research methods, and debunks some of the myths surrounding behavior analysis in the contemporary research methods literature.

SCIENCE AS A DIRECT OBSERVATION, DESCRIPTIVE ENTERPRISE

Very broadly defined, the term *science* is synonymous with the quest for knowledge (Sharpe & Hawkins, 1992a, 1992b). Again, according to Mach the term *science* implies the direct observation of things so as to produce data with a high degree of intersubjective agreement, or objectivity (Neale & Liebert, 1973). If we are to subscribe to the importance of objectivity as a necessary characteristic of science, then "doing science" includes in its definition concepts such as operational measurability, reliability and replicability of description and explanation, and systematic testability of a variety of treatments. Simply put, research in the psychological, social, and education sciences should be based on directly observable empirical evidence and reasoned argument rather than on the opinion and perspective of experimental participants (Mayer, 2000). Mayer (2001) offers two important rationales for this view of science as follows:

1. Science is self-correcting, so that unproductive theories eventually can be discarded on the basis of mounting evidence and reasoned argument. The alternative view that all forms of discourse—including art—are equally valid leads our field to [unbridled] relativism.

2. Rejecting science [in the traditional sense of the definition] will not garner much respect from the [larger] scientific community. Given the generally low credibility of [educational and social science] fields (Levin & O'Donnell, 2000), turning applied research into a non-scientific enterprise is unlikely to improve the situation. (p. 29)

It is in the context of such rationales that a brief epistemological overview of some important philosophical traditions is presented here to give the reader a better understanding of the importance of a direct observational approach to doing science.

How knowledge is defined and generated, and how researchers construe explanation, varies across research methods. In our judgment, researchers can benefit by a discussion of (a) the philosophical foundations from which various research methods originate, and (b) the main competing research methods approaches, including some of their main advantages and shortcomings. Table 1.1 is provided as an overview of

Table 1.1   Philosophical Traditions

Essentialism (Galileo, Newton)

1. is the strongest proponent of causal inference, of which there are three necessary conditions:
   (a) contiguity between presumed cause and effect
   (b) temporal precedence of the cause specific to the effect
   (c) constant conjunction (i.e., causal presence whenever the effect is obtained)

2. posits that causal inference assumes dependency between presumed cause and effect; a mechanistic, push-pull philosophy

3. proposes that cause does not have to precede an effect, but that the two variables must be related

4. asserts that causal inference and explanation are synonymous

5. has experimental variables explain a phenomenon in terms of their necessary and sufficient presence for the event to occur

6. assumes powerful prediction and successful forecasting

7. is highly aligned with an activity theory of causation in that it posits that causes are what we can manipulate

8. is a proponent of closed-system research, from which all known extraneous forces are excluded

Rationalism (Bunge, Descartes)

1. clearly identifies causal relationships

2. proposes that causal relationships exist outside the human mind and cannot be perceived with total accuracy by our imperfect sensory and intellectual capacities

3. asserts the existence of a special survival value to knowing about manipulable causes

Empiricism (Locke, Hume)

1. divorces the notion of causality from explanation, without abandoning the notion of cause

2. posits that all knowledge stems from experience or sensory perception, as opposed to rationalism, which proposes that knowledge may stem from sources outside of human perception

(Continued)

Table 1.1 Continued

3. asserts that knowledge is limited to what can be experienced and that what we experience is accurately and universally perceived, which places primary emphasis on our power of observation

Probabilism (Suppes, Toulmin)

1. proposes that the real cause of effects is not certain

2. posits that presumed causes have relative probability and de-emphasizes causal inference

3. asserts that presumed causes are fallible rather than inevitable

4. proposes that empirical observations can be explained in terms of an infinite number of hypotheses

Pragmatism (Dewey, James, Peirce)

1. posits that explanation that is useful in a practical sense is the only viable scientific pursuit

2. seeks to mediate between opposing philosophical perspectives

3. deplores the search for ultimate cause or absolutes

4. asserts that nature is the reality beyond which we cannot go

5. settles for a pluralistic multiple-perspective approach

6. is aligned with relativism

Positivism (Comte, Russell)

1. de-emphasizes the notion of cause in its entirety

2. posits that knowledge of cause is unnecessary because it is not implied by functional mathematical relationships

3. takes a descriptive, noncausal approach to explanation

4. asserts that correlation does not imply causation

5. emphasizes probabilism and pragmatism

Falsificationism (Popper)

1. is diametrically opposed to the descriptive "confirmationist" position of positivism

2. stresses the ambiguity of confirmation, in that corroboration gives only the comfort that the presumed cause has been tested, has survived the test, and is thus not yet disconfirmed

3. implies a skeptical probabilistic nature

4. proposes the inescapable predicament that we cannot ultimately prove a causal proposition

6. establishes cause via elimination of rival-case possibilities

Idealism Versus Realism: A Philosophical Subcategory

1. *Idealism* (Plato, Berkeley, Kant, Hocking)
   (a) couches causal inference in terms of the laws of thought, consciousness, and "hidden" meaning rather than by methods of objective science
   (b) asserts that reality consists of ideas, thoughts, minds, or selves rather than material objects and forces
   (c) posits that all we are aware of is perceptions; therefore, perceptions become reality, which is closely related to metaphysics
   (d) is aligned with phenomenalism, which involves a search for meaning behind the observable and the distinction between the appearance of reality in consciousness and reality itself
   (e) is aligned with existentialism, which involves humans' attempt to describe their existence in terms of inner conflict and its origin (e.g., Kierkegaard, Nietzsche, Sartre).
   (f) asserts that relativist and pragmatist camps are threatening to traditional science, for if the truth is relative to individual perceptions, there is no consensus

2. *Realism* (Aristotle, Macmurray, Whitehead)
   (a) posits that the state of being is existent, as opposed to that which is metaphysical or in our thoughts
   (b) asserts that the objects of our senses are real in their own right and exist independently of their being known to, perceived by, or related to mind
   (c) is most highly aligned with essentialism and causal inference due to its proposing the unchanging nature of the physical realm and the existence of universals apart from our sensory experience

SOURCE: Sharpe and Hawkins (1992a), based on Bakker and Clark (1988), Cook and Campbell (1979), and Titus, Smith, and Nolan (1986).

philosophical and epistemological traditions to guide discussion. Although there may be disagreement among scholars regarding some of the finer points in the table, Table 1.1 provides a good general introductory summary to the philosophical traditions.

It is important for researchers considering a particular research method to understand that method in the contexts of both other methods and the philosophies that guide the method (compared to the philosophies that guide other methods). Integrally related to philosophical understanding is epistemological familiarity. In other words, when a researcher chooses a method of data collection and analysis, what is really chosen is the explanatory adequacy of a particular set of procedures. "Doing science," then, refers to the investigation of events by purposeful and strategic observation. A philosophy of science concerns the study of science itself, or the question of the relative utility and legitimacy of a particular research method. We therefore have a continuum of philosophy, epistemology, scientific activity, and ultimately the application of scientific results in professional and cultural settings. For the purpose of this discussion, we will look at the elements on the continuum in reverse order. At one end of the continuum is a technology of application, which does not test scientific propositions but assumes them in order to design practical applications to benefit certain individuals or groups. Adjacent to technology on the continuum is science, which builds knowledge and information structures based on the systematic observation and analysis of data. Philosophy and epistemology are last on the continuum and concern themselves with the legitimacy of the scientific method and the logic of that method's scientific practice and scientific explanations.

We argue within a behavior analysis framework that direct observation, description, and the resultant explanation are all necessary and central components of doing science. A traditional definition of *explanation*, based in essentialism and rationalism philosophies (refer to Table 1.1), has been that it is what most clearly identifies a cause for something. Applied social and psychological scientists throughout the 20th century routinely and predominantly employed research methods aligned with these two philosophical perspectives. This causal perspective is also integral to Skinner's behaviorally based three-term contingency model.

However, current methodological debate in the social, educational, and psychological sciences centers around the supposed inappropriateness of adopting the types of philosophies and related research methods just summarized. One issue being debated is the notion that the strategies and tactics used to generate knowledge from the non-human or laboratory culture of science ought to be somehow different from the strategies and tactics used to generate knowledge about human interactions in applied settings. While we bring into question adopting an essentialist or rationalist philosophy as the most appropriate foundation for engaging in scientific activity, we don't do so by arguing that studying applied settings and human interaction is somehow fundamentally different from studying nonhuman phenomena in controlled laboratory settings. At issue for us is the importance of understanding the foundational philosophies that guide particular scientific methods, and in particular those that guide Skinnerian and Kantorian behavior analytic methods in relationship to those that guide other potentially compatible methods of data collection and analysis.

For example, leading empiricists such as Hume and Locke argued against a purely causal view of science as a viable construct (Hendel, 1963). Those who have accepted this empiricist position tend to de-emphasize the search for independent cause as the appropriate model for explanation. A more extreme position has been taken by some philosophers who are generally associated with the positivist school and who doubt our ability to ever know the causes of events with any certainty and therefore advocate that scientists minimize or even abandon the notion of causality altogether (Russell, 1929). Instead, simple description of events of interest as they naturally occur is equated with explanation, with any reference to one event causing the occurrence of another removed from the scientific enterprise.

We argue, however, that the total rejection of causality is unwarranted. Like Suppes (1970) and Toulmin (1961), we promote the idea that causal connections between directly observed events are more accurately characterized as "probabilistic." The methods provided in this book are aligned with Cook and Campbell's (1979) conception of cause that avoids an essentialist or purest explanation and instead recommends the scientific probing for high probability causal connections, using description (e.g., visual inspection of data graphs) as the primary data analysis vehicle.

Essentially, we promote an empirical view of research that de-emphasizes, but does not entirely reject, the notion of cause. Though most philosophies respect the idea that scientific activity is designed to explain human experience, essentialism and rationalism identify such explanation with the location of causes, while empiricism tends to divorce the notion of causality from explanation without completely abandoning a causal conception. We argue that scientists should perhaps take more seriously the proposition that all we know scientifically we learn from direct observational experience, and couple it with the judgment that experience tells us "that" something is the case rather than "how" or "why" it is the case (Hendel, 1963). This philosophical position leads to the intriguing possibility that explanation is very similar (if not identical) to "description." If we are to agree that explanation is constantly evolving toward more accurate scientific descriptions of the world around us, and that the most plausible explanation of an event at a past point in time may prove to be erroneous at present and even change again in the future, then perhaps the best we may hope to achieve scientifically is accurate, all-inclusive description of our world. Science, then, can be argued as a largely descriptive enterprise, with researchers primarily engaged in reporting and organizing objectively observed events.

A final proposition that we take seriously, and one that is a fundamental component of behavior analysis methods, is that an adequate scientific description/explanation is one that is deemed useful and beneficial, or pragmatic, to a particular individual or group. Especially important to education and clinical psychology practice is the idea that the best scientific theories are those that offer practical or therapeutic advantages. Many clinicians in the psychology profession have repeatedly voiced that much of the research available is of little use in guiding effective clinical practice (Bergin & Strupp, 1972). Part of the problem with the research lies in the preponderant use of large-group comparison methods, with assumptions of ultimate cause, rather than methods more amenable to focusing on challenges with individuals and documenting specific strategies that may be of therapeutic benefit. Typically, the practicing clinician or educator is confronted with challenging situations at the individual level (Kazdin, 1982), and "it is at that level that empirical evaluations of treatment need to be made" (p. 14). With regard to education, the most scientific explanation in teacher effectiveness research is the one that helps us best integrate a teacher's intent; the content being taught; and the context, process, and outcomes of particular teaching practices; it also assists in looking for ways to improve all of these components (Metzler, 1989). The focus of this book, then, is to provide contemporary research methods in a behavior analysis framework that are probabilistic, empirical, and pragmatic as well as deemed helpful to understanding more of what may be therapeutic for particular individuals in applied settings.

TOWARD A MULTIPLE RESEARCH METHOD COMPATIBILITY THEORY

Although this book is designed to explain how to perform behavior analysis research, and we advocate its use for a variety of research and evaluation activities, we also recommend that behavior analysis methods be used in concert with other research methodologies. In other words, although we explain and recommend one method, we feel that it should not be used to the exclusion of, or independently of, others and that other methods may benefit from the addition of a behavior analysis component. Clearly, this is an important topic for those who are being trained in the activity of engaging in applied science. If this position is adopted, then researchers should be supported by being adequately armed with all of the data collection and analysis tools necessary to match specific research questions with the most appropriate combination of scientific practices.

Support for most applied education and social science research activities has not always been forthcoming from the basic or experimental laboratory science community. Indeed, the basic or laboratory science community often views many of the published forms of education and social science in applied settings with great skepticism. In some ways, this skepticism is the result of the difference between what the basic science community thinks of as "art" and what it views to be genuine "science." Long marginalized by mainstream laboratory scientists, researchers in education and social science, and to an extent the psychological science, have wrestled with the challenge of how to accurately and inclusively describe and analyze applied settings in a quantitative way. This has been particularly the case with those settings in which a host of complex behavior-behavior and behavior-environment relationships are ongoing with high frequency and in simultaneous or overlapping fashion.

Simplistically put, there have historically existed the two broad categories of qualitative and quantitative research methods in the social, educational, and psychological sciences designed to meet these challenges (Shulman, 1987). In the most radical case, some (e.g., Barone, 2001) have seriously proposed that applied education research in particular should become nonscientific, so that, for example, artistic productions would be considered to be educational research studies. The argument goes something like this: By turning away from traditional quantitative science, education researchers would become unfettered by the annoying requirement to base arguments on directly observable evidence. Relativism would be the foundational philosophy (refer to Table 1.1), in which all individual opinions become equally valid explanations for phenomena. We argue, as does Kerlinger (1986), that opinion and authority are the most problematic and flawed ways of gaining information of value. However, we also argue that there are a range of research methodologies that are compatible with the applied analysis of behavior. We discuss these methodologies here from a compatibility perspective to foreground the remaining chapters of this text.

The two general categories of research methods have been more often opposed to each other than seen in terms of their potential compatibility. One category is qualitative research, of which ethnographic narratives and self-report questionnaire-type efforts have generated the most interest and are the most well-known examples. This family of research draws heavily from anthropology, sociology, and linguistics. It relies on an interpretive focus and utilizes a largely subjective perspective (Smith & Lytle, 1990). The other general category is quantitative research, which includes behavior analysis as well as a variety of descriptive, correlational, and experimental methods.[2] Discussion both in the contemporary applied literatures and at professional conferences has been devoted to the rhetoric of qualitative versus quantitative research; more typically than not promoting the incompatibility of each category due to intractable differences in their underlying philosophies (Firestone, 1987).

Two dominant systems of thought in the education, social, and psychological sciences—social constructivism and radical behaviorism (subsets of the larger qualitative and quantitative research methods categories, respectively)—have tried to meet the challenge of combining qualitative and quantitative methods and have consequently provoked a degree of resistance within the larger scientific community and have been subjects of attack (see Binder, 1994; Brown, 1980; Glaser & Strauss, 1967; and Morris, 1984, 1992 for a more complete discussion of these issues). In addition, Newman's (1992, p. 13) point remains the case—"proponents of . . . these [two] viewpoints have rarely accepted the other as valid, and have been at philosophical war with one another" since their respective inception. We agree with Newman when he goes on to say that these two methodologies contain more common characteristics than differences and that perhaps each could help with the often cited criticisms of the other. Also, behavior analysis methods, as a subset of quantitative research methods, may prove to be a bridge across the two larger categories of qualitative and quantitative research.

Qualitative Research

Most qualitative research stems from the field of cultural anthropology. In this method, the research setting is a catalyst for stimulating interest in the researcher in inductive ways. The researcher is an active participant and an integral part of the study. The focus has typically been upon the relationships between the environmental events that occur within natural settings and relevant participant responses. A rigorous set of scientific procedures has been developed to collect and analyze narrative descriptions of a variety of natural settings. A similar set of procedures has also been developed to collect and analyze various types of interview responses designed to gain insight into the participant perspectives and cognitions believed to be operating within those settings (see LeCompte & Preissle, 1993, and Miles & Huberman, 1984, for a detailed discussion of such methodological procedures). This research category provides a potentially inclusive description of behavior-environment events, and potentially provides data related to thinking and mind, getting at what many behavior analysts term *private events* or *covert behavior*.

A lot of confusion, however, surrounds those who discuss qualitative research, in that it has often been regarded as if it were one approach (Lutz & Ramsey, 1974; Magoon, 1977; Rist, 1977; Smith, 1983; Wilson, 1977). Jacob (1988) and Smith (1987) provide detailed discussion of qualitative research methods across a broad classification of types and strategies and into the general areas of: (a) human ethology, (b) ecological psychology, (c) holistic ethnography, (d) cognitive anthropology, (e) ethnography of communication, and (f) symbolic interactionism. Important to this discussion is that the central theme of all of these qualitative strategies is participant observation of as many behavioral and setting variables of interest as possible. The desired database for all of these strategies is a synthesis of extensive narrative fieldnotes. For qualitative methods, however, participant observation may be, at the same time, a primary advantage and a major shortcoming.

Due to the strategy of narrative synthesis with a single case or small group, qualitative research involves a highly reductive data analysis based in large part on researcher intuition, with conclusions couched within the inherently value-laden perspectives of the researcher and the study participants. In other words, the final data analysis is in large part dependent on the subjective way in which certain data are gathered and used while other data are overlooked or discarded during the data synthesis process. Although qualitative methods may provide important insight into the form and character of an experimental setting, direction regarding what should be studied, and participant (or social) validation of the researcher's perspective on a particular treatment, the nature of the data collection and analysis process makes it inherently difficult to distinguish cause from effect, with overall experimental coherence becoming a challenging determination.

The main weakness of this method, therefore, lies in the need for grounding the descriptive narrative data collection efforts in research techniques that can provide a more objective means of data analysis. In essence, the qualitative descriptive details from which the intuitive conclusions of the researcher stem are in need of criteria for consistent data interpretation across studies.[3]

Quantitative Research

Quantitative research has a longer formal history than its qualitative counterpart and consists of many forms, including descriptive, correlational, and experimental methods and the behavior analytic procedures that are the focus of this text. The chief advantages common to this variety of data collection and analysis strategies are a more objective data collection and analysis process and a clearer demonstration of causal connections or potential functional relations among variables. This category of research methods, however, is not free of methodological challenges either, although many myths and misconceptions have been cast upon these methods during contemporary methodological debates in the literature (see the Some Myths About Behavior Analysis Debunked below for more on this). Historically, quantitative research in the applied social, educational, and psychological sciences has passed through overlapping phases ranging from efforts to simply describe existing states to correlational activity among behaviors and events within a particular setting to large-group comparisons across distinct participant groups that each receive different types of treatments. An accompanying array of parametric and nonparametric statistical analyses of numerical data have developed in complexity and sophistication over the years to accommodate the needs of quantitative data analysis. Although behavior analysis has not received the same legitimacy in mainstream quantitative methodological circles as other forms of quantitative research, it is included in this research category due to its thoroughgoing quantitative character, and even though it also employs many characteristics of qualitative methods (including intensive study of individuals or small groups and a focus on the direct observation of the behavior and environment events that occur in the settings in which certain individuals operate). In this regard, behavior analysis may be viewed as a compatible or collaborative bridge across quantitative and qualitative research methods.

Behavior analysis is a more focused avenue of study than its qualitative counterpart. In similar fashion to most quantitative methods, however, by stipulating quantitative behavior and event category systems prior to data collection, researchers may to some extent be imposing their own ideas on a setting, because data collection is preceded by knowledge of what a researcher wishes to observe. One of the most pressing traditional constraints to quantitative and behavior analysis strategies lies in the practice of isolating behaviors and events from the complex stream or chain of events in which they naturally occur in applied settings. This is a particular challenge to behavior analysis methods in light of the claim that behavior analysis is aligned with the philosophical school of *contextualism* (i.e., the view that all behavior and event activity must be studied with sensitivity to the particular context and setting within which it occurs; Morris, 1992). What will become apparent in later chapters is the challenge that more Skinnerian and lineal mechanic behavior analysis methods have been faced with when certain behaviors and events under study are removed from the larger context of an experimental setting due to the method of data collection and consequent analysis. The response to this is the sequential and interbehavioral behavior analysis methods that will be discussed in detail in later sections of this text. These strategies are specifically designed to take into account more inclusive description of multiple characteristics of multiple behaviors and events, and detail in quantitative ways the time-based connections among behaviors and events as they actually occur in an experimental setting.

Another principle that challenges the legitimacy of the logical positivist philosophy on which most quantitative methods are based arises out of the dilemma concerning the quantitative methodological process of confirming scientific theories (Garrison, 1986). Confirmation of anything from grand theoretical statements (T) to the most basic hypotheses (H) consists of drawing a logical or causal implication from the hypothesis or theory to an experimental conclusion (E). In the quantitative research tradition, this is stated using the following structure: If T or H is true, then E will be observed; and, consequently, if T or H is not true, than E will not be observed. If the experimental conclusion is observed under the appropriate research conditions often enough to be statistically significant (i.e., occurring more often than would be assumed by random chance) through use of an acceptable statistical analysis technique, then the theory or hypothesis that is the focus of a study is said to be verified. The problem is that this structure is logically flawed, representing what has been called *the fallacy of affirming the consequent* (Garrison, 1986; Johnston & Pennypacker, 1980). For example, a particular theory or hypothesis may be true and the experimental conclusion nonetheless false due to other explanations and impacting variables. In contrast, a particular theory or hypothesis may be false but supported as true due to experimental conclusions that are connected not to the theory or hypothesis but to some other variable or group of variables that was responsible for the experimental result that was recorded. This provides the inherent danger to quantitative research of statistically confirming a variety of theories and hypotheses through inappropriately connected experimental conclusions and the resultant explanations.

Methodological Compatibility

Although both general research categories that we have presented provide clear advantages for particular research questions and related research study designs, some challenges to each may be outlined as follows:

1. Qualitative research is
   (a) extremely broad in focus, producing a rich, descriptive database. The database, however, may be value laden as a function of how a researcher collects the data, which in turn impedes the probability of a completely objective data synthesis and analysis process when reporting research results.

(b) founded philosophically in relativism and phenomenology, encouraging researchers to ascribe larger meanings to behavior and event occurrences. The objectivity of the data is not checked, resulting in an oftentimes unbridled subjective and intuitive data analysis process.

2. Quantitative research is
   (a) explicitly objective in data collection and analysis; however, many time-based interactions among variables in an experimental setting are oftentimes ignored or excluded through methods intended to simply control for the potential effects of variables not under direct experimental analysis.
   (b) a largely deductive process with regard to data analysis, with the presupposed methodological structure and procedures of a particular experiment inappropriately providing untoward emphasis on the ultimate conclusions derived from a data analysis of experimental conclusions.

Again, debate currently centers around the perceived necessity of qualitative and quantitative research methodologies remaining separate due to their supposed incompatibility (Howe, 1988). The main argument in this debate centers around how closely particular research methods must be tied to their respective philosophical foundations. Firestone (1987), for example, provides an appealing argument that philosophical ties are rhetorical at best. We know that quantitative methods express the assumptions of positivist philosophy, which holds that behavior can be explained through objective data. In quantitative methods, design and instrumentation persuade by showing how bias and error are eliminated. On the other hand, qualitative methods express the assumptions of phenomenological philosophy, which states that there are multiple realities that are all socially and perceptually defined in a variety of ways by particular individuals and groups. Rich description persuades through a researcher, who, having been immersed in a setting of interest, provides enough verbal detail to enable an audience to make intuitive sense of the situation. Firestone (1987) proposed that although the two methods are rhetorically different, their results can be complementary and therefore compatible.

Finn (1988) and Shavelson and Berliner (1988) emphasized the need for using alternative combinations of research strategies in the social and educational sciences that draw from the advantages of each particular research method. For example, quantitative research methods may count up the number and duration of deviant behaviors in a classroom situation and find that certain teacher practices diminish those behaviors, whereas qualitative research methods may discover some of the reasons behind the incidence of that deviant behavior and the relative receptivity on the part of the teacher to implement practices designed to reduce the unwanted behavior. Finn, as well as Shavelson and Berliner, stress that the major ailment of applied research in general is the public's great skepticism toward it. Although education and social science research, and even much psychological research, yearn for the attention and respect given the laboratory-based physical sciences, the physical sciences have gained respect due to the enormous practical difference they have made through their technological application in the lives of people. We argue that in some respects the lack of public respect for education and social science research is due to a lack of research methods collaboration, and that this lack is related to the lack of impact of separate efforts on the public (and professional) good. In essence, the lack of research methods collaboration and a proactive and supportive research community may serve to limit the fruitfulness of education and social science research in practical terms.

During the past three decades, the scientific community's opinion of qualitative methods in educational research has evolved from ridicule to appreciating its utility in provisional exploration to wholehearted acceptance of it as a valuable alternative in its own right to seeing it as a method that should receive priority in terms of scientific legitimacy. We argue that what is necessary is a return to perceiving all research methods as equally important in the context of the types of questions that they are best suited to answer, and that qualitative methods should be viewed as potentially compatible with quantitative strategies.

A major concern of those who argue for incompatibility is that capitulation to what works experimentally ignores the supposed intractable incompatibility of the competing realist and idealist philosophical outlooks (refer to Table 1.1) that support quantitative and qualitative methods, respectively. However, Howe (1988) and Newman (1992) propose an appealing pragmatic alternative. They argue that no incompatibility between quantitative and qualitative methods exists at either the level of practice or the level of epistemology. Taking a pragmatic stance, they further argue that there are no reasons at the level of scientific activity for applied research to resist forging ahead with what works due to the many commonalities of qualitative and quantitative research at the level of data collection and analysis—in particular with regard to behavior analysis and qualitative methods.

We feel that research methods compatibility rests upon two points. The first point involves the domain of research practice. In practice, differences between quantitative and qualitative data, design, analysis, and interpretation may be accounted for largely in terms of differences in research interests and judgments about how best to pursue them. For example, if a teacher wants to know how many correct responses students are making with respect to a particular method of teaching reading pronunciation, then a quantitative data collection method is most appropriate. If the same teacher, on the other hand, wants to know how receptive his or her students are to the type of instruction being used, then a qualitative data collection method may be more appropriate. If differences can be accounted for by research interests and how best to pursue them, it prompts suspicion about the need to promote different conceptions of reality and different philosophical underpinnings as the rationalization for using different research methods.

Our second and related point is a bit more elaborate and depends on acceptance of the first point. Researchers who argue for intractable incompatibility admit that problems arise not so much at the level of scientific practice as at the philosophical level via the following rationale: Realist and idealist philosophies underlie respective quantitative and qualitative methods. These two philosophies are purported to be incompatible due to their contradicting premises. Therefore, the two methods are incompatible. Our response to this is that a principle implicit to incompatibility argument—that abstract philosophy should determine research methods in a one-way fashion—is erroneous. Research methods, in our view (and also implicit in a behavior analytic view), must demonstrate their worth in terms of how they inform, and are informed by, their respective audiences and clientele to potentially therapeutic ends. If such a two-way relationship is viable, then research methods, and potential combinations thereof, must be evaluated in terms of how well they correspond with the demands of research practice, and, if warranted, the idea of the intractable incompatibility of methods must vanish.

Although each research method has a different philosophical foundation and different and unique data collection and analysis procedures, each also has particular benefits that may complement the other. Due to the ability of qualitative and quantitative methods to each potentially negotiate the obstacles of the other, alternative strategies that incorporate some of the benefits of both research categories may be valuable (refer to Jacob, 1982, for a more complete discussion of this). Bliss, Monk, and Ogborn (1983) provide an early example of a categorical quantification system used in qualitative research and designed for methodological compatibility. Experimental efforts required the coding of direct behavioral observations into categories while still preserving the inductive nature of the data. Data analysis took the form of a tree diagram, a pictorial representation that showed related, independent, and conditional categories. Such a tree structure provided an important aid in organizing large sets of descriptive categories into a structured quantitative system as well as in enhancing the clarity of qualitative research reporting and interpretation. Brown's (1980) Q-Methodology provides another specific illustration of the prospects of coupling qualitative methods' ability to uncover subtle influences in a setting context with a quantitative structure to more objectively determine behavior-environment relationships. There also exist a host of contemporary published applied behavior analysis studies that rely on qualitative techniques for socially validating the quantitative support for a particular educational treatment (e.g., Sharpe, Lounsbery, Golden, & Deibler, 1999).

Some Professional Recommendations

We believe, as do Heward and Cooper (1992) and Sage (1989), that the lack of equal and thoroughgoing exposure of researchers to a variety of research methods is due in large part to the narrow focus of traditional research methods courses in graduate programs in the educational, psychological, and social sciences. Most typically, graduate students are taught a very traditional quantitative version of knowledge production, or, alternatively, a primarily qualitative approach to science, as the only legitimate way to engage in research. If alternative forms of applied research are mentioned at all, they are more often than not presented in a less than desirable light. Instead, a convincing case needs to be made in these courses that there is a broad array of viable forms of scientific inquiry. We caution, as have others (e.g., Schutz, 1989), that strong advocacy of one particular research method, to the overshadowing or exclusion of others, only encourages new researchers to adopt the "have method, need problem system" (p. 31). Of utmost importance is the need for the careful and reflective development of the research question prior to framing it within an appropriate data collection and analysis method. The most prominent interbehavioral theorist in psychology, Kantor (1979), maintained that any science that insists on the priority of a particular research methodology is not yet true science. In our view, that the research question ought to dictate the method of investigation is perhaps the most self-evident, yet most often ignored, principle of science. It is in this context that the methodology materials are compiled in this text in what we hope forms a resource for those interested in the principles and practice of applied behavior analysis and quantitative approaches to direct observation of behavior-event relationships. Prior to jumping into a detailed recipe for these methods, however, we believe that it is important for us to discuss some of the prevalent myths that surround behavior analysis methods.

SOME MYTHS ABOUT BEHAVIOR ANALYSIS DEBUNKED

The following statement by Silverman (1996) provides a pointed illustration of how most professionals who operate outside the university setting—those the university-based research information is designed to reach—view the research process: "The best way to have people avoid you at a cocktail party is to tell them you teach statistics and research methods" (p. 36). If this quote is any indication, a significant challenge of bridging the gap between research information and its professional application remains great and is potentially becoming worse. In addition, this challenge appears specific to the social and educational sciences. Landrum (1997) illustrates this by showing that physical science data is generally trusted; for example, when boarding an airplane there is typically inherent trust that reams of experimental data have been consulted in the construction and flying practices of each airplane to ensure optimal safety and effectiveness. When a physician is consulted by a patient, she or he will often support a proposed treatment plan by referring to the latest medical research. However, when teachers and clinicians in the social sciences are consulted, they rarely provide descriptions of research supporting a particular practice used by a teacher or social worker.

There are many potential reasons for this continuing challenge to the scientific professionalism of those in education and the social sciences. First, data tend to be ignored, with many professional practices contradicting data-supported effective procedures. Kauffman (1996) provides an example in mathematics education in which the currently popular constructivist approach to teaching math skills has been widely adopted despite clear evidence that "it is not the most effective and efficient instructional approach for most students" (p. 56). This is evidence of a larger cultural challenge, again according to Landrum (1997), which is our society's general trend of belief that applied scientific data do not matter in terms of providing any guidance to educational and clinical practices.

There are some items that we feel it is important to discuss here in relation to the pervasive nonuse of scientific data in making professional decisions. These involve the potential reasons for the nonuse of data, in general and in relation to some of the appealing features of behavior analysis research methods, and some pervasive myths concerning applied behavior analysis that are detrimental to acceptance of the method as a legitimate partner in the community of applied scientific methods.

One potential reason for the nonuse of data is that American society tends to place great distrust in information presented in quantitative formats. This is probably due in large part to the knowledge that our news and marketing media consistently manipulate information in ways designed to meet oftentimes self-serving ends antithetical to an increased quality of life. In addition, a traditional mechanistic causal model for conducting research may not be the most appropriate or capable method to use in determining effective educational or clinical practice due to the host of variables that are operating in applied instructional settings. In education, isolating one independent variable, such as teacher feedback, and selecting one dependent measure for its relative effect, such as appropriate subject-matter engagement, without taking into account the myriad other variables that may also have an effect on subject-matter engagement, will often provide for misleading, albeit data-supported, conclusions (as mentioned earlier in our discussion of theories and hypotheses not necessarily being appropriately connected to experimental conclusions).

Another challenge to the use of data-supported professional practices is that there may simply be too much ongoing data generation for professionals to feasibly keep abreast of it. This is due to recent advances in technology that have facilitated data access, coupled with the basic governing principle for the relative success of research faculty professionals to produce as much data-based publication activity as possible. This ever-increasing activity means that there is an overwhelming amount of information to sift through. This abundance of data, and ready access to this data, provides the professional with the added challenge of reviewing and determining sound data from that produced simply for the sake of research faculty advancement and without scientific merit.

A third challenge is the dangerous assumption promoted by currently popular qualitative methodologies that there are no universal truths to be discovered, that individuals construct their own realities and beliefs, and that each of these variable individual constructions is equally valid and true. If we take this approach to applied research (and we by no means wish this challenge to be interpreted as a criticism of qualitative data collection and analysis methods, for we believe these methods to be legitimate and important contributors to the applied scientific literature), then as research faculty professionals we may be inadvertently dismissing the importance of adherence to objectively supported professional practice. In other words, if one does not strive for the data-supported discerning of static and generalized truths, then no one professional method of doing anything can be argued as a relatively more or less effective method, and therefore data collected in a particular situation with particular individuals and on a particular professional practice will have little relevance for any other situation.

We believe that using the principles of applied behavior analysis based on sound behavior analysis research is one means of overcoming the nonuse of scientific data. For this to occur, however, it is necessary for researchers to combat some popularized negative opinions about behavior analysis as a viable research method. Negative opinion can be countered with a variety of arguments.

A first and important assumption of behavior analysis research is that it must have a therapeutic or utilitarian criterion. All information to be gathered must be designed to help improve the quality of life of the participants in positive ways, and ideally all research activity should be conducted collaboratively with groups of interagency professionals, including faculty-level researchers and the professional practitioners who operate in the situations to be studied (Sharpe, 2001; Sharpe, Lounsbery, & Templin, 1997). Pragmatic questions, such as how we want professional situations to function and how we can get them to be that way, are of paramount importance in such research.

Although behavior analysis is of potential appeal because of its pragmatic stance, and many researchers have called for greater use of data-supported principles in professional practice over the past two decades (e.g., Hrycaiko & Martin, 1996), many myths and misconceptions have halted the method's optimal impact in the education, social, and psychological sciences. These misconceptions can be categorized into five general areas (see Aeschleman, 1991, and Kazdin, 1982, for a detailed discussion of this): behavior analysis lacks internal validity, behavior analysis lacks external validity, behavior analysis uses a visual inspection of data that is not scientific, behavior analysis does not take cognitions into account, and behavior analysis is a technocratic and robotic enterprise. Each of these myths is discussed below.

Myth 1: Behavior Analysis Lacks Internal Validity

Behavioral methodologies have evolved into a complex offering of designs arranged to specifically control for most traditional internal validity concerns. These range from multiple baseline designs, in which treatment is provided to different matched participants at different points in time, to multiple treatment and component treatment reversal designs, in which treatments are provided in different sequences to different participants, to multiple treatment introductions and extended maintenance and nontreatment phases, to a variety of multiple-measure, multiple-variable alternating treatment designs (all of which are detailed in later chapters of this text in relation to validity concerns).

Myth 2: Behavior Analysis Lacks External Validity

Behavior analysis methods operate on the premise that scientific study should hold as most important the discovery of how professional participants and the environment in which they operate may be arranged to be most therapeutic for the various participants in that specific environment. Thus, behavior analysis methods emphasize discovering what might help a variety of professionals and their clientele in particular situations and with particular challenges. This is effected through careful replication of an original study that includes a potentially effective treatment, and by careful manipulation of the characteristics of participants and environment from study to study, making rigorous generalizability of findings possible over the course of a series of focused studies.

Myth 3: Behavior Analysis Uses a Visual Inspection of Data That Is Not Scientific

This misunderstanding is potentially the most damaging to behavior analysis methods because traditional statistical analyses have a subjective warrant of translating into *good research* by the very function of their use in the eyes of many researchers and research consumers. In this regard, then, visual inspection of data represented in graphic form is considered an illegitimate form of analysis (Huitema, 1986). A contrasting argument is that all that a large group statistical comparison may hope to show through disproving a null hypothesis based on a traditional statistical manipulation is that "something" differed across experimental groups during a particular study. What a statistical analysis does not show, and what is a great leap of faith on the part of researchers using such analysis, is that this difference is actually and explicitly due to whatever treatment or independent variable was introduced to a particular experimental group. In addition, and little understood by those unfamiliar with behavior analysis methods, a sophisticated set of visual inspection practices and procedures are required to argue favorably for a treatment effect, including mean and level magnitude of change analyses, trend and latency rate of change analyses, and a variety of appropriate nonparametric statistically based data comparisons. Also, visual inspection of readily discernable data changes contained on a graph is viewed by the behavior analyst as beneficial, especially in relation to the challenge of more complex and less discernable statistical information. Changes due to a particular treatment, for example, may be more receptively argued for use by practicing professionals as a function of the relative ease with which the data may be accessed and interpreted from a graphic representation. Barlow (1980) argues that the gap between important data-supported information and its use by professional practitioners will not be narrowed as long as researchers continue to slavishly insist on traditional large-group factorial designs, multivariate statistics, and predetermined levels of significance, for these types of information will never be viewed with receptivity by professional practitioners in real-world settings.

Myth 4: Behavior Analysis Does
Not Take Cognitions Into Account

Another argument against the use of applied behavior analysis methods is that the data collection and analysis procedures implemented do not take into account what experimental participants think, feel, or perceive in relation to the behaviors and events documented by the method. In response, Skinner (1945) provided the concept of what behavior analysts term *private events* (i.e., events that take place inside people and are not detectable by direct observation). From a theory of behavior perspective, both private and publicly observable events operate according to the same Stimulus→Response→Consequence laws, with the difference being one of the relative feasibility of data collection and analysis of those respective events. Although mental explanations are de-emphasized in behavior analysis methods due to the challenge of collecting data on private events, the use of questionnaire and self- report data is recommended in concert with public event data to provide supporting information on private events (these are typically called *social validation* procedures).

Myth 5: Behavior Analysis
Is a Technocratic and Robotic Enterprise

The applied analysis of behavior has been traditionally thought of as a very mechanistic and rule-governed approach to collecting information, in which two or three behaviors are isolated for analysis from a larger experimental situation. In this traditional model, a relationship between two behaviors is hypothesized in a general sense, data are collected in a particular situation to support that relationship, and then general rules are promoted to guide the instruction and application of the behavioral relationship to be supported. In education, connections are made among these fragmented behaviors, in which isolated teacher events, which presumably affect student practices or student achievement in some mechanistic or additive way, are aggregated over time (Doyle, 1990). As will be seen in our detailed description of behavior analysis methods as evolved and unpacked, many computer-supported comprehensive description and sequential analysis methods have been designed and developed to discover the multiple relationships among multiple teacher and student behaviors and events in particular situations (see Morris, 1992, for a detailed discussion of emphasis on behavioral "discovery" and "understanding" rather than simple behavioral "demonstration"). More sophisticated behavior analysis methods have been developed as a function of researchers requiring more sophisticated tools capable of discovering the multi-event conditions that characterize effective and not-so-effective professional practice in particular situations and of providing information to alter those conditions and encourage those professionals in more effective practice in the context of challenging client behavior.

OVERVIEW OF BEHAVIOR ANALYSIS
PRINCIPLES AND PRACTICE

The remaining two chapters contained in the first part of this book provide an important introduction to the main principles of applied behavior analysis, with the remainder of the book detailing an introductory to intermediate-level cookbook approach to the activity of engaging in applied behavior analysis research in a compilation of most of its many methodological and procedural forms. The order of information is structured to facilitate the reader's familiarity with the steps necessary to conduct behavior analysis research that would logically be taken when engaged in the actual research process. As the preface detailed, the remaining chapters in Part I focus on some of the basic principles and terminology necessary to the navigation of applied behavior analysis methods, and detail some of the important specific principles of contemporary systems-oriented and sequential methods. Part II of this book provides a detailed procedural primer for constructing a coding scheme for particular research or assessment purposes, including the many assumptions and limitations that should be taken into consideration when conducting behavior analysis research. Reliability and treatment fidelity issues and procedures are discussed in detail, and close attention is paid to the steps of criterion standard development, staff training, interobserver reliability, and treatment implementation accuracy. A series of category system illustrations taken from a variety of education, social science, and psychology disciplines provides the reader with hands-on familiarity as to how behavior analysis efforts in these respective areas has been implemented with success. Part III of this text includes a variety of reported and generally accepted techniques in the areas of collecting, analyzing, and visually representing data. Application procedure details and their potential advantages are provided and related to some contemporary techniques for recording in real time, overcoming validity challenges through more sophisticated research design types, and issues regarding graph preparation and the use of statistical analysis support for descriptive and inferential purposes. The last part of this text provides recommendations on how applied behavior analysis methods may be used to enhance a variety of research and development, professional or clinical assessment, and instructional applications across a variety of education, social science, and psychological activities. We have included detailed illustrations of field-based professional evaluation activities, research and development opportunities designed to uncover information not previously available to other research methodologies, and laboratory simulation activities heretofore unavailable through other methods and without the aid of behavior analysis-supported computer technology.

As computer hardware development moves forward with increasing speed and sophistication, our potential for as yet unrealized quantitative description and analysis of the world around us is greatly enhanced. Those of us engaged in the development of increasingly capable observational instruments are continually amazed at not only the wealth of additional information that is becoming available but also the opportunity afforded to look at things in new and different ways. In these contexts, we want to provide researchers, educators, and clinicians with a quantitative means to more capable and inclusive description of highly complex and interactive settings. In compatible software publications (our BEST software, described in Appendix B and advertised in the flyer included with this book; Sharpe & Koperwas, 2000), we provide tools capable not only of such a task but also of being programmed for the unique observational interests of a host of professionals working within a wide variety of situations and settings. To provide a theoretical foundation for these materials, we draw on the conceptual work of pioneers in observational and field theory for support for some of the alternative lenses we discuss that can be used to view and analyze the rich and varied information that state-of-the-art computer-based data collection tools are capable of providing. Finally, we include conceptual and procedural information that may help those interested in the direct observation of complex phenomena as they undertake the challenges of such an endeavor.

NOTES

1.   The Association for Behavior Analysis (ABA) is currently located near Western Michigan University and can be contacted as follows:
ABA Offices
1219 South Park Street
Kalamazoo, MI 49001
Telephone: (269) 492-9310
Fax: (269) 492-9316
E-mail: Mail@abainternational.org
The ABA website is http://www.abainternational.org

2.   It can be argued that even quantitative research that has been characterized as psychometric or cognitive can be behavior analytic in framework. The behaviors or the products of behavior of the experimental research participants are typically reported or inferred using these methods, though the results of study are typically interpreted in nonbehavioral terms using nonbehavioral approaches to data analysis.

3.   It is important to note that qualitative research methodologists do not regard the narrative descriptive process as a weakness. They believe that the bias, subjectivity, and relativity contained within qualitative databases are meant to be encouraged and exploited rather than restrained through a mechanism for objectivity. Intersubjective agreement or data objectivity is viewed as irrelevant. Our intention is not to denigrate these views, but rather, to point out the potential drawbacks and challenges to this approach and to contend that a rejection of intersubjective agreement and objectivity as a necessary component to scientific practice is to potentially alter the nature of science in very dangerous ways.

2

A Behavior and Sequential Analyses Primer

In language, clarity is everything.

— Confucius (cited in Titus, Smith, & Nolan, 1986, p. 495)

"Then you should say what you mean," the March Hare went on.

"I do," Alice hastily replied; "at least—at least I mean what I say—that's the same thing, you know."

"Not the same thing a bit!" said the Hatter. "Why, you might just as well say that 'I see what I eat' is the same thing as 'I eat what I see'!"

— Carroll (1946, p. 78)

After reading this chapter, you should be able to define the following terms and provide the information requested in the study guide below.

TERMS

General principles (as contained in the terms list in Table 2.1)

Specific procedures (as contained in the terms list in Table 2.1)

Objectivity

Therapeutic criterion

Sequential behavior analysis

Metaphysical

Field systems

STUDY GUIDE

1. Explain the definition of the term *science* in relation to behavior analysis methods.
2. List and discuss the core features of applied behavior analysis as enumerated by Hrycaiko and Martin, Mahoney, and Day.
3. Provide an illustration of how a researcher might go about analyzing a situation of interest using traditional behavior analysis procedures versus a more field or sequential orientation.
4. Explain the relationship between description and explanation with regard to behavior analysis methods.
5. Discuss how a behavior analyst handles the concepts of thoughts, feelings, and cognitions, in light of current criticisms of behavior analysis in this regard.
6. Explain and discuss the terms and definitions contained in Table 2.1 that provide a summary of general principles and specific procedures regarding applied behavior analysis methodology.

N ow that you are familiar with the historical development of behavior analysis research methods, we will present some basic terms and definitions that are frequently used when discussing research methods and when discussing independent and dependent variables used in research activities. The developers of the methodology of applied analysis of behavior have constructed a very specific and rigorous language to adhere to when engaged in analytic activity. Many believe that the terms and definitions developed by behavior analysts can be daunting and unfriendly to both scientific and lay audiences (Morris et al., 2001). In response, some methodologists have begun to construct alternative language systems to provide a more user-friendly way of connecting with these audiences; for example by replacing unique behavior analysis terms such as *reinforcement* and *punishment* with alternatives such as *selection* and *deselection* (Brown & Hendy, 2001). However, Jack Michael (Morris et al., 2001) illustrates the need for familiarity with, and use of, the original language designed for behavior analysis research with the following example:

This reminds me of someone encountering a physicist at a cocktail party and asking, "What do you do?" The physicist replies, "I work in the area of quantum mechanics." The other person asks for more information: "What is quantum mechanics? Explain it in everyday language that I can understand." A physicist who wants to be perfectly honest could say, "I cannot explain it to you in everyday language. It does not follow from everyday language. We have to go to a technical language, in this case the language of mathematics. How are you with calculus, and especially with differential equations?" Well, it is the same with behavior analysis. . . . I do not think we should worry that our technical behavior-analytic language is not user-friendly, that is, not user-friendly to people without requisite training. When possible, we should of course provide language appropriate to the listener's background, but we should not change our language to something less appropriate to our technical needs. (pp. 143-144)

Important to providing applied behavior analysis methodology materials is, therefore, the provision of an introduction to the language used in the scientific literature that reports behavior analytic studies. This chapter first provides such an introduction based on Skinner's rigorous and complete terminological accounting of functional relations and on the field-systems and sequential analysis contributions of Kantor and subsequent methodologists such as Bakeman and Gottman, and Ray. We provide a list of terms that introduces a core language for those unfamiliar with behavior analysis terminology. Additional detailed information on terminology can be found in journals such as *The Behavior Analyst,* the *Journal of the Experimental Analysis of Behavior,* and *The Analysis of Verbal Behavior.*

SOME INTRODUCTORY TERMS

As Cooper and colleagues (1987) attest in their introduction to applied behavior analysis, the task of describing, changing, and predicting behavior in applied settings is a challenging activity. When focusing on social science, education, and applied psychology settings, behavioral study becomes even more challenging due to the typical complexity of human repertoires that are exhibited in these settings and to the many potential interactions among these repertoires and the environment in which they are operating. To provide a scientific database designed to support the use of a variety of educational and therapeutic strategies, the language used to conceptualize behavioral activity must be well understood. In this way, more rigorous and relevant scientific study may be constructed according to the methods and procedures detailed in this text. Table 2.1 is a list of the commonly accepted terms and procedures that are important to applied behavior analysis methods.

The terminology list in Table 2.1 is broken down into the two general categories of general principles and specific procedures. Terms and definitions are presented in a logical order of introduction, rather than alphabetically. The table first provides an overview of the *general principles* of behavior analysis, which originated in Skinner's pioneering work and are necessary to conceptualize a science of behavior. It then lists the *specific procedures* used in behavior analysis, that is, the technological procedures that are well-supported by existing behavior analytic studies as being effective for a variety of clientele. This language provides a foundation for continuing our understanding of human behavior in applied settings through the use of the scientific procedures that facilitate observational description, control, and prediction. Many textbooks are currently available with detailed discussion of the general principles and specific procedures language we have summarized in Table 2.1, thus we have not provided detailed illustration and explanation of it here. Those interested in a more sophisticated understanding of the language summarized in the table should consult the sources at the end of the table. In addition, *The Behavior Analyst* journal[1] is an excellent resource for continuing dialogue over the finer operational points of the scientific language of applied behavior analysis.

BEHAVIOR ANALYSIS UNPACKED

In Chapter 1, we provided a behavior analysis–friendly definition of the term *science* as the act of describing the observable world around us in a systematic and controlled manner (Kerlinger, 1986). If scientific activity is regarded as a descriptive enterprise, then it is also necessary to systematically and empirically ensure the accuracy of the descriptions, and systematically and empirically test for changes in those descriptions based on the introduction of certain behaviors and events (i.e., experimental treatments or interventions) into the descriptive mix. What is ruled out, according to this definition of science, is the explanation of relationships among observable behaviors and events using metaphysical or unsubstantiated beliefs. Peirce (cited in Buchler, 1955) stated that the scientific method satisfies all doubts or competing

(Text continues on page 54)

Table 2.1   Behavior Analysis Terms and Procedures

General Principles

Behavior: Any directly measurable activity an individual engages in. To be categorized as a behavior, it must result in directly detectable changes in the individual in relation to his or her environment, and those changes must be quantitatively measurable.

Behavior modification: The act of using documented experimental procedures to change an individual's behavior in a desired direction within a particular setting and with intent to generalize the behavior to other, similar settings.

Equivalence class: A complex behavior package that consists of reflexivity or identity matching, symmetry or functional reversibility, and transitivity or the equivalence of the three stimulus characteristics.

Stimulus: Any physical object or event that may potentially affect a behavior of an individual. Stimuli may be internal or external to the individual.
1. **Antecedent stimulus:** A stimulus that precedes or accompanies a behavior and exerts discriminative control over that behavior.
2. **Unconditioned stimulus:** A stimulus that evokes a response without the individual's having had any prior experience of it.
3. **Conditioned stimulus:** A stimulus that evokes a response after a few pairings with another stimulus already known to cause a particular response.
4. **Discriminative stimulus:** A stimulus that an individual perceives a strong likelihood of receiving reinforcement or punishment for having a particular response to.

Response: Any behavior that an individual engages in as a function of being exposed to a particular stimulus or group of stimuli.
1. **Unconditioned response:** An individual's response that is evoked by a stimulus without any prior experience with that stimulus.
2. **Conditioned response:** An individual's response that only occurs after pairing a stimulus with another that is known to evoke that response.

Consequence: Any behavior or stimulus that is a direct result of an individual's response to a particular set of stimuli.

Contingencies (functional relationships): The relationships among stimuli, responses, and consequences. Contingencies can occur naturally or can be experimentally induced.

Three-term contingency: The Stimulus→Response→Consequence relationship advocated by Skinner to describe prediction and control relationships in human behavior. The three components of what occurs prior to an individual's behavior (antecedent stimulus), the behavior itself (response), and the activities and behaviors that ensue as a function of the response (consequence), which provide for experimental observation of all behavioral relationships.

(Continued)

Table 2.1 Continued

Control: When a condition consisting of a functional or causal relationship between an individual's behavioral performance and a particular event or experimental treatment exists. To make a case for control, alternative explanations of the individual's behavioral performance have to be ruled out.

Compliance: When an outside reinforcer successfully controls an individual's actions, *and* the values and belief systems of the individual in relation to that action have no influence on that action.

Matching law: A phenomenon in which individuals are said to behave or respond in choice situations in proportion to the relative amount of reinforcement provided for each choice.

Prediction: The general case whereby through multiple research replications a database is produced in support of a behavior←behavior or behavior→event relationship across a variety of operationalized situations to the point of being able to stipulate with confidence that certain relationships will occur given a certain set of behavioral circumstances.

Field system: The placing of tasks, individuals, and environment and setting events into a logically interconnected unit to achieve a somewhat complex and inclusive explanation of individual behavioral function.

Fatigue: When an individual briefly slows down or stops using a behavior, and when the behavioral inactivity is clearly observed for a substantial period of time and then followed by a return to the previous level of behavioral use.

Satiation: A reduction in the power of a reinforcing event for an individual due to repeated and frequent exposure to the reinforcer.

Spontaneous recovery: When a particular response by an individual reappears after not having occurred for an extended period of time. This phenomenon, which is sometimes termed *resurgence*, occurs as a function of an individual's past behavioral history in the context of present circumstances.

Adaptation: A gradual change in an individual's behavior as a function of a change in environment or new stimuli being introduced to an existing environment.

Habituation: When an individual is repeatedly presented with a stimulus over a short period of time that is designed to evoke a response, the desired response will diminish as a function of repeated stimulus presentation.

Habilitation: The degree to which an individual maximizes use of behaviors designed to receive reinforcement, and minimizes use of behaviors perceived to evoke punishment.

Learning: Any enduring change in an individual's behavior over time that occurs as a result of behavioral experience. All phylogenetic and ontogenetic development occurs as a function of respective evolutionary and individual behavioral learning.

Emotion: Temporary physiological changes in an individual as a function of exposure to certain stimuli.

Private event: All feelings, emotions, perceptions, and cognitions experienced internally by an individual; however, operating according to the Stimulus→Response→Consequence laws that govern external behavior.

Phylogenetic development: The view that humans have developed from earlier life forms over time through evolutionary processes; and the complimentary view that over time more complex communal behavioral structures and functions develop culturally and are designed to serve particular situations more effectively.

Ontogenetic development: The description of the development of a single individual during that individual's lifetime, and the related view that over time an individual will develop more complex behavioral repertoires designed to function more effectively in particular situations.

Specific Procedures

Reinforcement: A change in the conditions, stimuli, or events occurring right after an individual's response and causing that response to be learned (i.e., used again in similar circumstances).

1. **Social reinforcement**: Providing reinforcement to an individual that involves another person's actions.
2. **Negative reinforcement**: An individual's attempts to increase the use of a particular behavior when faced with potentially receiving something aversive. This term also refers to an individual's increasing a particular behavior to potentially terminate an already existing aversive stimulus.
3. **Positive reinforcement**: An individual's attempts to increase the use of a particular behavior when faced with potentially receiving a reward or reinforcing condition.
4. **Continuous reinforcement**: Providing an individual with a schedule of reinforcement in which all occurrences of a designated response class are reinforced.
   (a) **Intermittent continuous reinforcement**: When an individual receives occasional rather than consistent reinforcement for a particular behavior. This terms relates to experimentation with alternative schedules of reinforcement.
   (b) **Differential continuous reinforcement**: When an individual receives reinforcement for one behavior instead of another, and when reinforcement is designed to extinguish one behavior over another. This includes a variety of procedures, such as ALT-R (differential reinforcement of alternative behaviors), DRD (differential reinforcement of diminishing rates), DRH

(Continued)

Table 2.1 Continued

(differential reinforcement of high rates), DRI (differential reinforcement of incompatible behaviors), DRL (differential reinforcement of low rates of behavior), and DRO (differential reinforcement of other behaviors; see Sulzer-Azaroff and Mayer, 1991, for a complete discussion of a variety of procedures).

Punishment (aversive stimuli): An outcome or consequence for an individual that is designed to reduce the occurrence of the behavior or actions that the outcome closely followed.
1. **Type I**: Punishment that involves the provision of an aversive consequence.
2. **Type II**: Punishment that involves the withdrawal or withholding of a reinforcer as a function of an unwanted behavioral occurrence.

Respondent conditioning: A direct change in an individual's response to certain events that is directly due to the reward that is provided after that response. This is commonly associated with the experimental procedure of pairing two stimuli that results in one stimulus (conditioned stimulus) acquiring the power to cause the response already caused by the other stimulus (unconditioned stimulus).

Operant conditioning: Changes in the likelihood of an individual's future responses due to the results of a particular response.

Imprinting: Changing a neutral stimulus into a reinforcing event for an individual by exposing the individual to that stimulus as a newborn.

Instinctive reinforcer: A reinforcing event for a response that either helps an individual to survive in a particular setting or helps other individuals familiar to the primary individual to survive.

Frustration: Withholding reinforcers from individuals in situations where they have been obtained by that individual before.

Motivation: Providing events for an individual that (a) increase the effect certain stimuli have as reinforcers, (b) increase the effect of these same stimuli as unconditioned or conditioned stimuli, and (c) increase the overall rate of behavior occurrence in an individual as a function of exposure to these stimuli.

Rule control: Providing rule-based statements for individuals that (a) describe the character of desirable or undesirable responses, (b) describe all relevant setting conditions for those responses, and (c) describe the results of particular responses in that setting. Stimulus control occurs when rule designations function as discriminative stimuli.

Shaping: A method of reinforcing successive approximations of a desirable behavior for an individual. Typically, an individual is taught to make responses that more and more closely resemble the ultimately desirable behavior by reinforcing responses that approximate the ultimate behavior. In experimental conditions, the definition of the approximated behavior is more and more narrowly defined with each series of successful approximation attempts on the part of the individual being educated.

Feedback: Providing individuals with specific information relative to task performance. Feedback may be designed to reinforce or punish or to serve a discriminative function.

Chaining: An experimental procedure in which existing responses of individuals are reinforced in a particular sequence (e.g., forward or backward) so that individuals learn a more complex response constructed of the existing responses.

Fading: An experimental pairing technique in which stimulus control is gradually shifted from a stimulus that is exerting control over an individual's present behavior to one that did not exert any control before the experimental procedure was employed. The procedure includes the introduction of the new stimulus in paired form and the gradual removal of the existing stimulus over time.

Prompting: When an individual receives a partial explanation or example of the desired behavioral outcome to facilitate behavioral performance. Typically, prompts are provided on an intermittent schedule until the behavior is successfully performed.

Imitation: An experimental procedure that includes (a) presentation of a model for the desired behavior that sets the occasion for a response from the individual, (b) instructing the individual to replicate the modeled behavior, and (c) reinforcing the individual for successful replication of the modeled behavior.

Response cost: An experimental punishment procedure in which an individual loses a certain amount of reinforcement as a function of a certain amount of displayed inappropriate behavior. The intent is to decrease future amounts of inappropriate behavior.

Extinction: Gradually withholding a reinforcer for a particular behavior from an individual until a gradual reduction and elimination of the targeted behavior occurs.

Over-correction: An experimental procedure in which individuals are exposed to repeated practice of positive alternative behaviors after having been observed in undesirable behaviors.

Time-out: An experimental procedure where an individual's opportunity to receive reinforcement is delayed for a short period of time because the

(Continued)

Table 2.1 Continued

individual committed an error according to the rules of the situation. The intent is to punish the individual and thus discourage future errors.

Good behavior game: A procedure in which individuals are divided into teams, rules are specified, and reinforcers are provided to team members who violate specified rules less frequently.

Discrimination training: An experimental procedure in which particular care is taken to reinforce only one particular response in the presence of only one discriminative stimulus. The intent is to successfully educate an individual to use only one response when presented with a particular stimulus.

Behavioral rehearsal: The procedure of reinforcing individuals when a complex skill is practiced successfully in simulated conditions.

Task analysis and task selection: The experimental activity of first breaking down a complex task to be learned into its logical and interconnected parts, and then presenting that task in component part form to individuals in such a way as to facilitate mastery of the entire task.

Behavioral objectives: A procedure, typically related to behavior contracting, in which specific goals are designed for clientele to include three essential elements: (1) target behavior definitions, (2) the specific situations and conditions in which the behavior is to be performed, and (3) the quantitative standard or measure of successful behavioral performance.

Behavior or contingency contracts: A procedure in which a series of behavioral goals is contracted in writing with a particular individual, goals are mutually agreed on by client and therapist, and rewards are selected as a function of successful contract performance.

Group contingencies: Experimental arrangements in which individuals are reinforced or punished as a group according to the behavior of individuals within the group.

Self-management: A variety of experimental conditions in which the individual response to be controlled is defined and the responses required to control the targeted response are identified and monitored. Typically, an educator or therapist provides a procedure by which an individual will self-monitor both the response to be controlled and the stimuli that are designed for control.

Correspondence training: The experimental condition of providing reinforcers to an individual only after both a verbal report of the behavioral activity by the individual and direct observation of the individual's performance of that activity have occurred.

Peer-mediated strategies: A variety of experimental treatments in which individuals who are similar in character to the target individual are trained and used to implement the educational or therapeutic treatment.

Token economies: A procedure in which reinforcers are exchangeable for activities when a task or series of behaviors is successfully completed or not engaged in over a period of time.

ALT-R: The differential reinforcement of alternative behaviors, one example of which is when an individual is reinforced for using alternative behaviors to the point of extinguishing undesirable behaviors that are no longer reinforced.

DRD: The differential reinforcement of diminishing rates, in which a schedule of reinforcement is provided to individuals for responses repeated below a series of gradually diminishing rates.

DRH: The differential reinforcement of high rates, in which reinforcement is given to individuals when a sequence of responses is successfully emitted in rapid succession.

DRI: The differential reinforcement of incompatible behaviors, in which individuals are reinforced for using behaviors that are incompatible with undesirable behaviors. This procedure is designed to curtail undesirable activities.

DRL: The differential reinforcement of low rates of behavior, in which individuals are reinforced for not using a behavior during a prescribed period of time, with the individual allowed to resume using the behavior after the prescribed period.

DRO: The differential reinforcement of other behaviors, in which individuals are reinforced for not using particular responses or engaging in particular activities. This procedure is sometimes referred to as *omission training*.

Deprivation: An extended period of time in which no contact with a particular reinforcer is allowed an individual.

Stimulus matching (matching-to-sample): When a stimulus is presented to an individual along with a set of comparison stimuli and reinforcers are given to the individual for correct responses in matching the selected stimulus with a comparison stimulus that is the same.

Generalization (or stimulus generalization): When an individual uses a response in one situation and that use increases dramatically the probability that the response will be used in other situations that are similar to the one in which the response was originally used.

1. **Unlearned response generalization**: The tendency for individuals to use new responses spontaneously in particular settings.
2. **Learned response generalization**: The tendency for individuals to use responses in a particular situation because they have produced a desirable result in past situations.

(Continued)

Table 2.1 Continued

Stimulus generalization gradient: Experimental conditions that provide new stimuli in different situations that gradually begin to differ from the original stimulus that produced a response, with the power of the stimulus to control an individual's response comparably lessened.

SOURCE: Chance (1998); Cooper, Heron, and Heward (1987); Malott and Whaley (1983); and Sulzer-Azaroff and Mayer (1991).

answers by collecting information in which our thoughts, beliefs, perceptions, biases, values, attitudes, and emotions—that is, *metaphysical* processes—have no effect on the data gathering process. In other words, and through nonreliance on any internal cognitive process, such as that just listed, a behavioral scientist endeavors to ensure the element of *objectivity* in his or her data collection and analysis efforts by only recording those events that can be viewed with the naked eye. In this way, it does not matter who performs the information collection or data analysis procedures, for if those procedures are followed correctly, the information and conclusions will be the same regardless of the particular direct observer and procedural user. In this regard, we agree with Kerlinger's proposition that although there exist a number of research methods (i.e., various quantitative, qualitative, and behavior analytic procedures) for collecting and analyzing information scientifically, there is only one scientific approach.

If we are to base a set of recommended data collection and analysis tools on the above definition of science, in particular tools to be used within the applied education, psychology, and social science domains, then these tools should have the capability to objectively and inclusively collect and analyze observable phenomena using traditional quantitative method (i.e., by counting the occurrence and duration of various events). An important feature of a behavior analytic approach to science is the ability to count or quantify particular behaviors and events so that others may gain an accurate representation of the experimental setting that is being described.

As discussed in Chapter 1, and reinforced in the Some Introductory Terms section earlier in this chapter, the applied analysis of behavior is a branch of psychology that attempts to discover and apply the ways in which particular behaviors are acquired and maintained in particular settings. Similar to qualitative methodologies, applied behavior analysis research, and the applied practice that is consequently supported by that research, must contain a *therapeutic criterion* that stipulates that the treatments designed for behavior change must benefit the client in some productive way. Applied behavior analysts have also developed, expanded on, and experimented with a variety of rigorous scientific procedures designed to describe and analyze settings of interest in behavior analytic ways. This methodology, which is based on the historical work of early scientific pioneers (e.g., Kantor, 1953, 1959, 1969; Skinner, 1989; Watson, 1970, etc.; see Figure 1.1), at its core proposes a behavior-behavior and behavior-environment Stimulus→Response→ Consequence relationship. Within this framework, a host of studies in a variety of applied settings have shown that multiple behaviors and events (stimuli) may be linked to trigger the same behavior (response) if repeatedly presented together; that stimuli may successfully be substituted for one another to produce the use of desired behaviors and the extinction of undesirable behaviors; that new behaviors (responses) can successfully be trained and maintained in the absence of that training within various natural settings; and that many behaviors may be generalized to situations outside of the primary experimental setting under the proper experimental training conditions.

The body of work generated by applied behavior analysis methods is also founded on efforts to provide a more rigorous quantification scheme for the study of human interaction in a variety of settings, and it is focused on overcoming the limits of more subjective methods of information gathering. Thus behavior analysis methods are necessarily limited to the collection and analysis of observable events that have a definite beginning and end time and are amenable to being described and counted in some quantifiably acceptable way. There are many methods of counting, which range from simple number or frequency counts to percentages of experimental time to rates in general (i.e., an average numerical count over a specified period of time; e.g. number per minute) to rates of acceleration or deceleration (i.e., changes in behavioral rates over specified periods of time). However, whichever method is used, the primary focus of behavior analysis is always to quantify observable behaviors and events.

In comparison to more traditional large-group quantitative research designs, behavior analysis methods have a number of appealing characteristics that according to Hrycaiko and Martin (1996) render these methods very user-friendly for a variety of professionals. First, behavior analysis methods focus on repeated measures of an experimental research participant's actions over significant periods of time, facilitating analysis of trends and variations in performance. Second, most behavior analysis designs expose all participants within a particular study to the treatment. This feature overcomes the resistance of applied professionals who may not wish their clientele to be part of a no-treatment control group and therefore miss out on a potentially beneficial experience. Third, a rigorous set of reliability procedures is required prior to the implementation of data collection procedures by behavioral researchers; and an equally rigorous set of reliability procedures is required to ensure that specified treatment procedures have been implemented with integrity and procedural fidelity. Both of these sets of reliability procedures go far toward ensuring the legitimacy and accuracy of data collected and consequent analysis interpretations of treatment effects in applied settings. Methodological priority also rests on the study of one participant or a small group of participants to come to a greater understanding of how to benefit the participant or participants in that particular setting as effectively as possible, and then the use of careful study replication over time with different participants and in different settings to come to a cautious sense of how generalizable the original study results may be.

The following composite summary of behavior analysis principles and methods is based on information in Mahoney (1974) and Day (1983):

1. an assumption of macroscopic determinism in which there exist universal truths that are capable of being discovered through objective and reliable data collection and analysis techniques

2. an emphasis on direct observation of behaviors and events of interest through reliable data collection procedures

3. a pragmatic adoption of operationism, in which independent and dependent variables are each clearly and objectively specified according to the procedures (operations) entailed in their measurement

4. a strong emphasis on falsifiability (or testability) as the cardinal feature of meaningful scientific hypotheses and legitimate empirical research (successful behavior analyses must be able to specify what data would have bearing on the truth value of a hypothesis.)

5. an emphasis on controlled experimentation as the ultimate means for accumulating and refining knowledge about behavior

6. a positive analysis of independent replication of original studies to provide generalizability of findings

7. a conception in which private events are either identified with verbal reports about them through qualitative social validation techniques or held to be incapable of playing any role in a scientific account of behavior

As a result of the very principles of this method of observational assessment, behavior analysis methods have often suffered in mainstream education, social science, and psychological methodology circles—in particular from those who take the perspective that such methods are too time-consuming and labor intensive to be feasible in highly interactive settings where multiple participants are engaged in a variety of interactions and within a changing environment. Many mainstream methodologists outside of the applied analysis of behavior argue that the behavior analytic data collection and analysis process often excludes many relevant behavioral events or environmental stimuli that potentially impact on the primary behaviors and events of interest in a particular research study. The fact that behavior analysts have historically observed and analyzed only a very limited set of behaviors or environmental events in an experimental setting, using cumbersome and time-consuming paper-and-pencil methods, has contributed to this argument. The use of traditional data collection and analysis tools has also fueled the criticism that behavior analysis as a method tends to fragment a naturally occurring interactive process in which isolated events are aggregated over time with presumptions being made about how those events may affect other events in some mechanistic or additive way (Doyle, 1990). In addition, many behavior analysis researchers, and consequently many readers of behavior analysis studies, have tended to make unwarranted assumptive leaps with regard to an explicit and oftentimes generalized causal link between various stimuli and responses operating within a particular situation. In other words, collecting information on the relative number of occurrences of a particular behavior or environmental event that is hypothesized to act in a stimulating way, and collecting the number of occurrences of a response that has a hypothesized connection with the stimulus under observation, does not necessarily support the explicit causal nature of such a connection—particularly when one is involved in the collection and analysis of data in applied settings with multiple participants who are all operating within environments that are subject to change.

In the past decade or so, many scientists focusing on the study of behavior in applied and experimental settings have been involved in developing enhanced data collection and analysis procedures designed to overcome some of these challenges. Many have also engaged in developing alternative ways of conceptualizing how behavior operates in applied settings and how it may be more effectively, accurately, and inclusively studied. One of the main efforts of this book is to present some of these developments in relation to more traditional behavior analysis practices so that they may be more readily applied to a variety of research and evaluation activities that focus on better understanding behavior. The two areas of greatest methodological development have been in field systems conceptualizations and in what is most frequently termed *sequential behavior analysis*. The former domain has proven productive in moving behavior analysis efforts toward a more inclusive focus when studying complex interactive settings, and the latter domain has provided a mechanism for making the functional analyses among behaviors as they occur in time-related sequence more explicitly quantifiable.

THE FOUNDATIONS OF FIELD SYSTEMS AND SEQUENTIAL ANALYSIS

A field systems perspective toward behavior analysis is, in large part, a technological and methodological evolution of the philosophical work of Kantor (Morris, Higgins, & Bickel, 1983)—work that was predicated on the pioneering efforts of Einstein and Infeld (1938). Kantor's most important premise in relation to behavior analysis is that all explainable phenomena arise from a single, vast matrix of events—*all* within the natural sensory (i.e., directly observable) realm (Lichtenstein, 1983). Thus the conceptual emphasis of any scientific practice is on answering the question of how an individual scientist can collect information to describe in more complete and inclusive ways the many observable behaviors and events that are occurring in a setting of interest. It is this question that Kantor, and other field theorists before him, felt must be answered first in gathering information about any situation in which multiple behaviors and events are operating and require greater scientific understanding.

Pronko (1980) defined the term *field* as "that complex or totality of interdependent factors [organismic behaviors and environmental events] that constitute or participate in a psychological [or behavioral] event" (p. 5). We define *field system* as the totality of elements (i.e., behaviors or environmental events) contained within a particular situation under study. A field system can also be viewed as dynamic and continuously evolving, and is considered relatively unique to each individual operating within a particular setting. A field system under study at a given point in time is also characteristically dependent on previous field systems and on the behavior and setting factors that have influenced individuals under study at previous points in time. Thus it is important to study field systems over periods of time and to provide a mechanism for inclusive description of the many behaviors and events that may act to determine the characteristics of a particular field system. Within this conceptual orientation, generality of scientific results is viewed with great caution; with generalized claims about scientific findings made only after very careful and extensive replication of a particular study over long periods of time and across a variety of carefully altered situations.

To effectively visualize a field system approach to the study of behavior, a model such as that in Figure 2.1 may help.

The field system contained in Figure 2.1 is very much akin to *dyadic interaction*, in which multiple organisms emit behaviors in one another's presence. According to Thibaut and Kelley (1959), the essence of any interpersonal or behavioral interaction among individuals is contained in the time-based character of the interaction, and not so much in the characteristics of the behavioral components of that interaction. Description of behaviors in this regard provides the possibility that each behavior of each individual in a particular situation has at least the possibility of affecting the behavior of the others. Most individuals in applied settings have a complex repertoire of behaviors from which to choose and to use accordingly, thus inclusive description and analysis becomes a challenging enterprise—an enterprise that moves from the consideration of single behaviors and events to that of larger analytic units or clusters of multiple behaviors used in concert. A complete field system first necessarily includes the historical events and background characteristics that are functionally related to current behavioral interaction, what in Figure 2.1 is labeled the "Preceding Event." Next, a configuration of relatively stable, but subject to change, setting events is necessarily part of the field configuration and

Figure 2.1   A generic field systems model

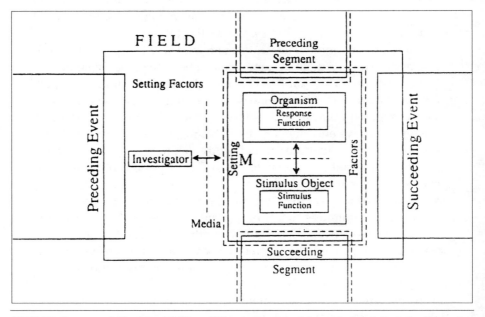

SOURCE: Sharpe and Hawkins (1992b, p. 79) and reproduced from *The Interbehaviorist*, Edward K. Morris (Ed.), *17*(1), p. 2. Reprinted by permission

must be taken in to consideration. Also included are all observable behavior and stimulus events currently in operation, akin to a multiple Stimulus→Response→Consequence framework based on Skinner's original model. Analysis must take the form of recognizing the many potential functional and interdependent relationships among all elements within a field system, although each element is not necessarily functionally related to every other element. The field system operates on the assumptions that (1) there exists a varying degree of control by the field participants of each behavior and event element, (2) that field participants at least partially control the functional nature of the larger field, and (3) that there is a degree of functional autonomy among the many elements within the field that gives each field a degree of operational flexibility. Thus in any behavioral field system, there are varying degrees of functional integration, there is relative stability with perturbations as the field moves through time, and there are potentially well-defined outcomes in relation to a variety of behavior←→event relationships that will functionally impact the future structure of the field system under study. Viewing behavior within a field system perspective provides for the inclusion of many homeostatic processes, through which characteristics such as macroscopic boundaries and rules of governance can be scientifically determined in spite of potential disruptive event occurrences. At the same time, a field system is assumed to be in a constant state of change, and we hope that through the scientific introduction of additional or alternative behaviors and events, it is being moved toward more effective and complete realization of the goals of the professional participants. Professional goal realization, or therapeutic enhancement, within a field system may therefore take place through changing the nature of the interaction among behaviors and events and by introducing new behaviors and events to the system.

This is quite a complex introduction to the field system, and the concrete example that follows may enable the reader to better understand the concept. The illustration we have chosen is of a teacher operating in a large public school classroom of 30 or so students of varying backgrounds and abilities, with an aide to help with her instruction. At the most basic level of analysis, and one similar to traditional behavior analysis efforts, the individual behaviors of the teacher that are felt important would be defined and described in relation to one or two behaviors of a particular student. For example, the questioning behaviors of the teacher might be documented in relation to types of subject matter responding of particular students. In addition, certain classroom management practices of the teacher, such as close proximity to a student and verbal praise, might be documented in relation to certain off-task or disruptive practices of particular students. In a classroom situation, however, there are a variety of behaviors that the teacher, the teacher's aide, and each student may use that have an impact on the isolated behaviors of interest we have just mentioned in our illustration. According to field systems theory, all of these potentially impacting behaviors must be described in a data collection effort in inclusive ways. Also, there are many setting arrangements that may impact on the primary behaviors of interest, such as the physical arrangement of the classroom, the objects and materials in the setting that may gain the attention of students, and a variety of visual and auditory stimuli that should be taken into account. All of these setting events are items that should be documented according to a field systems analysis perspective because of their potential impact on the primary behaviors of interest. There are also a variety of historical experiences on the part of the teacher, the aide, and each student that may affect the primary behaviors of interest. For instance, a teacher's past work experiences, past educational training, and past positively and negatively perceived interactions with students may affect her or his present behavioral interactions in the classroom with certain students and with the student body as a whole. In addition, each student and the entire student body have a variety of past educational and larger life experiences that may affect their use or nonuse of certain behaviors. Clearly, students who come from disadvantaged home environments or those who have not had exposure to enhanced educational and social experiences will react in very different academic and social ways from those who have benefited from certain past out-of-the-classroom activities. Essentially, a field systems orientation to behavior analysis recommends inclusive documentation and analysis of historical or preceding events, setting factors, and immediate occurrences of a variety of behavioral events among all setting participants. A field systems orientation also recommends the use of multiple measures to describe the behaviors and events that are occurring in a particular setting, as well as the use of measures that describe the time-based connections among those behavior and event occurrences. In this way, a more complete understanding of the specific behavior, event, and setting arrangement relationships may be discovered in relation to certain behaviors of interest, and larger configurations or behavior-event packages or clusters may be determined to be functionally related to certain behaviors.

This theoretical orientation is reminiscent of Gestalt traditions in psychology, which posits that individuals do not exist in isolation but are integrated into interactive wholes (Marx & Hillex, 1963). For example, when we look at a building we do not typically first see the bricks, wood, mortar, and glass of the building structure, but rather, we view a particular house. In much the same manner, most professional practitioners do not see individual stimulus and response elements in isolation—instead, they view a professional setting in action and interaction in a particular context. This integrated system is then studied in terms of its many component parts and the specific manner in which those parts are functionally connected in time. What distances field systems theory from earlier Gestalt orientations to psychological phenomena are the use of (a) a quantitative scientific method of analysis, and (b) a variety of mathematical equations and rule-governed visual analyses of data to map interactive behavioral situations.

Another component of field systems theory, also predicated on the pioneering work of Kantor, is the importance placed on experimental analysis of the many behaviors and events within a particular field system in the context of their time-based relationships with one another as each behavior or event of interest actually occurs. Kantor used the term *interbehavior* to describe his recommended emphasis on analyzing these time-based connections. Essentially, Kantor argued for an additional emphasis to Skinner's Stimulus→Response→Consequence methodological development, which entailed describing behaviors and events not only in terms of the quantitative characteristics of the events themselves (e.g., number and rate of occurrence, duration, percentage of experimental time, celeration, etc.) but also in terms of the relative probability with which certain events occur in time-based proximity to certain other events. In our classroom example, the issue becomes one of not just analyzing the number of teacher questions and student responses, or the duration of each, but the timing of each occurrence in relationship to each and every other occurrence.

It is in the area of time-based probability of occurrences between and among behaviors and events that a call for greater experimental specificity has been made (see, e.g., Espinosa, 1992) and largely answered (see, e.g., Bakeman & Gottman, 1986, 1997; Sharpe, 1997a). The probability of a behavior or event occurrence as a result of particular stimuli is important to Skinner's radical behaviorism (Skinner, 1944, 1953); however, Skinner never explicitly defined how to quantify this probabilistic relationship outside of explicating a variety of event specific characteristics, such as number of occurrences, length of occurrence, and amount of time that elapses between occurrences (see Skinner, 1938). Indeed, Skinner (1957) stated that "Probability of responding is a difficult datum" (p. 344) and left it at that. In answer to this dilemma, the pioneering philosophical addition to behavior analysis methods that Kantor recommended has evolved over time, and oftentimes independently of Kantor's influence, in the past decade or so under the methodological umbrella termed *sequential behavior analysis*. This type of analysis has developed a variety of methods to quantify the relationships in time among behavior and event occurrences. Sequential analysis has also been developed in large part to provide a methodological means to making functional relationships among particular behaviors and events of interest quantitatively explicit through the use of mathematical equations that describe the conditional probabilities of a next behavior or event response in time-based connection with a particular stimulus. This type of analysis can perhaps be thought of as similar to the quantification of a musical score used by a conductor to better view all of the elements contained within a particular musical system as they are temporally related to one another.

There are many potential advantages to the addition of field system and sequential analysis components to the applied analysis of behavior, some of which include the following:

1. The researcher's use of appropriate data collection tools provides for a more inclusive and comprehensive documentation of complex interactive environments.

2. Field system and sequentially focused analysis techniques enable a researcher to view and analyze a larger behavior$\leftrightarrow$ environment system in action and interaction in quantitative ways.

3. The addition of time-based locus and extent of behaviors and events (i.e., start and stop time data on each and every event occurrence) provides a mechanism for making time-based functional connections among particular behaviors and events of interest more explicit.

4. Such techniques facilitate a highly inductive process in which a very sensitive and inclusive analysis of observable events specific to particular settings is made available, with generality established through the use of the same observation systems across a variety of experimental settings.

When behavior analytic data are collected in complex interactive environments within which multiple behaviors and setting events are continuously interacting, we feel that two important additions to more traditional Skinnerian activities are (a) efforts toward more inclusive data description of the characteristics of all potentially impacting behaviors and events that are operating within a given field system, and (b) stipulating a time-based conditional probability among behavior and event occurrences for the immediately and proximally preceding and succeeding presences and absences of other behaviors and events of interest (to better capture the many relationships among particular behaviors and events). Morris (1992), in an important published presidential address to the Association for Behavior Analysis, provided an important rationale for moving in the two methodological directions we have noted. Morris advocated that movement forward from Skinner's important three-term contingency prediction and control model toward a multiple and bidirectional Stimulus$\leftarrow\rightarrow$ Response$\leftarrow\rightarrow$Consequence model of behavioral understanding be undertaken. Morris (1992) provided the important illustration from data-supported behavior analysis technology that follows: "Discovering the [myriad of complex] conditions [within and across situations] that control inappropriate behavior and altering them may take more time and effort [and alternative data collection and analysis tools] than demonstrating that a particular behavior-change techno-logy (e.g., time-out) can suppress disruption [within one particular situation]" (p. 9). It is in this regard that the science of behavior must evolve to include appealing components—such as a field systems view and a sequential analysis technology—to move forward with the act of scientific discovery and understanding rather than to remain with simple technical demonstration within the control of a particular situation. In our view, discovery and understanding involve the challenging activity of bringing behaviors and events of interest under the control (i.e., making appropriate and effective time-based connections among behaviors and events) of certain clientele in particular situations well beyond the primary experimental training setting.

But before we move forward to detail the specific principles and practices of the quantitative direct observational methods we recommend, a brief discussion of what we consider two of the major characteristics (and often wrongly characterized criticisms) of the applied analysis of behavior—that the method is descriptive and how it conceptualizes mental events—is warranted.

BEHAVIOR ANALYSIS AS A DESCRIPTIVE/EXPLANATORY ENTERPRISE

Many in the larger mainstream education, psychology, and social science methodology communities view behavior analysis methods as only descriptive in nature, and use this position to argue that a behavior analysis study should not be interpreted as causal, explanatory, or predictive (Lichtenstein, 1983). This concern is, of course, based on the conceptual distinctions that could potentially be made between description and explanation. We, however, argue that description and explanation should be viewed as roughly synonymous, although we do believe that this idea should be qualified by Kantor's (1953, p. 34) view that "as a rule explanations constitute elaborate descriptions, typically those relating some event to one or many others." We have not found an adequate answer to the question "In what sense can an applied scientific method do more than provide a relatively complete description of behaviors and events, the conditions in which they operate, and the mathematical relationships among them?" If description and explanation are viewed as one and the same, then repeated descriptions of similar behaviors and events operating on one another in similar ways across a variety of situations become high probability explanations of why certain behaviors and events operate in a certain way. Hence, a predictive capability is also made available from rigorous and inclusive descriptive data sources, for high probability occurrences of particular behavior←→event relationships across a variety of settings provide important information for the probability and hence prediction of future similar occurrences of the documented relationship.

In this regard, we view larger causal claims in relation to how a particular behavior or event may impact on another as perhaps too strong an emphasis and therefore as often unwarranted claims. Rather, and as we articulated in Chapter 1, a more appropriate perspective may be that the best we can endeavor toward scientifically is more and more accurate and complete description of the world around us, and through this description come to a heightened probability-driven view of how we might predict and control a variety of behavior ←→event relationships. In our view, and as a specific argument in favor of the use of behavior analysis methods over statistical analyses of experimental and control groups, a preponderant emphasis on statistical significance to prove that certain events caused certain other events is oftentimes unwarranted. This is due to the assumption of statistical methodology that there is a causal link of a particular behavior or event with other particular behaviors or events—a causal link based on proving that something (as opposed to nothing) occurred in relation to null hypothesis theory. This approach neglects to explain with specificity the potential relationships among a variety of other contributing variables outside of those specifically defined in an experimental relationship. These variables are potentially operating to the point of having a functional effect within a given experimental setting of interest.

HOW BEHAVIOR ANALYSIS CONCEPTUALIZES MENTAL EVENTS

Another pervasive concern that is often used to criticize behavior analysis methodology, and the theoretical foundations on which it operates, has to do with how behavior analysis conceptualizes and articulates the existence and operation of mental events. A particular challenge to thoroughgoing receptivity for behavior analysis methods, in the larger culture of education, psychology, and social science research methods, is the idea that behavior should be explained by a variety of conscious or unconscious mental events. A mentalist explanation of behavior has been more receptively welcomed in applied scientific circles in recent years, and has become a satisfactory answer for many lay and research professionals across a variety of disciplines and across a variety of experimental studies. The pioneering work of Skinner, and, relatedly, the methods of behavior analysis, are often accused of defining human beings as organisms devoid of all thoughts and feelings, and are thus accused of an abject denial of consciousness. A closer read of the set of assumptions that underlie behavior analysis provides an important response to these unwarranted claims.

First, behavior analysis assumes that behavior occurrences do not happen randomly or by chance, but that they occur according to a set of static laws. In other words, behavior must operate according to a set of rules or laws in order for us to be able to predict and control behavior, and behavior must be assumed to operate according to a set of rules and laws if scientists are to come up with a set of procedures (i.e., a technology of behavior change) designed to change behavior toward more therapeutic or productive ends. Second, the explanation of behavior consists of describing directly observable physical events to determine the functional relationships among those events over time. Physical events are broken down into two basic categories—biological events (e.g., the role of genetics, heredity, and physiological development) and environmental events (e.g., behavioral and environmental experience)—with both categories taken into account for a thorough and complete analysis of behavior. Third, and most important to countering a criticism of behavior analysis for lacking a cognitive or mental dimension, is that behavior analysis assumes that thoughts and feelings do not act to explain behavior, but that thoughts and feelings are an integral part of the behavior to be explained and operate according to the same laws that govern observable behavior. Chance (1998) provides a nice example of this assumption with the following:

> A person may feel angry and slam a door, but he does not slam the door because he feels angry. Both feeling angry and slamming the door are part of being angry and must be accounted for in terms of the history of biological and environmental events. To say that a person slams a door because he is angry, amounts to saying that he is angry because he is angry. Similarly, to say that a person solves a problem because she has insight into it is to say that she solves the problem because she solves the problem. Such statements are absurd because a phenomenon can never explain itself. (p. 32)

Behavior analysis implies that no information is required other than that derived from directly observable data collected through normal sensory perceptions. In accounting for thoughts and feelings, behavior analysis does not deny their existence, but simply states that they lie outside of the current capability of two independent individuals to directly observe them and that therefore a reliable accounting of thoughts and feelings cannot be made available. If a reliable accounting cannot be made, then the phenomena of interest must fall outside of the realm of scientific activity. This challenge, again, means not that thoughts and feelings do not exist, nor that they do not operate according to the same general laws that govern directly observable behavior, but that they are at present difficult to document according to scientific practice. An individual's thoughts and feelings are often as important as how an individual behaves; however, while we currently know something about the biological functions of direct observation, we know very little about the biological functions of why individuals feel the way they do. Here is another illustration from Chance (1998):

Feeling is a kind of sensory action like seeing or hearing. We see a tweed jacket, for example, and we also feel it. That is not quite like feeling depressed, of course. . . . We can also feel *of* the jacket by running our fingers over the cloth to increase the stimulation, but there does not seem to be any way to feel *of* depression. (p. 33)

Essentially, thoughts and feelings are conditions of an individual's body that operate according to sensory laws similar to those of seeing or hearing, but they are conditions that are not well understood as yet from the standpoint of how to scientifically document them. The difficulty for the behavior analyst when arguing for the legitimacy of the methodology thus lies in the wrongly presupposed denial of the realm of cognition, unconscious mental events, and the metaphysical domain by those not familiar with the theoretical premise of behavior analysis. Often, *behavior* has been defined as a muscular or glandular response, rather than as the response of the individual as a whole. If we were to generalize, we would say that psychologists have most often identified behavior with physical movement and have therefore given the impression that mental and intracerebral events (i.e., metaphysical events) have no place or do not exist in the behavioral realm.

Kantor (1922), on the other hand, provided a philosophical foundation for the idea that behavior analysis may study both overt behavior and mental experience. He objected to the position that behaviors are limited to the actions of muscles, nerves, and glands. He further provided the assumption that a behavioral occurrence is the *total* interaction of an individual with his or her environment, with physical movement playing an important but not exclusive defining role. If we are to accept Kantor's definition of behavior, it becomes possible, and even necessary, to embrace thinking, feeling, and perceiving within the behavioral framework, though we have not, as yet, found an effective means of scientifically and systematically observing them.

Some important tasks now remain to us as authors of this textbook. First, we must continue to stress that the scientific legitimacy of quantifying directly observable behaviors and events is equal to that of more subjective ways of information gathering when performing educational, psychological, or social science. Next, we must provide a set of concrete methods and procedures for the technical feasibility of a quantitative method of data collection and analysis in complex interactive settings—*and* we must tie these technical procedures to a compatible scientific theory that explains the manner in which behavior-behavior and behavior-environment interactions occur and that supports the importance of quantitative observation as a way of learning more about a particular behavioral phenomenon. The primary focus of the remaining chapters contained in this book is, therefore, to provide an amenable and appealing means of quantifying directly observable behaviors and events within the larger umbrella of the scientific enterprise.

One means for us to use in accomplishing this objective is to provide user-friendly tools that both new and experienced members of the research and development community will be receptive to, and that various professionals will see the advantages to using when held up against other popular scientific (and sometimes pseudoscientific) methodologies. John Gottman (Bakeman & Gottman, 1986) summarizes well the importance of direct observational methods with a behavior analytic component as follows:

> Observational methods deserve a special role in our measurement systems. First, we think that the descriptive stage of the scientific enterprise is extremely productive of research hypotheses, models, and theory. Second, the time is ripe for a reconsideration of observational techniques because we now know a lot more about what to observe, how to construct reliable measurement networks, and how to analyze data to detect interaction sequences. (p. xiv)

We thus emphasize both traditionally used and recently developed methods in the direct observation of behavior. It is the latter point raised by Gottman that challenged us to develop the software tools that facilitate the methods detailed in this book (see the description of BEST software in Appendix B and the flyer advertising it that accompanies this text). We hope that through making this methodology text available in the context of providing facilitative computer technologies that the appeal and resultant use of applied behavior analysis will increase in the education, social science, and psychology communities and spread so that a growing number of professionals use quantitative direct observation approaches for their chosen research and evaluation tasks.

NOTE

1.   *The Behavior Analyst* can be subscribed to by contacting
The Behavior Analyst
Association for Behavior Analysis
1219 South Park Street
Kalamazoo, MI 49001
Telephone: (269) 492-9310
Fax: (269) 492-9316
E-mail: mail@abainternational.org

3

An Interbehavioral
Multi-Event Perspective

*In order that an important invention may be successful, two
conditions must be favorable. First: It must be possible, that is, the
scientific principle on which it is founded must be known. Second:
the invention must be wanted.*

— Henry (1886, p. 306)

After reading this chapter, you should be able to define the following
terms and provide the information requested in the study guide below.

TERMS

Technology   Sequential data
Models   Conditional probability
Interbehavior   Field system
Static data

STUDY GUIDE

1. Explain and illustrate the relationship between the terms *science* and
   technology.
2. List and discuss the three important aspects of providing scientific
   models for research and development.

3. Provide an illustration that highlights the differences between and potential benefits of using questionnaire data, static behavioral measures, and sequential data when studying interactive situations.
4. List and discuss the four education and social science research trends that may benefit from use of an interbehavioral or sequential analysis.
5. Describe what is meant by *conditional probability* in relation to time-based sequential data measures.
6. Provide a simple unconditional and conditional probability statistical illustration using example data.
7. Explain the importance of multiple event thinking to the study of situations using behavior analysis methods.
8. Discuss the three primary benefits of computer technology in data collection and analysis activities.
9. Discuss the advantages of, and some cautions regarding, computer-assisted data collection and analysis activity.
10. List and discuss the four main reasons for using computer-based approaches with applied behavior analysis methods.
11. Explain the assumptions and limitations of conducting direct observation and behavior analysis activity.

Joseph Henry, one of the leading North American pioneers of the scientific and industrial revolution at the turn of the 19th century, was aware that in order for scientific knowledge to be of value, it must make a positive difference in people's lives. This practical difference relates specifically to the relationship between science and technology. And this relationship is particularly important to behavior analysis, given the methodological priority it places on research information's need for positive application and therapeutic value for the individuals to be served by such research.

FROM SCIENCE TO TECHNOLOGY

The practical relationship between science and technology has been described by Moxley (1989) as symmetrical, with the two activities ideally interacting in a reciprocal, two-way relationship. This concept is integral to behavior analysis methods, for the primary intent of studying phenomena behaviorally is to provide data-supported technologies that will be of therapeutic benefit to a particular individual or group. Also, the provision of a particular technology can stimulate additional research into other, related efforts to provide even more effective procedures for those for whom the original technology was designed and implemented. Some of the education research literature provides a nice illustration. Sometimes education research is a source for practical technological applications, and sometimes the practices of a particular instructional technology are a source for extending research efforts. However, the character of each enterprise has a lot to do with the way that relationship functions in our culture. A brief discussion of the nature of this practical relationship will lay a foundation for what we consider to be reasonable expectations for how applied behavior analysis as a research method (and therefore as a scientific undertaking) may impact on professional practice (a technological venture).

Science is the quest for additional knowledge. The term also implies the observation of phenomena in such a way as to produce data with a high degree of intersubjective agreement, or objectivity (Neale & Liebert, 1973). Further, the relative objectivity of science presupposes such concepts as operational measurability, reliability and replicability of description and explanation, and systematic testability. Accordingly, there are many characteristics inherent in the process of doing science that bear on its relationship with technology. Among these are its slow, patient, tentative nature and largely inductive approach to gaining new information. Due to these attributes, the time lag between a scientific discovery and its practical application can be quite lengthy. Mosteller (1981) has illustrated this point by showing that lemon juice was discovered as a cure for scurvy in 1601, almost 200 years before the British Navy began to use citrus juice regularly for the cure and prevention of the disease. Further, another 70 years passed before this method effectively eradicated scurvy in the mercantile marine.

The long latency period between discovery and application is not always something to be deplored. History is replete with examples of technological applications that have been mixed blessings (e.g., television, nuclear power, and the revolution in chemical engineering). Sometimes technological advances have even been harmful (e.g., the widespread proliferation of infant formula as a substitute for breast feeding in the third world during the 1970s). Oftentimes the loose connection between science and technology surfaces in the education and social sciences as well. Pointed evidence of this has been provided, for example, in the revision and re-revision process experienced by mainstream public education over the past three decades. Unks' (1986) scathing remarks concerning the typical state of mainstream education reform efforts make this point quite well:

> It is no news to those who watch educational policy that there is an abundance of repair-people around [researchers] . . . who [each] promise that he or she has "the answer" to our school problems. We have seen it all before. How many ideas [i.e., scientific discoveries] have had their way . . . promising everything and delivering very little—movable seats, audio-visual materials, team teaching, programmed instruction, and many more? Some were harmful, others innocuous, and a few were silly—deserving of the public ridicule that they ultimately received. (p. 242)

Although science is a slow and often painstaking process, it remains important to disseminate data collection and analysis methods that help in making explicit connections between scientific discovery and professional technological practice. If such an endeavor is not undertaken, then scholars and professional practitioners alike are left with information that is lacking in measurability, reliability, and testability. Without a scientific foundation, the quality of what passes for technology would be questionable at best and detrimental at worst.

Many scholars and practitioners (for a variety of articles on the topic refer to Gardner et al., 1994, or Morris et al., 2001) have argued in favor of making greater professional use of the principles and practices that have emerged from the science of behavior to help strengthen the connection between science and technology. A first task, however, is to understand and facilitate a proper relationship between knowledge production and its practical application. *Technology* may be broadly defined as the application and extension of the knowledge gained from the scientific enterprise (Bohme, Van Den Daele, & Krohn, 1978). By its very nature, technology is closely tied to science, although it is primarily concerned with professional practice. In other words, technology needs to accurately reflect the knowledge gained from research and must also be experienced as user-friendly by those for whom it was designed. Although this relationship is a fairly straightforward one, there remains a longstanding outcry by professionals in the education, social, and psychological sciences for a mechanism for strengthening the tie between research and practical application. Research on knowledge utilization, for example, indicates that many practicing professionals in these areas tend to rely primarily on colleagues and other local sources of information rather than on the knowledge disseminated from scientific investigation (Kazdin, 1982; Landrum, 1997; Lloyd, 1992). As a result, researchers normally see practitioners as uninformed, and practitioners see researchers as out of touch with reality. To bridge this gap, researchers need accessible aids to properly conceptualize and appropriately implement scientific findings in practical settings (Richardson, 1990).

Lawson (1985) has suggested that researchers and practitioners have different knowledge systems and that what practitioners prefer is not scholarly scientific knowledge but working knowledge that blends selectively perceived scientific knowledge with professional ideology and experiential knowledge. Others in the education profession have suggested that for research to influence practice, the two must be more closely connected with research questions emerging from practice and research designs that address the contextual realities of practical situations (Berliner, 1986; The Holmes Group, 1990; Lawson, 1990). If, as researchers, we are to have an impact on practice, perhaps we need to abandon the traditional one-way, hierarchical relationship that exclusively regards the researcher as the disseminator of information and the practitioner as the consumer of that information. Instead, the symmetrical relationship between science and technology ought to become more functionally tied (refer to Sharpe, Lounsbery, & Templin, 1997, for a detailed discussion of one such symmetrical model). This approach would allow practitioners to use easily conceptualized scientific models, and it would provide the scientific community with the feedback and technological resources to continue the quest for additional knowledge.

We have established behavior analysis research methods as scientific in character, by virtue of their largely objective use of observable data and with regard to the patient way the method inductively generates knowledge. Another challenge, then, is to provide support for behavior analysis data generation utility in terms of technological application. This is the final challenge and the ultimate test for any scientific enterprise. In other words, for a researcher's scientific efforts to be thought complete, it is important for him or her to be able to answer the question "How have our data gathering and analysis efforts impacted on technological implementation by a variety of professional practitioners?"

We feel that the answer to this question lies in the construction of simplified and readily understood models of scientific knowledge generation, complete with a clear terminology with which users can make appropriate, feasible, and readily understandable applications of research. Most scientists perceive *models* as simplified analogies that enable theoretical knowledge to be visualized and understood more easily. Models are also thought to have three important functions (Schmidt, 1988). First, due to their capacity to enable visualization, they suggest predictions that might be overlooked using only deductive logic. These predictions then suggest further experimentation. Second, models are excellent instructional devices. Finally, models are an ideal vehicle for lay application of relatively complex scientific knowledge. They have a unique capacity in this regard for the organization and simplification of scientific data. One of the intentions of this book is, therefore, to provide a readily understandable direct observation research model founded in the principles and practice of behavior and sequential analysis.

DIFFERENCES IN ASSESSMENT: MODELING AN INTERBEHAVIORAL LENS

As direct observation methods further develop and add to existing data collection and analysis strategies, a detailed explanation in the form of a data-based illustration or model is in order. We feel that the scientific act of quantifying things using direct observation data gathering approaches is an activity that should enjoy equal exposure with other data collection and analysis methodologies in the applied research communities. Given some of the criticisms of direct observation and behavior analysis that we have mentioned, many researchers in this area have searched for and developed methods that may provide a more capable direct observational lens. Even early scholars working during the formative years of a thoroughgoing applied behavior analysis methodology as applied to education and social science concerns (e.g., Rosenshine & Furst, 1973) articulated a cautionary perspective with regard to methods that focused on the descriptive counting of behaviors and setting events in particular situations. They voiced uncertainty with respect to the ability of traditional behavior analysis methods to discriminate between relatively more or less effective professional practices within and across particular situations. This caution included the perspective that it may be possible that the discrete characteristics of particular behaviors and events may be so complex and idiosyncratic to particular applied situations that specific interactions may not be adequately described using these techniques, thus making generalization efforts difficult for those engaged in prescribing more broadly based therapeutic recommendations. This is similar to the more contemporary argument by Doyle (1990) that although quantitative knowledge of specific professional practices is important, what has oftentimes occurred through applied behavior analysis methods is the counting of only a few behaviors in isolation and the inappropriate fragmenting of a larger interactive process into discrete elements that are presumed to affect target behaviors or events in some causal way. To avoid rendering the study and evaluation of education and social science settings simplistically generic, and to ensure that behavior analytic approaches remain in the mainstream of applied science, developing alternative methods of direct observational data collection and analysis may be necessary that are capable of quantifying the repeated occurrence of multiple variables and their many setting-specific interactions. This latter recommendation is what has largely comprised development efforts by researchers using inter-behavioral and sequential methods who work in the area of direct observation and applied behavior analysis. In addition, recent developments in the area of computer technologies have significantly added to direct observation research capabilities and have facilitated the development of alternative data collection and analysis techniques once thought of in only conceptual terms. Computer-based innovation has facilitated the contributions from pioneers in the field of behavior analysis concerning what can and what should conceivably be observed (e.g., Heward & Cooper, 1992; Morris, 1992; Skinner, 1968; Sulzer-Azaroff & Mayer, 1991), more capable measurement systems that have been developed in the area (e.g., Bakeman & Gottman, 1997), and methodological and statistical applications for quantifying time-based sequences of behavior have been developed (e.g., Gottman & Roy, 1990; Ray & Delprato, 1989; Sharpe & Hawkins, 1992a).

Education research provides an important illustration of an *interbehavioral* and sequential lens. These methodological developments in direct observational practice are important to the study of settings such as education classrooms due to the challenges of studying multiple participants within highly interactive settings in which multiple behaviors and events are repeatedly occurring. At the first level of educational analysis, an approach might be to ask a teacher to fill out a qualitatively oriented questionnaire (e.g., Likert scale normative data or open-ended response data) and from the responses of that teacher to provide information on a topic such as job performance or job-related satisfaction by assigning individual scores to the teacher response data gathered. This type of information might then provide general indicators of possible relationships among job performance and relative satisfaction with experiential dimensions (such as a teacher's past professional and personal experiences or particular work setting characteristics). This type of data gathering and analysis effort is probably most frequently cited in the education and social science literature; however, this type of *static data* measure (i.e., a measure that does not include how events are connected to one another in time) does not tell us much about how a particular teacher interacts with his or her student clientele on a regular basis, nor does it tell us much about how those interactions impact on the relative quality of professional behavior (in terms of educational effectiveness or relative personal satisfaction with professional roles). An appealing research and evaluation alternative to learning more about a particular teacher, therefore, may be to describe and analyze the dynamics of how a teacher interacts with his or her students on an immediate and daily basis.

When a researcher uses a direct quantitative observation method to study a particular teacher, the potential contribution of an *interbehavioral* or *sequential* lens (i.e., a measurement focus that makes the relationships in time among behaviors and events explicit) to the data collection and analysis process becomes readily apparent when it is used in addition to the more traditional static measures of the characteristics of teacher and student behavior. When studying a teacher in a classroom situation, for example, a *static* measure (i.e., the discrete characteristics of behaviors and events themselves, such as the relative number of questioning, instructional, feedback, or interpersonal behaviors used) could be collected and the percentage of class time that students are engaged in behaviors (such as skill practice, management and organization, waiting for an opportunity to interact with materials, or active responding) could also be measured. This approach is in line with most behavior analysis techniques and is an approach that would provide important information regarding how a particular teacher and his or her students tend to use their time in a particular educational situation. In addition, many of these kinds of immediately occurring behaviors have been documented as highly correlated with long-term measures of learning and achievement in particular subject matters and skills to be learned. They may, therefore, be used as relatively effective indicators of the general effectiveness of a particular educational situation. For example, a variety of behavior analysis research has been conducted that focuses on one or two potentially effective teacher behaviors as independent variables and uses a single measure of student behavior such as ALT (Academic Learning Time; Metzler, 1989). Although some research designs have been developed to examine the behavior of more than one person, rarely have these types of studies focused on the time-based character of behavior← →environment interactions among multiple individuals (Wampold, 1992).

As such, we agree with Doyle (1990), Kantor (1969), Morris (1992), and others that four recommended research and evaluation trends in the education and social sciences are apparent, and that these trends are compatible with the more capable data collection and analysis tools being developed in the direct observation and behavior analysis arenas. First, behavior← →behavior and behavior← →environment relationships are a very complex set of phenomena that need to be more thoroughly and inclusively examined. Second, emphasis must be placed on ecological validity, or analysis of the functional differences across a variety of settings in which certain relationships are relatively more or less productive. Third, analysis emphasis must be placed not just on the discrete characteristics of behavior and environment events (e.g., number or frequency, percentage of experimental time, rate, etc.) but also, in a complete analysis, on the form and character of the multiple stimuli and response relationships among multiple behaviors and events as they actually occur in time in particular situations. Fourth, emphasis must be placed on the discovery of behavior← → behavior and behavior← →environment relationships that have been repeatedly documented as having predictive therapeutic ends within and across particular professional situations.

This brings us to explanation of the appeal of an *interbehavioral* or sequential addition to the direct observation of behavior in applied settings. This appeal has partly to do with the inability of the more static approach just illustrated to always fully explain the explicit time-based interactive connection between what a particular teacher does in a specific educational situation and how a particular student or group of students responds to the behaviors of that teacher. For example, documenting how often an instructional or organizational behavior is used by a teacher, or the relative amount of time a particular student devotes to skill practice, does not tell us much about how each teacher and student behavior is explicitly connected in time-based sequence and may therefore be functionally related. Discrete characteristics of teacher or student behaviors collected without regard for the time-based connection among other behaviors and events also does not tell us much about the immediate instructional and social interactions a particular teacher may use to either facilitate desirable student prac-tices or inhibit undesirable student activities. The type of data-based information gathering that is recommended by the interbehavioral conceptual contributions of Kantor (1969, 1979), for example, and made possible by the sequential methods contributions of individuals such as Ray (Ray & Delprato, 1989) and the authors of this text (Sharpe, 1997a; Sharpe & Hawkins, 1992a) are the type of data gathering that may be used to answer the types of information gathering needs just illustrated. These individuals recommend that although study of the characteristics of individual behaviors to discover more about the interactive relationships among humans is important and productive, there is another dimension of human interaction that is as important to explore—the transactions or connections among behaviors that are studied using time-based measures.

A time-based analysis is performed not due to a need to alter a typ-ical behavior analytic observational coding system in some way but due to the need for adding an alternative measure to be used in such a way that the data to be recorded are conducive to capturing behavior sequences. *Sequential data* provide an additional level of *interbehavioral* information about an interactive setting under observation, and such data provide information that is not accessible without specifically including a sequential observation lens in the data collection and analysis process. In education research, a sequential data set could, for example, help answer questions about just what students tend to do after being exposed to certain types of instruction and whether those teacher behaviors helped to improve student skill practice. Sequential data may also help in answering how certain students might charac-teristically respond to certain types of interpersonal interactions. Answers to these types of sequentially based questions require a dif-ferent type of observational lens and an additional way of collecting and looking at observational data. Although nonsequential, or *static*, behavior data can provide information related to how much instruc-tion or how many interpersonal interactions should be used by a teacher for general effectiveness (based, for example, on a general per-centage of student skill practice time), sequential data substantially help in making explicit the specific functional relationship of how a variety of student responses are emitted over time as a function of time-based exposure to different kinds of teacher behaviors.

For several years during and after Kantor's contribution to research and practice in the social sciences, the major criticism of his work was that his recommendations for behavior analysis methodology remained at the conceptual stage—without specific data collection and analysis strategies to support those recommendations. In other words, although an argument that favored looking into the sequential nature of behavior← →environment interactions was rigorously constructed, and many researchers and clinicians saw the potential importance of this argument, an appealing and user-friendly means of collecting and using this type of data remained largely unavailable. This is no longer the case. Computer-based procedures are now available to be applied to observe and analyze highly interactive applied settings. This study involves an explicit focus on what behaviors and events tend to precede or follow what other behaviors or events, and which of these sequential connections tend to be most productive in meeting particular educational or therapeutic ends. Some general illustrations may help the reader visualize just what we mean by an alternative lens.

Illustrations From Education

The following illustration, based largely on Crosbie's (1993) work on time-series analysis as it relates to applied behavior analysis data, is suitable for both computer-based collection of time-series data and machine transduction of data (in which the data collected are automatically detected or recorded without the need for a human observer). Many examples of the latter method can be found in recent issues of the *Journal of the Experimental Analysis of Behavior* and the *Journal of Applied Behavior Analysis,* in which study is focused on animal behavior in a structured laboratory setting. The following diagram provides the focus of the illustration:

and so on...

In this illustration, particular behaviors of interest are listed in the left column; moving across the illustration from left to right the passage of time is represented, typically noted with a particular metric measure (e.g., seconds, minutes, etc.); and onset and offset of the behaviors is demarcated with a raised line in between them to indicate the respective start and stop time of each incidence of each behavior in the ongoing record. Using this illustration, a traditional behavior analysis might focus on a measure of teacher instruction (behavior 1) and record both the number of occurrences and the length of each occurrence. In addition, a measure of student responding (behavior 4) might be recorded in the same way. This illustration adds, however, a measure of time, or an explicit quantification of when each behavior occurs relative to the time placement of that behavior in relation to the time-based occurrences of all of the others contained in a descriptive category system. From this representation a variety of measures may be extracted, including traditional measures (of number, individual and aggregate duration, percentage of total experimental time, and so on) and measures that specify the time-based occurrence of certain behaviors relative to others (e.g., number and conditional probability of time-based occurrence). Viewing our diagram again, it becomes apparent that teacher instruction (behavior 1) is consistently preceded by behavior 2 (perhaps the incorrect practice of a student) and followed by behavior 4 (student responding). Also, the time-based behavioral cluster of $2 \rightarrow 1 \rightarrow 4$ tends to occur in the presence of ongoing behavior 3 and to a lesser extent behavior 5 (perhaps particular setting events). The subcluster of $2 \rightarrow 1$ also consistently occurs in the presence of behavior 6 (perhaps a secondary instructional aid such as a focus on overhead materials). From this type of illustration, it becomes clear that any situation in which behaviors and events are ongoing and highly interactive may be more completely described, and the potential relationships among behaviors and events may be made more explicit, through the use of a time-based measure of behavioral occurrence.

At this point, some additional data-based illustrations may help the reader visualize how direct observational data may differ when a sequential or time-based component is added to a behavior analysis effort. Experimental and applied researchers interested in various behavior-behavior and behavior-environment relationships have consistently stated that the aim of behavior analysis has been the prediction and control of behavior through describing the quantitative characteristics of individual observable events and applying that knowledge. However, throughout the research history of behavior analysis, provided in Chapter 1, a predominant experimental research emphasis has been on demonstrating the effect of potentially controlling events (*potentially* is defined here as a rather loose connective thread that is largely assumed between documented stimulus and response activities due to a lack of time-based connective data) on particular client behaviors within a particular experimental or training situation, typically in a very narrowly prescribed linear or mechanistic fashion (Delprato, 1992; Morris, 1991). Although perhaps viewed as a subtle difference at first glance, a more and more frequently seen and potentially appealing and productive approach to the analysis of behavior is one that emphasizes the discovery of the multiple conditions that tend to control various behaviors and how one may go about productively altering those conditions toward therapeutic, behavior change–oriented ends. In addition, and related to the emphasis that a field or interbehavioral perspective on the analysis of behavior brings to the mix (see Einstein & Infeld, 1938; Lichtenstein, 1983, and Ray & Delprato, 1989, for detailed discussions of respective field and interbehavioral theory), is an analysis focus on the probable interactions in time-based sequence among behaviors and events.

A series of articles from the education literature (Sharpe & Hawkins, 1992a, 1992c; Sharpe, 1997a; Sharpe, Hawkins, & Lounsbery, 1998; Sharpe & Lounsbery, 1998) serve to specifically illustrate the appeal of adding a sequential data component to a direct observation of behavior effort.

A Descriptive Example

Data from a study by Sharpe and Lounsbery (1998), with additional discrete and sequential data comparisons by Sharpe, Hawkins, and Lounsbery (1998), provide one example at a descriptive level. This body of work involved the behavioral description of undergraduate teachers-in-training using both static characteristics of select teacher behaviors and sequential data related to how those same behaviors tended to follow one another over time. Essentially, both static and sequential behavior data were provided from the same experimental settings to demonstrate the additional information made available by a computer-based sequential behavior analysis observational lens, and to provide implications and applications for additional research as a function of using this type of observational lens in the study of teacher training and educational practice. Illustrative data are contained in Figures 3.1, 3.2, and 3.3 that respectively show static data of specific teacher behaviors, sequential data of those teacher behaviors, and related static data on select student behaviors.

The four teacher-trainees represented in Figures 3.1 and 3.2 included four undergraduates enrolled in a one-semester practice teaching experience. Data on student performance were also collected in this body of studies (as shown in Figure 3.3). The practice teaching situation was conducted in an actual school setting and was supervised by university faculty using computer-based data collection and analysis tools designed to provide static and time-based teacher and student data measures. The data representations in Figures 3.1 and 3.2 show the same teacher-trainees during the same practice teaching episodes and included teacher-trainee receipt of qualitative feedback only during baseline conditions, sequential or time-based behavior feedback during the experimental phase of the data illustrations, and then no feedback of any kind during the maintenance phase of the data illustrations (for a complete discussion of the different forms of teacher-trainee feedback and the specific procedures for static and sequential behavior data collection, analysis, and presentation as teacher feedback, see Sharpe, Hawkins, & Ray, 1995, or Sharpe, Lounsbery, & Bahls, 1997). Figure 3.3 shows student data during these same teaching episodes under observation. Teacher-trainee and student data are presented over the course of the entire semester, with the circled days on each figure representing when each participant received the sequential behavior feedback protocol.

The static observational data shown in Figure 3.1 include numerical counts of Instruction, Specific Observation, Feedback, and Encouragement for each entire observed practice teaching episode illustrated. These behaviors are clearly representative of traditional direct observation studies in education and are behaviors that have been documented as highly correlated with long-range student achievement indicators. As the data contained in Figure 3.1 demonstrate, very little change appears to be occurring in relation to a variety of visual inspection techniques (see the Visual Inspection section in Chapter 9 that details visual methods of analyzing data graphs). If a particular researcher was content to use only the analysis of these types

Figure 3.1   A discrete view of number of occurrence of select teacher practices using traditional observational measures related to effective instruction (Instruction, Specific Observation, Feedback, and Encouragement)

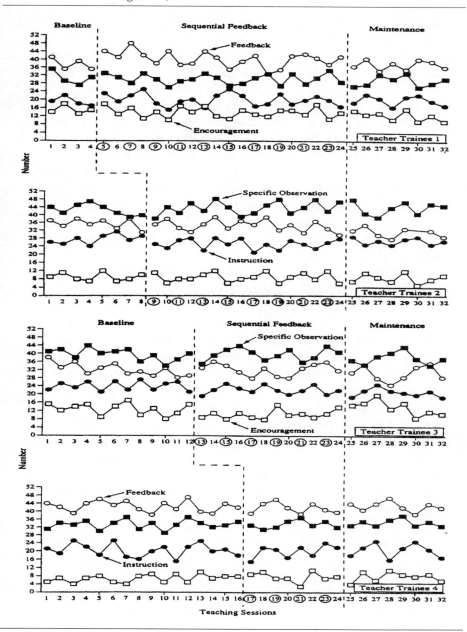

SOURCE: Sharpe, Hawkins, and Lounsbery (1998). Reprinted by permission

of static behavioral measures in his or her behavior analysis of these teachers-in-training, that researcher might reach a conclusion of no effect or no change.

Figure 3.2 provides sequential behavior data on these same four teacher-trainees operating in the same settings as in the data representations in Figure 3.1. The alternative measures of Instructional Opportunities (IO) and Appropriate Instructional Action (AIA), taken in the time-based sequential context of IO incidents, were used to generate the data shown in Figure 3.2. These measures are global in nature and provide only one of many potential illustrations of variables designed to focus explicitly on the sequential connections among behaviors and events of interest. IO incidents were defined as any student activity in which a particular student or small group of students was practicing a skill to be learned and was either experiencing difficulty executing the skill correctly or was engaged in prolonged periods of trying to figure out how to execute the skill to be practiced. AIA was defined as including (a) teacher-trainee provision of a particular behavior or set of behaviors to a student in time-based proximity to an IO incident, and (b) return to successful skill practice by the student receiving behavioral interactions from the teacher. The sequential data contained in Figure 3.2 were recorded in time-based sequence (see the BEST software flyer provided with this text for detail of the data collection and analysis tools used in this body of studies) by recording each incidence of an IO and then recording whether or not the teacher-trainee faced with that IO responded according to the recommended practices (i.e., emitted an AIA) of the cooperating teacher and the university supervisor who observed that lesson. In other words, the critical difference between the data in Figure 3.1 and that in Figure 3.2 was this: In the static data of Figure 3.1, no explicit connection was made between the teacher-trainee and student performance, whereas in the sequential data of Figure 3.2, a direct time-based connection was made explicit between a student having difficulty with the subject matter skills to be learned and how the teacher-trainee responded when faced with that difficulty.

This lack of explicit connection remains true even when static data are provided on student behavior. Figure 3.3, for example, provides data on representative students who were operating within the respective teacher-trainee settings represented in Figures 3.1 and 3.2. Target behaviors included the traditional measures of Activity Engagement, Organization and Off-Task that have been documented as correlated

Figure 3.2   A sequential view of teacher practices using number of appropriate instructional actions (AIA) relative to number of classroom occasions when appropriate action is necessary (IO)

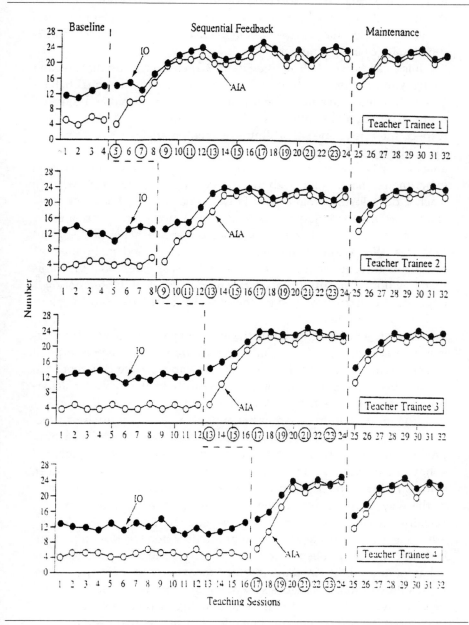

SOURCE: Sharpe, Hawkins, and Lounsbery (1998). Reprinted by permission

with the relative effectiveness of an instructional situation in relation to student learning and achievement. Although it is clear that the behaviors shown in Figure 3.3 are changing in positive directions over time, it is not as clear just what teacher practices, setting events, or outside-of-class variables may be functionally related to (or to some, "causing") those changes in student behavior.

It is clear, however, from the Figure 3.2 representation that striking changes in how teacher-trainees sequenced their instructional behaviors in the context of student behaviors (i.e., IOs) occurred as a function of the experimental treatments provided in this body of work. In this respect, the importance of adding a sequential analysis lens to behavior analysis study is demonstrated. Through the use of a sequential analysis of behavior, the assumptions that many direct observation experiments have made—about the relationship between what a teacher does instructionally and how the behaviors of students may change as a function of such teacher practices—are overcome by making explicit time-based connections between teacher and student practices. When comparing the static data contained in Figures 3.1 and 3.3 to the sequential data in Figure 3.2, it is apparent that the information gathered in support of a particular experimental intervention is dependent to a great degree on the observational lens used to collect and analyze that data.

In our teacher education illustration, using a traditional static measure to assess changes in teaching practice due to a particular type of teacher training method did not yield any appreciable differences in teacher behavior over the course of a study that exposed teacher-trainees to multiple forms of feedback on their teaching. In other words, simply counting the number of times a particular teaching practice was used yielded little information on possible changes in teaching practice due to a particular educational treatment. When a sequential behavior lens was used to analyze the same teaching settings, however, some striking differences in teacher-trainee behavior due to changes in the way feedback was given to teacher-trainees became apparent. Looking at teacher-trainee practices sequentially (i.e., scrutinizing what teacher-trainees tended to do or not do when faced with particular student behaviors) showed that they tended to alter their teaching behavior around the IOs that presented themselves in their classrooms. In this illustration, a time-based sequential analysis of teacher-trainee behavior yielded important information that would not have been uncovered if just a set of static behavioral measures had been used.

Figure 3.3   A discrete view of percentage of class time devoted to select student practices using traditional observational measures related to learning and achievement (Activity Engagement, Organization, and Off-Task)

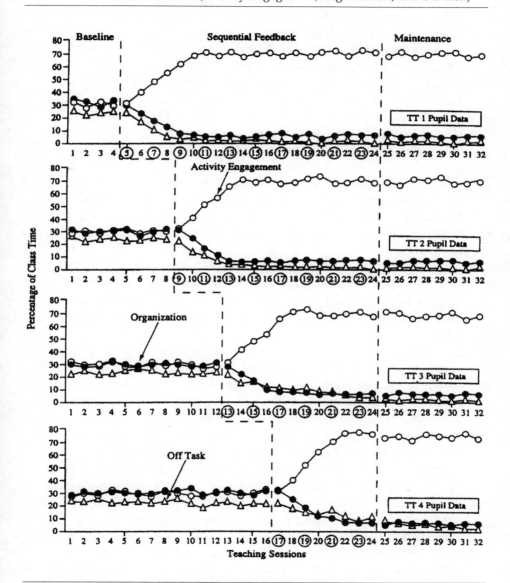

SOURCE: Sharpe and Lounsbery (1997). Reprinted by permission

A Statistical Example

Another illustration of the potential appeal of a sequential lens when conducting behavior analysis study can be provided in the area of statistical analysis. This example is founded on the work of Bakeman and Gottman (1986, 1997), and Gottman and Roy (1990), from which a variety of recommended methodological application illustrations have been provided in education (e.g., Sharpe, 1997a), psychology (e.g., Espinosa, 1992), and the area of ethology and animal behavior research (e.g., Astley et al., 1991; Ray & Delprato, 1989). The use of statistical models to describe and analyze the time-based sequential organization of behavior has frequently appeared in the literature over the past three decades. The methods have included, for example, Markov chain analysis (Chatfield & Lemon, 1970), information theory (Bakeman, 1978), cross-spectral analysis (Gottman, 1979a), grammatical inference (Rodger & Rosebrugh, 1979), and the most frequently used sequential behavior analyses founded on Bakeman and Gottman's statistical developments.

Our statistical example is linked to probability theory or *conditional probability* measurement, in which mathematical equations are developed to make quantitatively explicit preceding and succeeding behavioral events in time-based relation to a particular target behavior of interest.

Such an effort is founded on Skinner's three term contingency equation of Stimulus← →Response← →Consequence, and it adds a double headed arrow to the equation to signify the potential bidirectionality of behavior relationships and the possibility of multiple stimuli, responses, and consequences (i.e., instead of simply one stimulus under study or one response, there may exist 1-N potential stimuli and responses that require analysis). The concept of conditional probability quantification of time-based behavior-event relationships provides an additional dimension of rigor to the visual and descriptive inspection of sequential data provided in Figure 3.2.

The concept of probability in mathematics and physics has experienced a long history, beginning with analysis of simple games of chance during the early 1600s. Put rather simplistically, *conditional probability* simply provides a quantification mechanism for relatively more or less probable outcomes within a set of all possible outcomes in a particular situation and given a finite set of possible circumstances. For example, flipping a coin has two possible outcomes and rolling a traditional die has six possible outcomes. If the wind is blowing in a certain way, or if a die is weighted (a typical method of cheating at the gaming tables), then the probability of a coin ending up on a certain side, or the probability of rolling a certain number, is increased or decreased based on an impacting circumstance. From these possible outcomes, and the variety of circumstances that surround each possible outcome, a method of determining the relative probability of each outcome must be developed. Another example may be taken from those who raise horses. If a breeder has white horses and black horses, and the white horses eat more oats than the black horses, he may want to know why so as to better predict how much oats to grow or purchase. One easy explanation is that this particular breeder has more white horses than black horses, though each individual horse eats the same amount. Another explanation is that even though the same numbers of white and black horses are in the stable, the white horses are larger or more active and hence require more food. Many other possible explanations exist, but the point remains that scientific discovery of the reasons why one set of horses eats more than another, and then determining a conditional probability for those reasons, may be helpful in recommending to the breeder what his future behavior should be (in this case, how much oats to purchase).

The most frequently used conceptualization of probability theory in relation to the analysis of behavior-event occurrences is that of *relative frequency theory* (von Mises, 1964). Simply put, a collective of possible event sequences is defined and from this collective numerical probabilities are assigned based on the conditions of particular occurrences in relation to the defined collective. In other words, probability is assigned as a function of the number of times a particular behavior or event occurs in relation to the total number of times it could conceivably have occurred. The predominant point of view with regard to a statistical approach to quantifying behavior-event sequences is that probability is a relative or conditional frequency count (Johnson & Morris, 1987). This view also assumes that behavior is dynamic and requires development over periods of time and thus that behavior occurrence is time dependent. Therefore, in relation to direct observation and behavior analysis efforts that use the statistical quantification of time-based behavioral occurrences, statistical probability may be applied to the analysis of behaviors and events as they occur after one another in time-based sequence. Essentially, a method is derived to determine the relative or conditional probability with which certain events may precede or succeed certain other events, given information related to the number of possible events that are operating in a certain situation and the relative tendency for certain events to precede or follow certain other events in certain circumstances. While collection and analysis of the characteristics of certain behaviors provides important information to the understanding of certain phenomena (e.g., how much instruction or teacher reinforcement tends to be present before a student behavior is modified), sequential data from a statistical base provide information related to the quantitative discovery of the probability with which certain behaviors will be present or absent given certain time-based circumstances (e.g., how different student behaviors tend to be present as a specific function of time-based proximity with particular teacher practices in particular educational situations).

Studies from the education literature (Sharpe, 1997a; Sharpe & Hawkins, 1992a, 1992c; Sharpe, Hawkins, & Ray, 1995) provide illustrations of a statistical approach to the analysis of the sequential character of educational behavior. In these materials, it is argued that one person's behavior is both a response to another's past behavior and a stimulus for yet another's future behavior and should therefore be examined sequentially. For example, a student's off-task behavior may be a response to a request from that student's teacher, as well as a stimulus to another student's withdrawal from the ongoing activity *and* a stimulus to teacher behaviors designed to curtail the off-task episode. Therefore, while two teachers operating in two very different settings may exhibit similar numbers, rates, or class time percentages of certain behaviors, they may exhibit very different teacher-student interactional patterns when their behavior is described sequentially. In an education research setting, then, it may be the description and analysis of the sequential nature of the behavior between a teacher and his or her students that may allow discovery of some important therapeutic relationships in the particular classroom setting under observation.

In the simplest case, using a sequential data collection lens enables the researcher to answer the question of whether one behavior follows another behavior more often than would be expected by chance. For example, the question "Does a particular student's off-task behavior increase the probability of a particular teacher's discipline practice and, if so, what does that teacher do in sequence to curtail future incidents of off-task behavior?" may be explicitly answered. In order to discuss how a question about behavior sequence might be answered, it is first important for us to introduce how this type of data might be collected.

In addition to traditional measures of the characteristics of individual behaviors and events (such as number, rate, or percentage of experimental time), a measure of a start time and stop time must also be recorded for each behavior occurrence in a data record. Adding this type of information provides a time-based sequence of behavior-environment occurrences from which all sequentially based statistical analyses may be extracted. Sample data from a comparison of an experienced public school teacher versus a novice (Sharpe & Hawkins, 1992c) helps illustrate the utility of a sequential data lens. For the sake of simplifying our illustration, if we suppose that observational focus is on only teacher instruction (event A) and student engagement in the subject matter (event B), then a representative sequential 4-minute data segment for a novice teacher might look something like the following:

ABAABABBABBAAABABBABAAABBAAABB

If we further assume for the sake of illustration that each behavior occurrence was of the same duration, a simple numerical count or *non-*sequential behavior analysis would yield that A occurred 16 times and B occurred 14 times. A sequential analysis of this same data segment shows (1) an unconditional probability of A to be p(A) = 16/30 = .53, (2) an unconditional probability of B to be p(B) = 14/30 = .47 and most important, as will soon be demonstrated, (3) a conditional probability of B given the occurrence of A immediately before B to be p(B/A) = .56. The intent of a sequential analysis here is to reduce the uncertainty of B's occurrence, given the knowledge of the immediately preceding event in a time-based sequential chain of events.

If we then compare an experienced teacher's sequential behavior chain, which includes the same behavioral events as those of the novice, emitted in a teaching situation similar to that of the novice teacher, the importance of sequential information is well illustrated. Suppose that in studying our experienced teacher our focus is also only on the behaviors of teacher instruction (A) and student engagement in the subject matter (B). If this is the case, then the following chain segment may be recorded for the experienced teacher for the same representative 4-minute time period (see Sharpe & Hawkins, 1992c):

ABABAABABABABAABABBABABABABABA

Observing this experienced teacher's observational data by traditional behavior analysis methods, A again occurred 16 times and B occurred

14 times. Stopping at this point in the analysis would yield no differences in novice and experienced teacher behavior. Viewing the unconditional probability of A and B (p(A) = 16/30 = .53; p(B) = 14/30 = .47) also yields no differences across the experienced and the novice teacher's data sequences. What is important to illustrate, however, is that analyzing the experienced teacher's data sequentially using conditional probability statistics provides a marked observed difference as follows: The conditional probability of the occurrence of B, given that A has occurred just prior to B, is the proportion of times that B occurs immediately after A—A occurs 16 times, and of those times B occurs immediately after A 13 times. Thus, the conditional probability of B occurring dependent upon A is p(B/A) = 13/16 = .84. Clearly, .84 is markedly different from the novice conditional and sequential probability of .56. On closer sequential analysis of the experienced versus novice teacher data this illustration draws from, potentially productive differences in the form and character of a complex variety of teacher and student behaviors, and the changing setting events that surround these teacher and student behaviors, might be more capably analyzed. For example, teacher observation and feedback practices in the time-based context of the variable quality of student subject matter engagement, the relative proximity of the teacher in relationship to the student involved in certain teacher-student interactions, and a host of other similar potentialities may become evident.

Although we only provide very introductory examples here, adding a sequential capability to the analysis of multiple occurrences of behavior-behavior and behavior-environment interactions as they naturally occur in time-based sequence allows quantitative description of the many different interaction patterns among different participants operating in various situations. In other words, to the degree that one interactive participant's behavior is dependent on the immediately preceding behaviors of another participant, that participant's behavioral response probabilities are altered as a function of the types of behaviors and environmental cues also operating in the setting under observation. In addition, a sequential statistical analysis is not limited to only the immediately preceding and succeeding events that surround a particular behavior of interest.

Using similar sequential logic and applied statistics, one can provide a quite complex and sophisticated analysis of the conditional probabilities of a variety of behaviors and events that tend to occur before and after an event of interest, and the conditional probabilities of events that occur at time lags other than those that immediately precede or succeed that particular event of interest. Complex mathematical modeling of just how each behavior in an observation system interacts in time-based sequence with others comprises a full-blown statistically based sequential analysis. In the complete mathematical equations, behavior-event probabilities need not necessarily be limited to the effect of the immediately preceding or succeeding event but, instead, may be dependent on much more complex patterns of interactive activity—patterns that a complete sequential analysis is capable of describing and analyzing using contemporary software-based tools and that the literature has begun hypothesizing as potential characteristics of effective professional practices across a variety of disciplines.

As a statistical model, *sequential analysis* focuses on the problem of identifying and quantifying immediate and more distant relationships among behaviors and events as they occur in time-based sequence. It provides a means for determining, in setting-specific ways, the probable effects one behavior or event may have on another based on their repeatedly close appearances together in time. Step 1 of the model is to compute the unconditional probability of occurrence for each of the behaviors and events defined within a particular observation system by dividing the number of occurrences of a particular event by the total number of occurrences of all events contained in the observation system being used to collect data. Step 2 of the model is to compute the conditional probability of each behavior and event occurrence (including itself) as a function of the successive lags (or steps) of each behavior or event from each possible event that it could precede. This step is accomplished using the same procedure as in our experienced versus novice teacher comparison illustration—by counting the number of times each behavior or event follows each of the other events in the observation system. Included in this count is the number of times an event immediately follows another (commonly termed *lag-1*), the number of times an event occurs one event away from the primary event (termed *lag-2*), and so forth, up to the largest sequential step or length of probability chain of interest. The sequential, or lag, probabilities are then computed by dividing the number of occurrences of each behavior or event at lag-N by the number of times the behavior or event to be considered occurred. This analysis can be accomplished whether the researcher is using mutually exclusive or overlapping observation systems (see Chapter 4, Constructing a Coding Scheme, for discussion of these types of observation systems).

Behavior and event sequential chains of interest within a particular behavior data record that is organized in time-based sequence are often referred to statistically in terms of suffixes and prefixes. These terms are essentially the same as speaking in terms of preceding or succeeding events. The *suffix* of a behavior-event chain is defined as the last behavior that appears in the chain; the *prefix* of a chain is the subchain obtained by omitting the suffix. For example, using an education illustration, Instruction← →Skill Engagement may be a prefix and KR Feedback a suffix in the behavior-event sequence Instruction← →Skill Engagement← →KR Feedback. A statistical Z-Score Table transformation is most often used to compute the statistical significance of a particular behavior-event sequence of interest within a larger time-based data set. The meaningfulness of a particular behavior-event sequence is then calculated with respect to all prefixes and suffixes that could conceivably have occurred within the possible universe of sequences that could have occurred in that data set. In other words, a particular behavior-event sequence of experimental interest is determined meaningful due to the larger sequential structure of the entire data set and the total number of behavior and event occurrences within that data set (for a detailed discussion of both statistical formulae used in relation to Z-Scores to determine the statistical significance of a particular sequence of events within a data record and to determine the meaningfulness of that sequence, consult our Sequential Analyses section in Chapter 9 or Bakeman & Gottman, 1986, 1997). In this manner, a two-step process of determining the statistical significance of a particular sequence of events is provided and followed by a formula for the determination of the validity or legitimacy of that statistical significance through statistically testing the meaningfulness of the first significance finding.

Our intent with this example is to provide a summary of the statistical applications available through the use of existing statistical formulae with a sequential focus. For a detailed and thoroughgoing discussion of these statistical applications, and a listing with examples and illustrations of the specific formulae, consult Bakeman and Gottman (1986, 1997) and Gottman and Roy (1990). Clearly, from our rather simplistic example it can be seen that a variety of research and development activity is possible with respect to learning more about directly observable phenomena using a sequential lens. One example of this includes the study of the sequential nature of schedules of reinforcement, punishment, and extinction. Another example relates to the documentation of behavioral theories (such as matching law; Davison & McCarthy, 1988) designed to model in complex sequential ways applied settings that originated largely in tightly controlled, laboratory-based experimental conditions. What we hope to do in ensuing chapters is to provide the basics of implementing a variety of this type of time-based sequential measurement study, and to tie this type of information to equally important information concerning the static characteristics of individual behaviors and events.

MULTI-EVENT THEORY IN THE APPLIED SCIENCES

The interbehavioral and sequential approach to the quantitative analysis of behavior, founded on the conceptual efforts of Kantor (1953, 1959, 1969) and the sequential developments of Bakeman and Gottman (1986, 1997) and Ray (Ray & Delprato, 1989), among others, is worthy of reiteration. It began with Kantor, who felt that despite the many contributions of the experimental and applied analysis of behavior literatures, its lack of an interbehavioral or sequential component left this methodological approach open to criticism. The inclusion of such a component in behavior analysis was, according to Kantor, an attempt to move forward from the strict lineal mechanics perspective of Skinner's Stimulus→ Response→ Consequence. To Kantor, the Skinnerian behavior-behavior and behavior-environment relationship model needed further measurement development, in that behavior and environment were described primarily in terms of the characteristics of the stimulus and response of interest, and causal assumptions were largely assumed and not explicitly supported.

At risk of undue complexity, and lacking a practical methodology for carrying out his theories in applied research settings, Kantor (1969) stipulated that behavior-environment relationships should be viewed as a *field*, which he defined as

the entire system of things and conditions operating in any event taken in its available totality. It is only the entire system of factors which will provide proper descriptive and explanatory materials for the handling of events. It is not the reacting organism alone which makes up the event but also the stimulating things and conditions, as well as the setting factors. (p. 371)

Stated in more familiar terms, Kantor proposed that although study of the characteristics of individual behaviors to discover more about interactive relationships was important and productive, the most important dimension to interaction was that of the transactions or time-based connections among multiple behaviors in setting-specific situations, and not the isolated character of each behavior as a stand-alone entity. Although rooted in behavioral psychology, Kantor's work and the work of those who expanded on this premise was intended to reach a broad audience of professionals with interests in studying and evaluating humans and other species at various stages of development and across many diverse interactive settings. The connective thread that Kantor and the materials in this text provide is a common interest in observing highly interactive social or educational behavior in applied settings. A primary component of the analysis of direct observation data is, therefore, what behaviors and events tend to precede or follow what other behaviors or events, and which of these sequential connections tend to be most productive in meeting particular educational or therapeutic ends.

A primary criticism of Kantor's contributions to the social and psychological sciences, however, is that what Kantor laid out as important to study stopped with the provision of a theoretical model and did not include an applied methodology. In other words, although an argument in favor of a more inclusive description of behavior-behavior and behavior-environment relationships (in terms of the importance of looking into the sequential nature of behavioral interactions) was rigorously constructed, and many researchers, educators, and clinicians saw the potential importance of increasing the availability of this kind of information, an amenable data collection method that allowed the description and analysis of more inclusive and sequentially based information in applied settings remained largely unavailable—until the last decade or so of methodological innovation and compatible technologies to facilitate the user-friendly implementation of such innovation.

Field and sequential thinking is, therefore, an attempt to add alternative measurement lenses to the existing data collection and measurement tools of applied behavior analysis. For example, in the traditional mechanical view, a single-headed arrow is typically used to show a one-direction cause and effect relationship between two behaviors or events of interest and all other events are seen as under experimental control. The field concept, however, offers a double-headed arrow (see Morris, 1992, p. 15) between multiple events and aspires to describe probabilistic connections in time-based sequence. Providing a set of data collection and analysis tools that can yield more inclusive quantitative descriptions of multiple concurrent events, which are observed and recorded as they take place, is what remains necessary to the application of a sequential- and field systems-based approach to education and social science concerns. As stipulated by Delprato (1992), such a tool must be capable of

(a) identifying, defining, and measuring far more than the usual limited number of variables, and (b) tracking the [sequential] status of these variables on a moment-by-moment basis. (p. 3)

If such a set of tools were to be made available, then we feel that their direct appeal to education and social science concerns is readily apparent. Clearly, teaching, professional preparation, and most social interplay between human or animal participants is highly interactive and behavioral in character on many levels. These types of interactions involve what each participant is doing behaviorally with, and in response to, the others. These interactions also involve more subtle behaviors indicative of a qualitative or interpretive character related to emotional communication and attachment (Ray, 1992). Such interactions are conceivably quantifiable given the proper data collection and analysis tools, for we may now be able to scientifically speak in terms of behaviors such as verbal intonation, rate of speaking and pausing, and nonverbal gestures—all challenging but approachable behaviors, given the proper combination of direct observation lenses with which to observe. Stated from the perspective of a scientist who is critical of social science activity, the "art" of teaching or social interaction does not have to remain the exclusive domain of artistic representation; it is conceivably amenable to a more traditional and quantitative "scientific" description and analysis if (a) the proper tools are provided for such a task, and (b) education and social scientists are receptive to such an undertaking.

Thus tools capable of collecting, describing, and analyzing a more inclusive volume and variety of behavior-environment data, and a tool that contains greater economy and flexibility of data display, should prove helpful to researchers and evaluators alike whose subject matter is complex behavioral interaction. As stipulated by Locke (1992), a quantitative tool capable of putting into practice what Kantor recommends should provide data concerning "exactly what we are doing, as opposed to what we have come to imagine we are doing" (p. 86). Locke goes on to provide an educational illustration of how such tools might overcome the illusion that we know in intuitive ways how we or others have behaved in certain situations:

> It is a telling fact that teachers (and researchers) are surprised by some of the things they find in descriptive accounts. The illusion that we know what we are doing is persistent. Our surprise is enhanced [by sequential analysis] because its capacity for simultaneous display of temporally ordered details from both teaching behavior and teaching context opens the door to a new dimension, a world containing events of such subtlety that they are invisible to our ordinary perceptions. . . . The raw power of [sequential analysis] to reveal the inner workings of skill instruction is impressive. Absolute duration of individual events, the relative size of summary durations over larger blocks of time, and the start/stop, order, and transition of teacher moves across time can yield valuable insights. A simple example of something that produced such an insight for me will illustrate what [researchers] can find for themselves.

> I noticed first [in the data] the familiar but always impressive complexity of a teacher's work. What the authors call velocity (the rate at which behavior changes) is supplemented by a startling amount of simultaneous action, to produce an overall impression of tremendous activity. As I [observed the data further] my attention was drawn to some unexpected juxtapositions. The teacher was modeling a skill and giving verbal skill instruction at the same time. This is not uncommon; and teachers often recite critical verbal cues while they demonstrate—particularly when they do so in slow motion. The [data] also revealed that while [the teacher] was modeling she also was observing an individual student and giving performance-specific feedback (apparently interspersed with verbal cues). Such a disparate combination of behaviors is not common at all (or so I thought), and my first response was to be incredulous. That is exactly what [sequential analysis] has an almost unique power to do—confront us with what is happening even when it differs sharply from our expectations. . . . I had never been conscious of [these] teaching moves, either in my own or in

other teachers' repertoires. On the very next day, however, one of the videotapes I use in the UMass undergraduate training program revealed several clear instances that could have matched the [sequential analysis] graphic perfectly. Had that been under my nose all the time? If so, why did it not make an impression on me? Is it an effective tactic, and under what conditions . . . ? Those questions show exactly what [sequential analysis] can do that other methods of [scientific] inquiry are far less likely to accomplish. (pp. 86-87)

Thus we feel it important to provide both a sequential analysis component to the historically existing complement of direct observation and behavior analysis methods available to us and an argument in favor of using helpful technologies to facilitate the thoroughgoing implementation of the data collection and analysis strategies recommended in this text. Locke (1989) has stated that "any kind of science can be done as rigorous and systematic inquiry, just as any can be done as a careless or dishonest contribution to the pollution of knowledge. . . . Superiority rests not in the method, but in the match with particular problems" (p. 11). While true, this observation begs the question of whether the standard methods of inquiry, done rigorously and systematically, still leave us with an inadequate understanding of complex interactive settings and, hence, with the need to discover additional means of data gathering and analysis. Alternative approaches may be necessary to surmount the current constraints that challenge applied research. The fact must be recognized that there are alternative approaches and applications of formalized data collection and analysis strategies. We believe that a larger repertoire of available research methods can only serve to enhance the quality of research in general. Good (1979) has stated that better conceptualizations of variables and alternative measures of human behavior are necessary if we are to continually increase our understanding of complex interactive settings. This, coupled with the potentially appealing additions to currently available data collection and analysis strategies, leads us to believe that the pursuit of these additions is warranted. If demonstrable conclusions are an outcome, a more substantive foundation will have been laid in establishing education, social science, and psychological research as enterprises contributing to the legitimate forwarding of scientific activity.

THE IMPLICATIONS OF COMPUTER TECHNOLOGY

Currently, many education and social scientists hold the position with regard to their respective research and evaluation tasks that until data collection and analysis tools are developed that are perceived to be time efficient, cost effective, and easy to understand and use in comparison to other methods, they will use those that are readily available and easiest to implement. According to a variety of quantitative scientists in the education and social sciences, and to most practicing applied behavior analysts, this will limit the variety of research methods efforts in the education, social, and psychological sciences to those that are perceived easiest to understand and use. When one compares the perceived ease of implementing an instrument such as a questionnaire in contrast to the direct observational recording of behavior and event characteristics with a stopwatch and paper and pencil or some other traditionally cumbersome method, the choice for most professionals (and in particular, aspiring professionals such as graduate students) is an easy one. We believe—like Bakeman and Gottman (1986), Binder (1994), and a host of other scholars—that this path of least resistance with respect to doing science has resulted in diminished use of some potentially useful research methods in education and social science. We are also firmly convinced that the recent explosion of computer software and hardware applications in our society has provided a strong catalyst for reconsidering the feasibility of many research techniques. This is due to our increasing sophistication of direct observation methods and measurement types and to statistical analysis procedures for the analysis of data and the analysis of how accurately we are collecting that data and implementing related treatments.

Specific to behavior analysis methods—prior to the provision of sophisticated computer tools designed to collect and analyze multiple behavior and event occurrences and to allow the viewing of the many possible static and sequential measures of those events—researchers and professionals interested in studying the relative effectiveness of a particular applied setting with a direct observation lens typically used traditional stopwatch and paper-and-pencil recording methods (see Kazdin, 1982, or Sulzer-Azaroff & Mayer, 1991, for a detailed description of traditionally accepted recording techniques). Although many in education and social science voiced interest in (a) studying and evaluating multiple events more inclusively and (b) the sequential aspects of interactive behavior, most settled for a static measure due to the limited capability of the data collection and analysis tools available to them.

For example, a researcher interested in recording the number of feedback statements used by a youth sport coach—and the related changes in the percentages of skill practice time by a representative athlete—could be accommodated using a moment-by-moment recording procedure. In this case, the observer would simply break down the athletic practice time into logically specified time frames (for example 1 to 2 minutes), and spend 1 minute recording coach feedback occurrences, 1 minute recording the amount of time an athlete spent in skill practice, and 1 minute in data management tasks. Such a procedure did not allow, however, the recording of multiple coach and athlete behaviors and did not provide a data documentation method to allow observation of the connections among coach and athlete behaviors in time-based sequence. With the advent of computer-based data collection and analysis tool development, this need no longer be the case. Computer tool development is providing the opportunity to look at interactive settings in more inclusive and different ways, using different measures, and thereby facilitating data collection and analysis of the time-based sequential nature of multiple behavior-behavior and behavior-environment relationships in a setting under observation.

It is important for us, as potential creators and users of computer-assisted data collection and analysis methods, to discuss some concerns we have related to the development of computer applications (or any tools for that matter) designed to potentially enhance research and development, educational improvement, and a variety of clinical assessment activities. Clearly, the explosion of computer application development in the social and natural sciences is becoming a reality. However, our current feverish cultural pursuit of new computer applications provides an inherent danger as follows. When one is intimately involved with computer application development, it is often tempting to move beyond developing an application to improve professional practice or extend a body of knowledge, and to develop that application for the pure sake of being able to do so. If we can manage to remain sensitive to the danger of developing computer-based applications simply because we can, we feel that the potential for computer applications to provide tools that may uncover information previously unknown, and the potential for far more effective research, educational, and evaluative enterprises as a result, provides support for forging cautiously and systematically ahead with such development.

The primary question (posed by Sharpe & Hawkins, 1998, p. 20) related to computer application development is therefore "How can we avoid becoming technology's servant, while at the same time explore how technology may better facilitate our educational ends?" Many examples exist in the education literature of avoiding such servitude and facilitating educational enhancement. Computer development in relation to direct observation activities has, for example, included the design and implementation of professional evaluation instruments in field-based settings, the development of laboratory experiences to enhance professional education activities, and the exploration of some previously unknown determinants of effective professional practice through enhanced data collection and analysis techniques. Such development next requires a broader definition of the term technology.

In this regard, we define *technology* as more than computer hardware, software, and electronic systems (which are so often confused in our contemporary culture as being the same thing as the end products of technology). Although they are necessary to a certain type of tool development, they are only the mechanical parts (much like an electron microscope is a mechanical part), which still require the trained professional to connect their use to the discovery of new and important information and to enhancing research, evaluation, and education-based applications. Relying again on the perspective of Sharpe and Hawkins (1998), the computer applications we currently see developing around us are merely tools and mechanical instruments, much like the stopwatches and paper and pencil were the tools of the direct observer before the advent of computer-aided data collection, or like mimeograph machines and chalkboards before the advent of advanced photocopiers and sophisticated computer-driven presentation software.

Related to a traditional view of the scientific method, computer applications only gain value through their fruitful employment for scientific purposes. One of the chief characteristics that some anthropologists have used to distinguish humans from other forms of life is their penchant for tool making. To the degree that categorizing humans in this manner is a legitimate determinant, and to the degree that computer application development is a form of tool building, we argue that computer application development is a naturally evolving part of our endeavors to learn more about the world around us and is therefore an appealing facilitator of the scientific enterprise—one that should ultimately aid us in direct observation of complex interactive settings. The danger to which we must remain sensitive is that of not crossing the line between tool-building for a redemptive purpose and tool-worshipping (Ellul, 1964; Nietzsche, 1892/1978), which tends to have a deleterious effect on science. As scholars and researchers continue to develop more capable computer-based lenses (such as that described in the flyer included with this text), we caution researchers to steer clear of what we feel to be the most dangerous enticements that computer application development provides—those of developing a tool simply because we can develop it and of becoming infatuated with these gadgets because they are interesting to our senses.

Perhaps Dwyer (1996) has provided the best articulation of computer application development in relationship to scientific practice: While technology may or may not add value to academic and professional practices in the long run, it will only realize any potential value if and when it becomes an integral part of a comprehensive and scientifically supported plan for professional improvement. Users of a particular computer application need to be prepared to both use it *and* provide data-based documentation for it with regard to its potentially effective contribution as a research or evaluation tool.

Behavior analysis researchers interested in applying developments in computer software and hardware have been concerned with (a) how to collect and store more complete time-based descriptions of multiple events that occurred rapidly and often simultaneously in interactive settings, (b) how to collect this information in real-time as defined by collecting information as it actually occurred without gaps or disruptions in the data record due to recording constraints, (c) how to provide for immediacy of view and sophistication of analysis using a variety of visual, statistical, and sequential data interpretation methods, and (d) how to incorporate multiple methodologies into the data analysis as a function of a multiple methodology data collection mechanism (e.g., quantitative behavioral recording coupled with qualitative social validation information). Kahng and Iwata (1998) provide a fairly complete review of the variety of computer-based tools currently available to those interested in facilitating their behavior analysis research activities, and we provide an appealing computer-based option both referenced by Kahng and Iwata and detailed here (see Appendix B and the flyer included with this book for information on BEST software tools).

Through the use of computer-facilitated data collection and analysis, very detailed time-based records are easily generated in live settings or from videotape by simply pressing a variety of alphanumeric keys on a computer keyboard to signify the start and stop times of various behavior and event occurrences. Embedded in the typical data collection platform are features for pausing, editing, and displaying various portions of the data record as it is being recorded; recording multiple overlapping events as they actually occur, and providing a host of qualitative narrative and numeric notations at any point in time in the data record to enhance particular descriptions of atypical or unique behavior or event occurrences. For analysis, a number of appealing computer-facilitated features are available. Multiple characteristics of multiple events are made immediately available for informational view, including traditional measures such as frequency, duration, average duration, percentage of experimental time, rate, and standard deviations of each behavior contained in a particular data record. Time-based characteristics of events are also readily available, including first and last occurrence times, time span between occurrences, shortest duration, longest duration, and latencies among behavioral occurrences. Multiple data representation formats may be immediately generated, including a range of tabular and graphic formats. Traditional statistical analyses of graphic data, including mean, standard deviation, trend, and regression lines of best fit, are incorporated into visual analysis of the data. Data sets on one particular observational episode, or logically ordered data set combinations, may be analyzed graphically to determine changes within one observational episode, changes across multiple behaviors and events, and multiple measures of those events over longer periods of time and repeated measures of those events over time. Sophisticated sequential analyses are facilitated by software that provides numerical count, conditional probability, and Z-Score transformations to determine the statistical significance of probabilities of occurrence. A computer-facilitated sequential analysis of behavior provides the capability for creating a powerful analysis form that enables explicit scrutiny of the time-based functional connections among any and all of the behaviors and events contained within a particular data set. Computer-facilitated research support features that are available include (a) powerful reliability applications enabling comparison across multiple data files using simple frequency, point-by-point, and Cohen's Kappa methods (see Chapter 5 for a detailed discussion of these formulae and related procedures) to determine criterion training or interrater reliability or to determine levels of treatment fidelity; (b) data file merging and time-based sorting to provide complex multiple event data records not feasibly collected by one pass of a videotape or live experimental episode; and (c) clipboarding and multi-software tasking procedures to manipulate data representations in a variety of ways and to use multiple software programs simultaneously. From even this summary description, we feel it is apparent that developments in computer-based hardware and software applications have great potential for enhancing our capability with regard to direct observation activities and for discovering a variety of new knowledge as a result of the application of such developments in the scientific domain.

SOME ASSUMPTIONS AND LIMITATIONS

If we are truly capable of enabling the type of description and analysis previously described, then some potential cautions in the form of some assumptions about and limitations of the methods discussed in forthcoming chapters are important to note. First, and as iterated in the previous section on computer technology, we hold to the position articulated by Sharpe and Hawkins (1998) and Sharpe, Harper, and Brown (1998) that when one is intimately involved with computer application development, one risks the danger of focusing not on developing an application to improve professional practice or extend a body of knowledge but on developing an application simply because one can. However, there are researchers and clinicians involved in these types of activities who have continually been interested in the development of data collection and analysis tools that might better serve their respective research, education, and clinical tasks, and in this text we have drawn on the wide variety of their efforts (e.g., the computer-based tools described in Appendix B and advertised on the flyer included with this text illustrate this, as they are compatible with the methods and procedures contained within these materials and have evolved based on a particular set of theoretical constructs and on a particular set of data collection and analysis needs).

A next set of cautions refers to the activity of constructing category systems for direct observation and behavior analysis activities. Prior to giving the reader a detailed explanation of the important considerations regarding category system construction for a particular use, we believe that some general cautions should be highlighted. We recommend that the reader remain sensitive to these cautions throughout not only the category system construction process but also all data collection and analysis efforts that are detailed in forthcoming chapters.

A first caution in this respect relates to the primary intent of "doing" science. If scientific practice is focused on providing an inclusive and accurate description of the world around us, then all that the data collection and analysis tools we provide succeed in accomplishing is various forms of description. The question that is answered by the static characteristics of certain behaviors and events is: "How often and how long do the behaviors and events under consideration tend to be present or absent in certain situations?" The questions that are answered by any accompanying qualitative narratives involve attempts at providing a richer description of the variety of contextual and situational features that surround the presence of particular behaviors and events. The question that is answered by sequential data is whether or not behavior B follows behavior A more or less often then would be expected by chance. If the frequency of behavior B following behavior A is sufficiently different from chance occurrence (as determined by Z-Score-based mathematical models), then a conditional probability is present between behavior A and behavior B. Whether focusing on the quantitative, qualitative, or sequential characteristics of particular behaviors, it would be unwarrantedly optimistic for a user of the methods we describe to state unequivocally that behavior A "caused" the occurrence of behavior B, for causation is a separate epistemological question (and one that we feel is important to separate from scientific description and delineate from a determination of the potential existence of probable or functional relationships among the behaviors and events of interest).

Regarding the collection and analysis of static quantitative data (e.g., discrete characteristics of behaviors and events such as frequency, rate, or percentage of experimental time), some assumptions are also important to note. First, just because a category system such as that to be described in Chapter 4 is used to guide the quantitative collection of behavior-environment data, the user should not assume that the reliability or accuracy of that data is ensured. It is in this respect that a rigorous set of rules and procedures should be implemented to increase the probability of reliable and accurate data records. A reasonably complete treatment of some recommended procedures is provided in the Chapter 6 reliability and treatment fidelity sections and should be read thoroughly by those unfamiliar with recommended reliability and interobserver agreement methods for legitimate implementation of direct observation methods.

A second assumption articulated by van der Mars (1989), and one that we agree with, is that while it is assumed in most methodological literatures that a category system approach to the collection of observable behaviors and events should be used, such a method must not necessarily be assumed to be capable of measuring only those events that can be detected visually or audibly. We agree with Friman, Wilson, and Hayes (1998) that it is a misconception to automatically rule out behavior analysis methods when one is interested in phenomena such as emotions, feelings, attitudes, and perceptions. For example, pioneers of behavior analysis (see Skinner, 1989) have made it clear that most feelings and attitudes (labeled *private events* in the behavior analysis literature) may be connected with a readily observable manifestation of those emotions. Van der Mars (1989) provides an illustration of this:

> If we assume that attitudes and feelings are somehow going to be reflected in observable behaviors, such behaviors can be categorized and defined. For example, attitude of an athlete toward practice might be reflected in his or her on-time behavior, the amount of time he or she spends taking extra practice, and so on. Although these and other behaviors may not say much about that person's general attitude, they function as indicators of his or her attitude toward practice. (p. 8)

Related to the sequential nature of the data collection and analysis tools we discuss, Wampold (1992) lists some important assumptions. A first assumption is that the probability that event A is emitted is independent of its position within the larger behavior-event sequence of interest and, according to the null hypothesis of randomness, is independent of the other behaviors in the event sequence to be studied. This assumption is referred to in much of the sequential literature as stationarity (see Espinosa, 1992). *Stationarity* implies that the patterns of interaction will not change over the course of the observation. However, this may not be true in all sequential interactions, particularly those among various participants in education settings. For example, a teacher may change his or her interactional pattern within a particular class period according to the lesson context and the different skills being taught. When a researcher is analyzing a sequential pattern in which stationarity is not uniformly present, it is recommended that the behavior-behavior or behavior-environment sequence of interest be broken up into smaller data segments that exhibit stationarity and analyzed as independent data records. For example, introductory and closing behavioral exchanges in an instructional lesson may be segmented from a sequential analysis of the interactions present during the body of that lesson. In addition, as the body of the lesson changes contexts (e.g., from seat work to cooperative activities), the data record should be segmented accordingly.

A second assumption listed by Wampold (1992), related to the assumption that behaviors are independent of other behaviors in the sequence, requires that behaviors under observation not be constrained structurally in any way by the method of data collection. One example of a common constraint in the more traditional behavior analysis literature in education includes sequences that are collected by a data mechanism that does not allow a behavior or event to be followed by itself. This type of sequence is collected when a mutually exclusive coding system is used that only records a behavior when a change of behavior occurs.

In keeping with examples from education research, oftentimes a teacher's instructional behavior will be recorded until that teacher changes to another behavior, such as management or observation. A teacher's instructional behavior is, therefore, not allowed to follow a teacher's instructional behavior, and, consequently, misleading conclusions may result (See Wampold, 1986, for a more detailed discussion of this issue).

There are some important limitations to conducting direct observation research with a quantitative component. One potentially limiting methodological characteristic brought up most often when discussing the relative merits of a category system approach to the observation of behaviors and events is its inability to provide prescriptive information. Once a behaviorally based descriptive data record has been compiled and analyzed, what a particular researcher or clinical supervisor does with that information is a function of that professional's interpretation. In other words, it is important to note that the data record in and of itself does not provide a prescriptive interpretation of the relative effects of behavior or environmental events. The data record only provides descriptive, and we hope accurate, information on which analytic and prescriptive judgments will be made. Clearly, this method for collecting and analyzing data does not alleviate the need for a trained and experienced professional to interpret the results according to recommended procedures. It is in this regard that it is important to adhere to a strict set of procedures when interpreting behavior-environment data—to avoid superimposing the beliefs and biases of the observer on the situation under analysis. The potential loss of objectivity in data analysis violates both the tenets of scientific practice, as we have defined them in previous chapters, and the primary rules of governance with regard to behavior analysis methods.

Another potential limitation of this type of work lies in the mischaracterization of it that is oftentimes promoted when direct observation of behavior methods are used for evaluation purposes. The following teacher-training example perhaps illustrates this point most effectively. Many teacher educators have argued against a category system approach to the quantification of various teacher and student behavior practices due to its perceived technocratic character. In other words, a technocratic argument against behavioral observation is that it is inappropriate because it provides rigidly defined behavioral competencies that are either displayed in a proper amount or not displayed in a proper amount in a general way. The argument then follows that teachers-in-training are therefore inappropriately held to a rule-governed approach to either demonstrating particular behaviors at a particular level of performance (e.g., minimum frequencies or percentages of class time) or failing their evaluation experience. Clearly, however, the data records generated by this type of approach are contextually bound. We caution against using the type of quantitative data records this method generates to stipulate minimum levels of teacher behaviors or student practices related to instructional effectiveness in some general or arbitrary way. What we do recommend when using this type of data for evaluation purposes is that the data record should be considered with respect to the situation in which it was observed and the background and experiences of the participants who were under observation. For example, it would be inappropriate to expect the same levels of behavior from a novice teacher who is in a different school setting each day and from an experienced teacher who is always in the same setting. It would also be inappropriate to expect the same behavior characteristics from the same teacher across different subject matters, with different classroom arrangements, resource needs, and activity requirements. Hence, the degree to which the data generated according to this method are helpful to particular clients is reliant to a great degree on the trained experience of the professional who interprets that data for evaluation or research purposes.

Given the potential appeal of a sequential approach to the collection and analysis of observed behaviors and events, we believe that some limitations specific to collecting time-based sequential data should also be highlighted. First, the construction of an amenable observation system for the coding of behavior and the actual data collection process consumes time and technological resources. Only a few computer-based software systems are currently available (again, refer to the flyer included with this text) to help in this challenge, and, of those, most are not available commercially. Therefore, resource availability in relationship to the hardware needed to support such an approach must be carefully considered before implementing this type of activity. Although computer hardware, and the operating systems that are typically included with most hardware, are becoming increasingly capable and increasingly less expensive, the expense issue remains important to consider.

Related to the expense limitation is that when a researcher is conducting research into the complex behavioral character of certain settings of interest, collection and analysis from videotape permanent records are methodologically desirable and in some cases necessary. Complex overlapping coding schemes require multiple passes through a permanent record to capture completely the data of interest. In addition, when training a large staff for consistency and accuracy of data collection efforts, videotape records and multiple computers are required to implement such an undertaking (refer to the sections in Chapter 6 on reliability and treatment fidelity for a more detailed procedural discussion of these issues). Despite potential equipment limitations, once coding system construction and reliability issues are addressed, a sophisticated category system approach to quantifying observable events is easily undertaken by even the relatively inexperienced researcher, due to the current sophistication of data collection and analysis programs such as that described at the end of this text.

A second limitation related to the sequential nature of our data collection and analysis recommendations is that this type of analysis should be limited to behavior-behavior and behavior-environment interactions that occur with relatively high frequency and relative immediacy. Important events that occur infrequently or very irregularly are best left to another method. A related and equally impacting issue is that of determining the unit of analysis (e.g., in education research, the question of observing the entire class, small groups of students interacting with one another, one problematic student, etc.). If the research or evaluation task using the methods we provide is not contextualized by a particular unit of analysis (see Silverman & Solmon, 1998, for a detailed treatment of this issue), then results from such an activity may not yield meaningful results, in the best case, or may yield confounding results, in the worst case.

A PREFACE TO BEHAVIOR ANALYSIS METHODOLOGY

Inherent in a direct observation and behavior analytic view of scientific activity is the idea that it is the daily practices, or interactions, of professionals (teachers, coaches, counselors, clinicians, managers, therapists, etc.) and their various clientele that are potentially the most important and impacting variable in determining the relative effectiveness of most education and social science activities. We argue that it is just these processes that are important variables for the researcher to consider and strive to understand when engaged in research or evaluation tasks in applied settings in which a therapeutic end is sought.

Direct observation and behavior analysis approaches to research and evaluation have experienced a long and productive history in the applied sciences, although their reporting is sometimes difficult to access and general receptivity on the part of mainstream professional groups has sometimes been lacking. Nonetheless, select disciplines in education and psychology have long used a behavior analytic approach as a dominant professional methodology. In the past 2 years, for example, education reform has focused on a performance- and competency-based approach to ensuring effective educational practice and effective preparation of teaching professionals. Such reform carries a central component of direct quantitative observation of actual teaching practice and student performance in specific educational situations or, simply put, a return to a behavior analysis approach to education concerns at the levels of classroom activity and teacher preparation.

Because of the appeal of performance- and outcome-based education reform and the resurgence of interest in behavior analysis methods for education and social science research and evaluation, and because of the enhanced data collection and analysis capability afforded by computer technology, the time is ripe for the introduction of contemporary and interdisciplinary applied behavior analysis methodologies. We hope that these materials illustrate how easy and helpful it is to implement contemporary behavior analysis methods that were once thought cumbersome and time consuming. We also hope that this book addresses the challenges of devising observational methods to completely and accurately describe and analyze highly interactive settings in quantitative ways.

Our goal is to teach the general and specific principles of contemporary, technology-supported applied behavior analysis methods in a clear and user-friendly manner. Although the book has an introductory flavor, it is nonetheless designed to include information and references that should prove useful for the intermediate and seasoned researcher as well as the introductory student. Throughout the following methodology sections, we provide concrete illustrations and examples to clarify, in a very practical way, the methodological practices described. References to a variety of software resources and websites (from which information and software tools may be downloaded) are also included where appropriate. More sophisticated algorithmic information and detailed methodological precepts are referenced to provide the intermediate-to-advanced audience with additional support materials that are covered elsewhere. Our overall intent is to provide an interdisciplinary audience with an introductory-to-intermediate level methodology text that may be used in concert with the BEST and BESTPCC software tools described in Appendix B and advertised in the flyer at the end of this text.

Part II

Constructing Observational Systems

4

Constructing a Coding Scheme

The worth of a scientific system lies in its "usefulness and economy."

— Skinner (1983, p. 127)

After reading this chapter, you should be able to define the following terms and provide the information requested in the study guide below.

TERMS

Coding scheme

Treatment fidelity or treatment integrity

Mutually exclusive

Clarity

Complete

Operational definitions

STUDY GUIDE

1. Explain the difference in direct observation purposes in relation to the terms *demonstration* and *understanding* as explained by Morris (1992).
2. Discuss some of the benefits of using an observation system focused on the sequential relationships of behaviors of interest.
3. List and explain some of the important defining purposes in constructing an observation system for evaluation and research activity.
4. Describe the three basic structural decisions that are necessary to the construction of an observational coding system.

5. Using examples, explain the difference between a physically based code and a socially based code contained in a direct observation system.
6. Describe the procedures involved in developing objective, clear, and complete definitions for each code to be used in a direct observation category system.

Constructing a set of terms and definitions to be used to collect and then analyze direct observational data is a necessary first step in conducting a behavior analysis. Such a set of terms and definitions is typically called a *coding scheme* or *category system*. For example, many category systems that focus primarily on the static characteristics of particular behaviors and events currently exist in the teacher education, psychology, and social science literatures and are helpful illustrations of such systems (in Chapter 5 we provide detailed examples from the disciplines of teacher education, school psychology, special education, clinical psychology, and ethology). For those interested in reading further examples of these types of category systems beyond what is provided in this text, we recommend Darst, Zakrajsek, and Mancini (1989) or Stallings, Needels, and Sparks (1987), as these materials provide a wide variety of direct observation *coding schemes* that range in focus from traditional educational measures to more nontraditional measures, such as motivational, interpersonal, and other social dynamic correlates with directly observable behavior. Many other nontraditional coding systems are also available in the literature and may provide additional insight into the wide range of applicability of a category system approach to a direct observation data collection effort. Some of these alternatives provide systems designed for the collection of measures such as power and involvement (Penman, 1980), control and support (Pett, Vaughan-Cole, Egger, & Dorsey, 1988), and emotion dynamics (Ekman & Friesen, 1978). The pioneering work of Flanders Interaction Analysis Categories (FIAC; Flanders, 1970) and the efforts of Dunkin and Biddle (1974) may also prove helpful to those in the education professions (although we have some methodological concerns about these referenced efforts).

Using education as an illustration, the use of traditional category system approaches to direct observation is supported by a productive literature and includes the improvement of (a) general professional practices (e.g., Ingham & Greer, 1992; Kamps, Leonard, Dugan, Boland, & Greenwood, 1991), and (b) specific client (i.e., student) competencies, such as pupil attending, classroom control, and peer interactions (Cooper, Thomson, & Baer, 1970; Cossairt, Hall, & Hopkins, 1973; Hall, Panyon, Rabon, & Broden, 1968; Page, Iwata, & Reid, 1982). For those interested specifically in behavior analysis approaches to teacher- and professional training, the physical education (e.g., Darst et al., 1989; Sharpe, Hawkins, & Ray, 1995) and special education (e.g., Miller, Harris, & Watanabe, 1991; O'Reilly & Renzaglia, 1994; Warger & Aldinger, 1984) professions are two teacher-training areas that have used direct observation approaches to the behavioral evaluation of professional activities with great success when they were implemented by university faculty instructors. These examples, while education specific, also provide insight into and ideas for potential applications in a variety of other professional areas.

The examples just provided are of static criterion-based observation systems, in which a variety of professionals-in-training have been held accountable to a target measure (e.g., number, rate, percentage of experimental time, duration and average duration, etc.) use of documented effective practices. In turn, the targeted behaviors of their prospective clients that were thought to be correlated with skill acquisition have been separately monitored (e.g., Carnine & Fink, 1978; Greer, 1985), oftentimes with functional or causal connections between professional and client behaviors inferred.

We agree with Morris (1992) that training individuals to criterion use of particular behaviors to be used in their professional settings falls under what he calls "demonstration" (p. 9), in which a rule-governed approach to applying theoretically effective behaviors is learned and consistently used by a client. Thus a potentially important additional component to direct observation and behavior analysis activities is the inclusion of a sequential analysis of behavior and event occurrences of interest. Adding a sequential analysis capability to direct observation data collection and analysis helps the researcher with the challenge of identifying multiple stimulating events that set the occasion for desirable and not-so-desirable responses (Touchette, MacDonald, & Langer, 1985). This type of observation and analysis may also help in the area of what Morris terms "understanding" (p. 9), in which emphasis is placed on discovering just which behaviors tend to facilitate or impede the use of other behaviors in time-based sequence and within and across particular situations.

A variety of sequential analysis methodologies have been developed to pursue the recommendations of Morris and have included

Markov chain analysis (Chatfield & Lemon, 1970), information theory (Bakeman, 1978), cross-spectral analysis (Gottman, 1979a), grammatical inference (Rodger & Rosebrugh, 1979), and, the most frequently used, sequential behavior analysis (Bakeman & Gottman, 1986; Gottman & Roy, 1990). Sequential behavior analysis was first conceptually developed by Sackett (1979, 1980) in infant development literature and was formalized by Gottman (1979a, 1979b; Gottman & Roy, 1990) in his development of statistical modeling equations. Sequential behavior methods have been applied with productive results to a variety of behavioral questions in the social sciences. Although this method remains unfamiliar to many researchers, a rich source of examples across a variety of disciplines does exist for those who are interested in exploring them. Some of the following references should prove helpful to those interested in category system examples containing similar behaviors and events to those that a particular applied scientist with a sequential behavior interest may wish to study. Examples include interactional rhythms (Scheflen, 1982), family therapy and marital interaction (Gottman, 1979b; Wahler & Hann, 1987), clinical psychology (Ruben & Delprato, 1987), school psychology (Martens & Witt, 1988a, 1988b), ecological psychology (Willems & Raush, 1980), health delivery services (Ray, 1983), general interpersonal skills (Faraone, 1983; Jacobson & Anderson, 1982), and communication ethology (Altmann, 1965; Mjrberg, 1972; Ray & Delprato, 1989). In addition, some of the work in microethnography (e.g., Erickson, 1982) in which short time frames are used to record in rich detail various subtleties of human interaction may prove helpful to researchers.

Although sequentially based contributions are relatively less frequent in the education literature, some introductory sequential analyses have been conducted that have experimented with this type of analysis. Examples include implementing a sequential method to describe various levels of teacher proficiency (Hawkins & Sharpe, 1992), to provide feedback and goal setting in undergraduate practice teaching settings (Sharpe, Hawkins, & Ray, 1995), and to increase the self-monitoring skills of practicing teachers (Sharpe, Spies, Newman, & Spickelmier-Vallin, 1996). In addition, some experiments have been conducted in the area of alternative variable construction in an attempt to make the interactive transactions between teachers and students in challenging instructional and organizational situations more explicit (Sharpe & Lounsbery, 1998; Sharpe, Lounsbery, & Bahls, 1997).

Part II of this book provides reference to, and illustrations of, a variety of category systems that might be helpful to those interested in behavior analysis approaches to their research and evaluation interests. The principles and practice of developing a coding system and ensuring the reliable collection of data based on that system are also covered. Thus Part II provides a general framework for category system construction for users developing their own particular direct observation systems for their own particular needs, and it provides some specific category systems that have been used with success for various research and development and related evaluation purposes in education and social science situations.

A PREFACE TO CATEGORY SYSTEM CONSTRUCTION

Clearly, the construction of a category system that best fits the description and analysis task one may wish to undertake is the scientific step requiring the most thought, deliberation, and reflection. Because using behavioral codes to collect and analyze behavior-behavior and behavior-environment data often reduces the richness of the interaction to a finite set of categories, the choice of a coding system that is sensitive to the form and character of the interactions among setting participants is critical. For example, if the research interest is in what a particular student is doing in a classroom in relation to that student's academic performance, a simple code such as "subject matter engagement" might be used to record all instances of interactions with a particular subject matter. The research interest may, however, need to be further delineated as to the type of engagement, such as responding to teacher questions; type of responses given in relation to factual, conceptual, or synthesis of materials; seatwork with educational materials; correct versus incorrect and successful versus unsuccessful engagement; and so on. In addition, reference to the types of behaviors that might precede or succeed subject matter engagement might need to be included as definitions for particular categories are developed. Because of this challenge with regard to using behavioral codes, it is also important at times to include a qualitative narrative in a direct observation study to contextualize atypical or unique behavior or event occurrences. For example, a category such as "student off-task" might be used when observing a classroom situation, and it might be defined as any time a student disrupts a classroom activity. In this regard, extreme violent episodes that could be recorded within this category may need additional narrative explanation due to their somewhat atypical character according to the category definition. The data collection and analysis software that is described at the end of this text includes an appealing narrative notation feature that allows the writing of additional notes tied directly in time-based sequence to a particular behavior or event occurrence, which facilitates the use of a multiple-method methodology for the direct observation of behavioral phenomena when it is warranted.

An observational approach to the static and sequential counting of behaviors and events provides many appealing benefits. First, a set of procedures is provided researchers for discovering, documenting, and quantifying how behaviors tend to be related to one another in situations largely comprised of interaction among many individuals. Education and social science settings, for example, in which the predominant component is the interaction among multiple individuals, are well matched with such an analysis. Second, a set of rigorous quantitative data collection and analysis procedures, driven by field systems and sequential conceptualizations of behavior-event occurrences, should also prove productive in overcoming what is often seen as the constraint of behavior analysis efforts—an undue focus on a limited number of behaviors or events in isolation. Third, providing a qualitative data collection component as a complement to quantitative data collection procedures should help researchers overcome the criticism that in behavior analysis the behaviors and events under study are context free.

The capabilities that a thoroughgoing sequential and systems-oriented behavior analysis effort provides also seems well suited for uncovering many of the more subtle behavior interactions unique to particular situations. Characteristics such as automaticity, contingency management, and response time, all documented using other research methods and argued as possible components unique to effective interactions, may be amenable to documentation and quantification using behavior analysis methods. Key interactive characteristics, such as rapidly changing rates of behavior occurrence and latencies of participant responding, may also be uncovered within and across specific settings using behavior analysis. Once this type of information has been documented, the types of interactions just mentioned may then be amenable to successful training and transfer by professional educators, thereby improving the effectiveness of a variety of professional practices and related client behaviors that require change to ensure more productive and effective professional situations.

If the researcher decides to implement the software tools described at the end of this text, in concert with the methodologies outlined in this book; we believe that the level of capability and complexity of that researcher's quantitative description and analysis of behavior will be limited only by investigative interest and the inventiveness of the category system developed to collect corresponding data. Once the decisions discussed in Chapter 3, such as determining appropriate units of analysis, overcoming the assumptions of behavioral independence, and gathering the required resources, are met, the appeals of this type of data gathering and data analysis are clearly many. It is now necessary for us to provide some general guidelines for, along with some specific examples and illustrations of, starting an actual category system construction for a particular application.

DEFINING PURPOSES

When beginning the task of putting together a set of terms and definitions to form a category system to be used for direct observational purposes, there are many things to consider. The construction process is particularly important because it is the terms and definitions of a particular category system that will guide all remaining data collection and analysis efforts. A logical first step in actual category system construction is to ask those who will be using the category system for the general purpose or goal of the projects in which the category system will be used. If the general goal is evaluation, then discussion needs to take place to identify the most important features of the instruction or training experiences. This is an important step, as the category system to be developed for professional evaluation, for example, is ultimately designed to document whether or not particular clientele behaviors are indicative of successful instructional or training effects. In other words, the purpose of recording behaviors and events in an evaluation effort is to develop distinct categories for data recording in relation to the important features of the education or training experience—so that a particular instructor may hold his or her trainees accountable for those behaviors for which training efforts have been made. This is an important step in that the terms and definitions in a category system will be indicative of what various clientele will be held accountable for as a function of exposure to a particular education or training experience. Careful thought concerning terms and definitions in relationship to larger education or training issues will ensure a clear connection between the larger emphases of the training program and the behavior and environment events in the related category system—events that clientele will be held accountable for demonstrating in certain ways as a function of being successfully trained.The same idea of following a stated purpose holds true for a research and development activity that uses a category system for the collection and analysis of behaviors and events of interest. In a research and development context, however, the purpose question is twofold. First, a set of terms and definitions should be provided that are capable of describing as completely and accurately as possible the educational treatment or experimental intervention that is being tested for its relative effects. Whether the treatment is systematically manipulated (e.g., introduced or withdrawn at specific intervals or points in time in a particular setting; see Chapter 8 on the construction of an appropriate research design) or exists as a natural part of an ongoing setting of interest, the issue is the importance of being able to completely and accurately describe the presence or absence of a particular treatment and/or its various component parts. The descriptive recording of the characteristics of a particular treatment is an important and, until recently, an often underemphasized dimension of the observational research process. In this regard, we want to gain a clear understanding of whether or not the treatment was implemented according to the recommended procedures or practices set up as part of the experiment. Collecting data according to the characteristics of a particular treatment to determine if it has been implemented correctly is termed an assessment of *treatment fidelity* or *treatment integrity.* If a treatment is not implemented according to its description, and if certain treatment variations are not recorded during a particular experiment, then what is called the relative treatment fidelity or treatment integrity of a particular treatment intervention is severely compromised. If treatment fidelity or integrity is compromised, then analysis results may also suffer compromise in terms of inaccurate or incorrect experimental conclusions. Chapter 6 provides detail concerning how one may go about evaluating relative treatment fidelity and integrity issues. Witt, Noell, LaFleur, and Mortenson (1997) provide a contemporary data-based illustration of how one might measure and analyze treatment integrity in an education setting; and detailed discussions of this issue are available in the applied behavior analysis literature for those interested in additional information on this subject (see Gresham, Gansle, & Noell, 1993, and Peterson, Homer, & Wonderlich, 1982).

Another question related to the purpose of a research and development activity concerns the measures chosen to determine whether or not a particular treatment or intervention was effective. It is important to construct a set of terms and definitions that will most accurately and inclusively represent what the researcher holds most important regarding the desirable effects of a chosen intervention. This is the case whether you are looking for evidence of the presence of or increase in certain behaviors or events as a result of a particular intervention or evidence of diminishing or absent behavior or event occurrences as a function of a particular set of procedures. Care in the construction of measurement-oriented terms and definitions is also important, whether the research question involves determination of the relative effects of a manipulated treatment or the effects certain behaviors and events may have on certain others in settings in which both the treatment and the measure are naturally occurring.

DETERMINING OBSERVATION
SYSTEM CHARACTERISTICS

While an explicit set of terms and operational definitions is being outlined for the purpose of constructing a definitive category system, some structural questions must also be answered concerning how a particular category system code is organized to capture the particular behaviors and events that a researcher may be interested in. The structural organization of a particular coding scheme is fundamentally related to the type and scope of information a researcher or evaluator wishes to gather in relationship to other behaviors or events of lesser or negligible interest. When determining a structure, three basic decisions must be made. The first relates to whether the terms and definitions to be used for collecting data will be mutually exclusive of one another, or whether certain behaviors and/or events will be recorded at the same point in time (i.e., potentially occur in concert or overlap in occurrence). The researcher's ability to make this type of decision has been facilitated by the data collection sophistication made available by amenable software programs for the collection and analysis of multiple-event data records. For behavior and event categories to be *mutually exclusive* means that if one of the behaviors or events in the category system is being recorded then all (or a specified subset) of the other behaviors and events in the category system being used must not be recorded as occurring at the same time. The necessity of making such a distinction depends on the type of data-based information that is desired. For example, if a researcher is interested in the incidence of self-injurious behavior of a particular client who has a history of physical disabilities and related learning delays, and the researcher wishes to treat that behavior using a specifically prescribed sequence of therapist behaviors, then a mutually exclusive observation system may be best suited to such study and evaluation. If, on the other hand, a researcher is interested in the variety of behaviors that best describe effective instruction in a particular educational situation, an overlapping coding scheme may be in order, in that most teachers are known to use multiple behaviors in concert to accomplish complex instructional objectives.

Collecting data in a movement education classroom provides another illustration of this decision-making process. If, for example, the researcher is interested only in how certain types of instruction impact on the relative success of student practices when the teacher is proximate to a student, she or he might opt for a mutually exclusive code. In this context, the researcher might logically separate verbal instruction from skill modeling, and separate these two instructional behaviors from the instructional behavior of physical guidance. Although modeling may also be defined to contain elements of verbal instruction, and physical guidance may be defined to contain elements of verbal instruction and/or modeling, in this example, data collection interest is on the relative proportion of each instructional behavior as a separate entity and should therefore be recorded separately. If, on the other hand, the researcher is interested in describing the various ways in which certain types of instruction (e.g., verbal, modeling, and physical guidance) may overlap with one another to form more effective or meaningful combinations of instruction for particular students, then these behaviors should be defined to allow the coding of more than one instructional behavior when two or more of these behaviors occur in concert or in overlapping fashion.

Another issue related to mutual exclusivity is more of a pragmatic matter and concerns whether a category system is being used to record data directly in a live setting as the behaviors and events naturally occur or whether data is being recorded from videotape records of the setting of interest. Clearly, if the behaviors are being recorded live, a mutually exclusive format is easier to implement. Using a mutually exclusive structure will heighten the probability of an accurate data record, for even if the researcher is using a computer-based method of recording multiple occurrences of multiple behaviors and events, only so many keys on a computer keyboard can physically be pressed at the same time, and only so many behaviors and events (keys) can be recorded with an acceptable level of accuracy as multiple events occur in concert or overlap with one another. With live recording, the complete and inclusive nature of the data record is oftentimes sacrificed to a certain extent for the sake of feasibility and accuracy. In recording data from videotape records, a much more complex and overlapping event record is feasible, one that may provide a much more accurate and inclusive representation of the complex overlapping nature of an observed setting's behavior-behavior and behavior-environment interactions. Software programs such as the one described in the flyer included with this text provide for videotape synchronization and amenable data record sorting and merging according to the time-based starts and stops of behavior and event occurrences, enabling an advanced level of sophistication and complexity in producing a complete data record of complex interactive settings.

Another structural decision for the researcher developing a coding scheme is whether the category system needs to be capable of an all-inclusive (or "exhaustive," as termed by Bakeman and Gottman, 1986, p. 33) description of any potential behavior or event occurrence within a setting of interest, or whether particular behaviors are the primary focus, with all others of lesser importance considered so to the point of not being specifically included in the category system. In the latter case, this situation is similar to traditional quantitative experimental models in which focus is only on a specific independent variable or treatment and a particular measure or dependent variable, with all other variables considered extraneous and controlled for as well as possible according to certain threats to experimental validity (see the section Validity Issues in Chapter 8 for a more complete discussion of this). For the purposes of this discussion, a category system is termed *all-inclusive* if any behavior or event that may conceivably occur in the setting being observed can be recorded in one of the specified categories in that system.

Examples from education again serve well to illustrate this step in the category system construction decision process. Suppose, for example, that a clinician in a resource setting for a severely and profoundly autistic and self-injurious clientele is interested in the effects of a particular set of instructional behaviors on the incidence of self-injurious episodes. If this is the focus of a data record, then a category system that includes (a) particular instructional behaviors, (b) the primary measure of self-injurious incidents, and (c) a broad category of "other" might be a most appropriate system configuration. In this way, all other behaviors and events in the setting may be lumped together in a general or anonymous way to retain the time-based integrity of the data collection episode, but for recording purposes specific behaviors and events of interest are focused on using a less than completely inclusive system. Suppose, on the other hand, that the same clinician is interested in describing the many possible interaction effects of all behaviors and environmental events operating within the same resource setting, for the purpose of determining which behavior-behavior and behavior-environment interactions might be relatively more or less therapeutic in the reduction of self-injurious behavior. If this is the case, then a more all-inclusive category system should be developed that provides explicit information regarding all of the behaviors and events operating in time-based proximity to the occurrences of the self-injurious events within that resource setting.

A third coding scheme decision-making level involves the size and complexity of a category system. In other words, the number of actual terms, or codes, in the system to be used must be determined. This decision is related to the decision of whether data collection will take place live in the setting in which behaviors and events of interest are occurring or from videotape records of that setting. We recommend some general rules of thumb. First, we agree with other methodologists, such as Bakeman and Gottman (1986) and Kazdin (1982), that it is always prudent to err on the side of simplicity rather than undue complexity when constructing a category system. Otherwise meaningful information may be lost in a sea of data if the category system is unduly complex in terms of the number of categories included for recording purposes. Our experiences have convinced us that once we go beyond a certain number of individual categories in a particular system, the marginal utility of the amount of information gained becomes increasingly less than the increasing challenge of ensuring the accuracy and reliability of the data record. In other words, we recommend avoiding the danger of infinite regress into potentially less and less meaningful discriminations among very similar behaviors and events as a category system becomes more complex and larger in number. In our experience, we have found with live recording that beyond a limit of 16 to 20 categories within a particular system, the quality of information ceases to meaningfully increase and the feasibility of recording information accurately and reliability drops off sharply.

In contrast, the ability to record from videotape records an increasing number of behaviors and events with finer and finer discriminations among behavior and event classes when using a particular category system clearly exists. Through various methods (e.g., collecting and merging separate data records containing logically grouped behaviors and events), it is possible to ensure the accuracy and reliability of the data when using very complex category systems that contain multiple codes (see Chapter 5 for some representative coding scheme illustrations). The computer-based tools described in the back of this text, for example, provide for 36 categories and the subgrouping of each of those 36 primary categories into 99 subcategories by using numerical notations within each primary category. Even though we are capable of such data recording complexity when using such computer-based data collection tools, we have found that the same law of diminishing returns applies to recording from videotape that applies to recording live. We have typically found that when recording data from videotape, expanding a particular category system beyond 30 to 40 events yields a minimal amount of meaningful information. For example, including a group of 4 or 5 questioning behaviors in a category system designed to study effective instructional practice in postsecondary settings may prove very helpful in determining not only which types of questions are most effective in facilitating productive student interactions but also the most effective sequencing of questioning behavior for optimal instructional practice. If we split these 4 or 5 questioning categories further, say, into 15 or 20 subcategories (by the inclusion of various verbal and nonverbal cues and various other contextually based dimensions for each primary questioning category), we may not gain much additional information in the typical postsecondary setting under observation.

It is important for the researcher to make a final decision about the optimal way of using the computer-based facilitation of collecting and analyzing behaviors and events in multiple ways. Most software programs, for example, provide multiple analysis capabilities with respect to (a) the individual or static character of behaviors and events, (b) the sequential or time-based nature of event occurrences, and (c) the qualitative character of the behaviors and environmental events under observation. Beyond the technical decisions of how to construct a category system and actually record behaviors and events in the most economical way (e.g., the press-and-hold, toggle, numerical notation, comment features, etc., made available through most software-based data collection mechanisms), research and evaluation decisions must also be made regarding the most informative measure in relationship to the observational purposes decided on for a particular application. It is in this regard that contemporary computer-based direct observation and behavior analysis methods provide the capability to collect the occurrence of and consequently analyze each behavior and event recorded across most of the measures explained in Chapter 7 in the Measurement Options section (e.g., number, rate, duration, percentage of experimental time, celeration, sequential probability, etc.). What remains, however, for the behavioral researcher is the challenge of reporting the most appropriate form of measurement data to a particular research audience to get a particular analysis or evaluation point across and reporting the most helpful and readily understandable measurement data to various clientele when using these tools for evaluation and feedback purposes. In addition to this text's materials on the subject, we recommend that more advanced audiences read Bakeman and Gottman (1986, 1997), Barlow and Hersen (1984), Cooper and colleagues (1987), Johnston and Pennypacker (1980), Kazdin (1982), Kerlinger (1986), LeCompte and Preissle (1993), Miles and Huberman (1984), and innumerable other behavior analytic or qualitative methodology texts for a thorough treatment of measurement choice issues.

RECORDING PHYSICAL VERSUS SOCIAL CODING SCHEMES

Another important part of category system preparation lies in whether a particular set of terms and definitions to be used to collect data is physically based or socially based. Bakeman and Gottman (1986) have made the distinction among these two categories of coding schemes as follows:

1. Physically based codes are those that can classify behavior with clear and explicit ties to an individual's or organism's physical action. Action may be verbal in terms of sound, or physical movement.

In other words, codes that are not open to interpretation across investigators.

2. Socially based codes are those that classify behaviors and events by the perceptions of the researcher who is collecting the information over some form of social process. This type of category includes an inference on the part of the researcher when that researcher records information based on a particular socially based code.

The following examples and illustrations should help the reader make the distinction between the two types of codes. This illustration comes from education: If a data collector were interested in the number or percentage of skill-based feedback statements that a teacher used during a particular lesson, then a physically based coding scheme would be most appropriate. Clear and explicit definitions of what constituted feedback could be constructed and data could be collected as a function of observing incidences of the direct physiological actions of the teacher that were related to the use of feedback statements to various students in that teacher's class.

On the other hand, that same data collector may be interested in the emotional impact on students of teacher use of skill-based feedback interactions. Emotional impact in this regard might concern how relatively positively or negatively a student responds to a particular skill-based interaction of the teacher. Although certain physically based elements of this dimension of student behavior would be included in this portion of a coding scheme (e.g., teacher proximity to an individual student, teacher verbal skill-based information dissemination, etc.), the recording of a student emotional state or outcome as a result of receiving some form of teacher feedback interaction is socially based. In other words, coding a positive or negative emotional outcome on the part of a particular student as a function of a teacher interaction requires the data collector to make some sort of inference about a subject's (in this case, a student's) feelings and perceptions.

The categorization of physically based or socially based coding schemes may seem to some, at least at first, to be an artificially contrived distinction. Many behavior analysis researchers would argue that if a set of terms and definitions to form a coding scheme to be used for collecting direct observational data were termed, defined, and organized appropriately, then there would be no need for any inferential capacity on the part of the data collector using the code. In addition, argument could be made that any inferential requirement on the part of a data collector with regard to the mental, emotional, or perceptual states of those individuals being observed is best left to another method of analysis. There may, however, exist some important scientific rationales in support of the researcher distinguishing between physically and socially based coding scheme structures when conducting a behavior analysis. For example, there are times when a socially based coding scheme may more accurately reflect the questions that a particular researcher may want to answer. In the education research illustration just provided, there may be times when answering whether a teacher is within a certain prescribed proximity to a student and whether a certain type of verbalization was emitted by that teacher is not enough to answer a research question of interest. Sometimes it may be important to answer questions like whether a student was trying to obtain a teacher's attention and what the disposition of a student was before and after a set of teacher interactions. Although many scientific phenomena may be captured using a physically based describe-and-analyze technique, not all scientific phenomena of interest are amenable to such categorization and analysis. Skinner has defined thinking and feelings (i.e., private events; for more on this, see the How Behavior Analysis Conceptualizes Mental Events section in Chapter 2) in terms of an individual's internal neural workings that relate to thinking and feeling and how they may act according to the same laws of behavior that govern public physical events; however, we do not as a scientific community at present have an amenable data collection and analysis mechanism that may directly observe those events. In the case where these types of events are the primary interest of a particular investigation, some form of inferential quantitative category system approach to the indirect observation of these events, such as intuitive or qualitative fieldnotes, might be preferable to other forms of data gathering.

Bakeman and Gottman (1986) use the study of children's play practices to provide an example of the sort of process involved in deciding whether to use a physically based or socially based coding system. When a researcher is determining whether children are playing alone or with others and whether they are engaged in parallel play or a genuinely peer-engaged state of play, a socially based coding system may be helpful to a complete analysis. At one level, an observer should have little trouble determining whether children are in close proximity to one another or far apart, and a physically based coding system is adequate at this level of determining play engagement. However, when observing children in close proximity, another question a researcher may have concerns what else might constitute that children are genuinely playing with others. These questions logically follow that question: Is "playing with others" simply a determination of proximity, or is it a function of a particular set of verbal or nonverbal interactions? Is it a function of some sort of ongoing eye contact and recognition of a common play interest? What types of things should be included in the definition of "playing together"? When considering these types of questions, a socially based coding system in which an inference is called for from the observer of children playing is helpful. In other words, the observer may not be able to rely on the physical dimensions of play alone (such as proximity, gesture, posture, verbal and nonverbal interactions, and so on) in making a determination of the type of play children are involved in—the observer must make an inference concerning each child's intent and the subjective experience of those children when coding playing alone, in parallel formats, or in a group structure. This example illustrates the potential variety of instances in conducting direct observational research when a socially based coding scheme would offer a researcher greater informational insight into an experimental or evaluative question of interest than a physically based coding scheme would—particularly when the researcher is dealing with complex interactive environments where the behavioral intent of the participants observed may have an impact on behavior change and behavior outcome.

The decision whether to use a coding scheme that is physically or socially based is also connected to how the individual collecting the data from that observation system is perceived. If, for example, a data collector is viewed by the strict definition of the term *collector* as one who passively and unobtrusively collects information on just what publicly occurs in relation to the coding scheme used, then the type of coding scheme used is probably physically based. In this case, the data collector is merely being asked to view and record what occurs based on her or his vision of a setting in relation to a very specifically predefined coding system. If, on the other hand, a data collector is asked to make some culturally or socially based distinctions, or inferences, concerning the setting observed; and not merely passively collect occurrences and nonoccurrences of particular physically based behaviors and events, then a socially based coding system is probably in use. The critical difference here is not whether or not clear and complete definitions of behaviors and events are provided in the coding scheme but whether or not the data collector is asked to make an inferential decision about the occurrence or nonoccurrence of some event based on the coding scheme definitions.

A good illustration of the socially based coding concept is the direct observation activities in the marital interaction literature. Many codes used to observe therapist and client interactions in this literature have an observer decide whether marriage participants are happy, sad, angry, or frustrated at certain points during a therapy session. The determination of such emotional states requires that an inference be made on the part of the observer collecting such data, as it is a difficult task to provide a physically based code that could completely describe all of the verbal, nonverbal, and posturing behaviors and events that comprise each of these emotional states in relation to therapeutic interaction.

CONSTRUCTING OPERATIONAL DEFINITIONS

Once the researcher has considered the many defining purposes and coding scheme characteristics above in relation to a particular observational activity, the next and perhaps most important consideration lays in just how to articulate the operational definitions of the terms included in a particular coding scheme. To ensure *operational definitions* of behaviors and events in a coding system, we agree with Kazdin (1982) that behaviors and events included for observational purposes need to be defined very explicitly so that they can be "observed, measured, and agreed on by those who assess performance and implement treatment" (p. 23). Successful description, and accordingly successful analysis, begins, according to Hawkins and Dobes (1977), with objective, clear, and complete articulation of behaviors and events of interest—that is, operational definitions. Here is an example that illustrates the importance of this point. For instance, if an observer was interested in collecting information on the feedback behaviors of a teacher in a classroom, he or she might define the code of feedback as follows:

Feedback: A teacher is involved in interacting with a student

This definition, however, lacks many of the elements of clarity and completeness in articulation, lending itself to the dangers of inobjectivity in data collection. Many features of a potentially clear and complete definition of the code of feedback in this case are not covered, leaving an observer guessing just what constitutes an occurrence or non-occurrence of the feedback behavior to be recorded. Elements such as teacher proximity to a student or students, how many students may receive the feedback interaction, what the interaction may constitute, and when it typically occurs within a teacher↔student interaction are necessary for a clear and complete treatment of what constitutes feedback. In addition, examples of specific statements might be included in parentheses to further clarify the definition. In an effort to provide a more satisfactory definition of the code feedback, a researcher may develop the definition further along the informational lines just suggested to state something like the following:

Feedback: In close proximity to a student or group, the teacher makes a verbal statement or physical gesture following an individual's or small group of students' (typically 3 to 6) subject-matter or organizational practice behaviors, which is clearly designed to increase or maintain the effectiveness of those student responses in the future. The statement or gesture must follow soon enough after the behavior (typically during a student skill practice or within 30 seconds afterward) that the student clearly associates it with the behavior being commented on. Feedback is delineated by, for example, encouraging statements that occur *prior* to the student behavior in question and those that occur *after* the behavior (examples include the statement of a teacher who in teaching basketball shooting says "Move your arm this way," coupled with modeling the movement, as well as teacher statements such as "Good job," "That's correct, now remember what you did the next time we practice this," and "No, let me show you how this is done," coupled with the teacher's demonstration).

According to Hawkins and Dobes (1977), and in the context of our two examples that define the code feedback, *objectivity* refers to limiting definitions to the observable characteristics of specified behaviors and events. If definitions are truly objective, then they should avoid all references to behavioral intention or to internal states or mentalistic perspectives on those behaviors (Barlow & Hersen, 1984). *Clarity*, on the other hand, refers to the ability of different observers who use the category system definitions to read, interpret, and articulate instances and noninstances of particular behaviors and events with a lack of ambiguity or disagreement. Finally, the characteristic of *complete* refers to ensuring the articulation of a boundary of conditions that delineate behaviors and events across categories in the observational system. In other words, a set of category system definitions is said to be complete (and clear) if it is plain and apparent to multiple observers how certain behaviors and events should be included in or excluded from a particular category, and hence recorded and included in a data record or not recorded and hence excluded from a data record.

The characteristic of complete with regard to defining behaviors and events to be used for data gathering in a particular category system is perhaps most important. To ensure the complete nature of behavior and event definitions, a set of rules needs to be generated that makes explicit how particular behaviors and events should or should not be recorded. According to Hawkins (1982), to ensure that a definition is complete, it must include all of the following:

1. a descriptive name

2. a general description of the behavior or event much like that found in a dictionary

3. a discussion of the critical components of the behavior or event that may be used for rulings on inclusion or exclusion

4. typical examples of the behavior or event for use in making questionable or borderline judgments on difficult calls when recording data from the category system definitions

If these four rules of category system definition development are followed with respect to each term to be used for data collection, then the definitions that meet these criteria are termed or classified as *operational*.

One helpful strategy to use in ensuring an objective, clear, and complete set of category system definitions (i.e., an operationally defined coding scheme) is to watch situations in which behaviors and events of interest occur often and to (a) form an inductive and general set of descriptions of each targeted behavior and event and (b) collaborate with others in coming up with examples that are helpful in making borderline judgments on potentially ambiguous occurrences of each behavior or event in question. If this procedure is followed, it is less challenging for the researcher to finalize a set of definitions that meet the operational criteria of Hawkins (1982) listed above.

The contents of this chapter should have made it clear to the reader that the process of developing a clear and complete set of terms and definitions to be used for recording direct observational data is a stage of the research or evaluation enterprise that requires great care and thought from the individual interested in engaging in direct observation activity. Despite what may seem to some like a rather large set of procedures for coding scheme construction, and a relatedly daunting list of category system construction decisions and definitional development recommendations, a direct observational approach to the quantifying of behaviors and events may hold great promise and appeal because its rigorous data collection and analysis process meets the objective and systematic quantification objectives of the scientific enterprise that have been defined in previous chapters. We have provided a representative list of references for various education, social, and applied science direct observation applications. To help guide those using the methods and materials contained in this text to construct their own category systems for their own particular needs, we have also included a general terms and definitions framework and some specific category system illustrations that emanate from that more general framework. Chapter 5 is devoted to a detailed presentation of these representative illustrations and examples that have been used with success in various disciplines. Chapter 6 then provides a discussion of the important procedural issues of ensuring the reliability of data collection efforts, the accuracy of treatment implementation, and the related activity of appropriate staff training.

5

Interdisciplinary Examples and Illustrations

One can picture a good life by analyzing one's feelings, but one can achieve it only by arranging environmental contingencies.

— Skinner (cited in Sulzer-Azaroff & Mayer, 1991, Dedication)

After reading this chapter, you should be able to define the following terms and provide the information requested in the study guide below.

TERMS

Category system
Teacher education
Ethology

STUDY GUIDE

1. Explain the seven general guidelines that should be followed when constructing a coding scheme for direct observational purposes.
2. List and discuss a variety of general behavior and event classes that should be considered when constructing a coding scheme designed to observe in inclusive ways a setting of interest.
3. Describe the relationship among the terms and definitions used in a coding scheme for data collection purposes, the type of data gathered using those coding schemes, and the relationship between data information gathered and data used for evaluation purposes.

4. Provide clear, complete, and objective definitions for a variety of behavior and event terms contained in a direct observational coding scheme.

This chapter provides a selected set of category system illustrations chosen particularly for their potential to help those relatively new to direct observation and behavior analysis research activities to design, develop, and implement category systems specific to an individual's particular research or evaluation activities. In this regard, the term *category system* is defined as a set of terms and operational definitions that guide the act of collecting direct observational data in accordance with the *categories* (i.e., terms and their definitions) that a particular *system* (i.e., collection of terms) has articulated. The chapter is organized according to an extensive compilation of coding schemes that have been used with some success in a variety of disciplines for both research and evaluation activities in applied and clinical settings. Some of the category system examples provided are quite detailed and offer illustrations of terms, definitions, and referenced lists of evaluation strategies based on the use of the category system. Other examples are limited to a summary of category terms because the definitions of the terms are fairly straightforward or substantially similar in structure to the definitions provided for other category system examples, or because more detailed illustrations are available in our list of references. All of the category system examples are provided with the hope of stimulating thinking about the types of terms and definitions that may be best suited to a particular research or evaluation task, and for the examples we thank the various contributors who have been receptive to having their work included in this text. The two category systems represented as examples of education assessment applications (Tables 5.2 and 5.3) are also contained in immediately usable file format in the recommended data collection and analysis software program described in the back of this text (i.e., BEST). We also recommend that readers interested in detailed examples and illustrations of the types of alternative coding systems summarized in the introductory pages of Chapter 4 refer to the sources referenced in those pages, for the observation systems in those references are representative of a variety of direct observation and behavior analysis applications beyond those provided in this chapter of category system examples.

A GENERAL FRAMEWORK FOR
DEVELOPING A CODING SCHEME

Table 5.1 provides a general framework for those interested in developing a coding scheme in the education and social sciences. The framework is provided to stimulate thinking about the many different possible general behavior and environment categories that might be important to include for various research or evaluation purposes. Some categories are time and behavior based, and some are not but still remain potentially important to a complete and inclusive description of a setting in which multiple participants are interacting in educational or therapeutic ways. We hope that using this framework as a general guide to stimulate constructive thinking will enable researchers to readily design and productively implement specific category systems.

It is clear from even a cursory look at the general framework contained in Table 5.1 that it is steeped in education and social science applications of direct observation and behavior analysis methods. This general framework, however, also provides for a fairly comprehensive view of the many setting or environmental events, professional (e.g., educator, therapist, or clinician) practices, client (e.g., student or trainee) behaviors, and potentially impacting historical events that occur prior to the particular setting under observation. These types of event categories are all important to consider when constructing a relatively inclusive coding scheme designed to describe and analyze highly interactive applied situations. The researcher who uses this general framework as a guide for developing a coding system for a particular research or evaluation activity will find that it is still important to follow the general guidelines provided in Chapter 4 regarding the following:

1. defining the purpose of a coding scheme in relation to an experimental or evaluation question of interest

2. determining the structure and specific characteristics of the coding system being developed

3. determining the physical and social dimensions of the coding system to be used for a particular application

4. constructing a set of operational definitions that are objective, clear, and complete and contain specific examples and illustrations

Table 5.1   A General Framework for Developing a Coding Scheme

Classes	Description	Examples
Environment		
Setting	Service delivery setting or research setting	Classroom, resource room, natural habitat or client environment, etc.
Content	Subject matter to be taught, treatment or intervention to be introduced, skills to be learned	Math or reading skills, positive social treatments, behavior reduction strategies, etc.
Content Stage	Temporal status of the observational setting	Beginning, middle, or end; lesson preview, body, or review
Materials	Physical resources	Educational equipment and materials, socially stimulating toys, client workbooks or folders, etc.
Participant Grouping	Physical arrangements	Large or small group, number and kind of participants, etc.
Method of Interaction	Stimulus method to occasion responding	Instructional or interactive styles, such as command, individual, or reciprocal
Transitions	Events signaling situational changes	Changes in participant grouping, in educational or treatment context, in physical arrangements, etc.
Teacher, Therapist, or Leader Behavior		
Behavior	Relative to student, client, or other setting participants	Observation, verbal and nonverbal instructions and directions, questioning, responding, organizational and interpersonal interactions, compliance, resistance, etc.
Physical Movements	Relative to position in setting	Sitting, standing, moving, reaching, waving, eating, sleeping, walking, bar pressing, physically guiding another person, etc.

Classes	Description	Examples
Focus	How behavior and movement are directed	To an individual or defined subgroup of participants
Setting Position	Relative proximity to other defined setting participants	Central or peripheral setting locations, proximity to or distance from defined setting participants, presence in or absence from setting

Student, Client, or Participant Behavior

Behavior	Active stimuli and responses	Activity engagement (successful and unsuccessful; desired and undesirable), supporting and instructional behavior, listening, waiting, off-task, behavior, disruption, responding, interpersonal engagement, etc.
Physical Movements	Relative to position in setting	Sitting, standing, moving, reaching, waving, eating, bar pressing, physically guiding another person, etc.
Focus	How behavior and movement are directed	To an individual or defined subgroup of participants
Setting Position	Relative proximity to other defined setting participants	Central or peripheral setting locations, proximity to or distance from defined setting participants, presence in or absence from setting

Historical

Contextual	Past and present setting factors affecting behavior performance	Physical arrangements, participant arrangements, setting materials, methods of interaction, etc.
Experiential	Participant background	Education, years and types of experience, cultural background, age, socio-economic background, interactive history

SOURCE: Adapted from Hawkins, Sharpe, and Ray (1994)

relevant to the actual behaviors and events to be described and analyzed as a function of coding system implementation

5. determining the form and function of particular codes contained in a coding scheme in relation to whether they are focused on the static characteristics of a behavior or event itself or on the time-based connections or sequences among certain behaviors or events

6. deciding on the type of measurement focus in relation to Item 5 above and in relation to those described in the Measurement Options section in Chapter 7

7. going over a variety of feasibility issues with regard to the practicality of implementing the coding scheme in the research or evaluation situations for which it is intended

Finally, in relation to particular direct observation interests, we recommend that the general framework provided in Table 5.1 be used as a general guide only in stimulating thinking regarding just what one may wish to include in a particular category system application to a particular direct observation activity. Once the researcher is familiar with the general guide provided, reading about one or a number of the specific category systems that follow may be helpful to further specific coding scheme development. In addition, the researcher may wish to consult the many alternative category systems referenced in the introductory pages of Chapter 4, which may provide him or her with additional aid in coming to a completely developed and operationalized coding system tailored to particular research or evaluation activities.

EXAMPLES FROM TEACHER EDUCATION

This section provides two category systems (see Tables 5.2 and 5.3) that, although they are relatively inclusive in structure, have been developed and defined according to traditional and frequently seen direct observational methods found in the behavioral literature in education. Each system was structured according to a mutually exclusive and all-inclusive set of structural decisions, and each was designed for evaluation purposes for use by teacher educators who are interested in collecting data by directly observing actual practice teaching settings that undergraduate teacher-trainees are operating in for the purpose of improving their instructional skills. In the case of using the types of category systems illustrated in Tables 5.2 and 5.3, *teacher education* is defined as the activity of preparing professionals for roles as certified teachers for K-12 and other alternative educational settings.

The definitions in the category system provided in Table 5.2 are representative of traditional definitions that focus on measuring the static characteristics of individual behaviors and events (e.g., number, rate, percentage of class time, etc.), although the category system is also amenable to the recording of time-based sequential information of those same behaviors and events.

The category system contained in Table 5.2 was designed for use in physical education and youth sport settings in which movement and active participation are desirable student behaviors and a variety of instructional and organizational behaviors are used by both teachers and students. A list of definitions is also provided with this example to give the reader some relatively complete illustrations of definitions that meet the objective, clear, and complete criteria discussed in Chapter 4. In addition, operational and explicit lists of feedback strategies are available in the literature regarding this type of category system used as a feedback and goal-setting tool in the preparation of physical education teachers and youth sport coaches. Referring to these references may help those who are beginning to explore the development and implementation of evaluation activities with a behavioral component in a variety of professional preparation programs with how to go about operationalizing a structured set of feedback and goal-setting strategies for use with professional clientele. When constructing a category system to be used for evaluation purposes, it is important to construct complimentary educational information for various clientele based on the behaviors and events in the category system that are designed for effective trainee practice and trainee accountability. For those interested in a detailed discussion of the feedback strategies used with the category system illustrated in Table 5.2 and in relation to a set of operationalized teacher training procedures, refer to Hawkins, Wiegand, and Landin (1985), and Landin, Hawkins, and Wiegand (1986). Similar sets of materials can also be made available from the primary author of this text upon request as well.[1] The category systems contained in Tables 5.2 and 5.3 are also available as downloadable observation systems in the software package described in the back of this text. For the observation system

(Text continues on page 152)

Table 5.2   Physical Education Teacher Education (PETEACH) Category System Summary

Physical Education Teacher Education (PETEACH) Categories

Teacher Behaviors	Student Behaviors
1. General Observation	M. Motor Appropriate
2. Specific Observation	M- F3-1-RETURN. Motor Engaged
3. Encouragement	S. Supportive
4. Positive Feedback	C. Cognitive
5. Negative Feedback	N. On-Task
6. Management	F. Off-Task
7. Verbal Instruction	I. Instruction of Peers
8. Modeling	W. Waiting
9. Physical Guidance	
0. Interpersonal	
A. Off-Task	

Contextual Elements (Toggled Keys in PETEACH)
T. Transition
P. Preview
B. Lesson Body
R. Review

PETEACH Operational Definitions

Teacher Behavior

1.   General Observation: The teacher is watching student groups engaged in any category of student behavior. This category includes passive supervision, and there is no relationship of the observation to an instructional focus. The teacher must also *not* be engaged in any other category of teacher behavior in order to record general observation.

2.   Specific Observation: The teacher is watching *one* student engaged in a subject matter task for the purpose of providing feedback related to performance. The teacher position must be proximal to the student position so that observation is clearly focused on a specific student who is performing. Specific observation *could* also be recorded when the teacher is watching pairs or small groups of students when the instructional focus is clearly on a group task (e.g., observation of five players executing a fast break during instruction on the fast break in basketball).

3.   Encouragement: The teacher makes a verbal statement *prior* to a student skill or organizational attempt, which is clearly meant to enhance the student's perception of his or her ability to accomplish the subsequent task. The teacher is not telling the student what to do (e.g., an instructional prompt—behavior 7) but is clearly trying to build confidence (e.g., by saying,

"You can do it," "If you did it last time you can surely do it this way," etc.). This category may also be recorded when encouraging behaviors are conveyed to the class population as a whole or to small groups of students.

4.   Positive Feedback: The teacher makes a positive verbal statement or gesture following an individual's or group of students' skill or organizational behaviors, which is clearly designed to increase or maintain such responses in the future. The statement or gesture must follow soon enough after the behavior that the student clearly associates it with the behavior being commented on. Feedback statements may easily be delineated from encouraging statements, for encouragement occurs *prior* to the student behavior in question and feedback occurs *after* the behavior.

5.   Negative Feedback: The teacher makes a negative or critical verbal statement or gesture following an individual's or group of students' inappropriate skill or organizational behaviors, which is clearly designed to decrease or eliminate such responses in the future. The statement or gesture must follow soon enough after the behavior that the student clearly associates it with the behavior being commented on.

6.   Management: The teacher is engaged in carrying out a non-subject matter organizational task (e.g., setting up equipment, taking roll, collecting papers, explaining station rotations, directing students to move to another instructional activity or station, etc.). This category may be conducted in a verbal or nonverbal gesturing manner.

7.   Verbal Instruction: The teacher is verbally describing to the students how to do a skill or is using a verbal prompt to direct a student or group engaged in attempting a skill or activity. To record verbal instruction, the student task must be a subject matter activity.

8.   Modeling: The teacher demonstrates to students how to do a subject matter task or participates with students in a subject matter task or activity. If the teacher uses a student to demonstrate a subject matter task, this category should also be recorded for the duration of the student demonstration episode.

9.   Physical Guidance: The teacher physically guides an individual or group of students through a subject matter task or activity. The teacher must make and maintain actual physical contact with the student in question for this category to be recorded (e.g., holding a student's arm on a balance beam in gymnastics, guiding an athlete's arms through a proper swimming technique, etc.).

0.   Interpersonal: The teacher talks to an individual or group of students about non-subject matter and nonmanagerial tasks in a manner clearly designed to foster a positive interpersonal relationship between teacher and student. A teacher commenting on a student's clothing and talking about what a student did over the weekend are examples of interpersonal behavior.

(Continued)

Table 5.2 Continued

A. Off-Task: The teacher is clearly *not* paying attention to the instructional and/or organizational responsibilities regarding the class. A teacher making notes on what to do during football practice during the course of a physical education class, flirting with the passing office staff, and daydreaming against the gymnasium wall are clear examples of off-task behavior.

Student Behaviors

M. Motor Appropriate: The student is engaged in a subject matter motor activity in a successful manner. Success is defined as the student meeting the lesson objectives of the teacher or coach. Examples of this include a student dribbling around cones with a basketball without letting the ball get away, exhibiting correct skill performance as defined by a coach in a practice setting, and so on.

M- (Number Notation - 1). Motor Engaged: The student is engaged in a subject matter-oriented motor activity, but the task is either too difficult for the individual's capabilities or so easy that student practice is performed poorly or incorrectly, clearly not meeting lesson goals. Examples of this include a student dribbling around cones with a basketball and letting the ball get away, shooting free throws in a basketball practice session but missing the basket, doing improper hand turns during a swimming practice set, and so on.

S. Supportive: The student is engaged in assisting others to perform a subject matter motor activity (e.g., spotting in gymnastics, feeding balls to a hitter in a tennis lesson, throwing a volleyball to a partner who is practicing set up passing, clapping a rhythm for a group of students practicing a dance movement pattern, etc.).

C. Cognitive: The student is attentively listening to the teacher or a visual aid describing an organizational or subject matter task being attended to by the student (e.g., verbal description of a game, watching a modeling episode, viewing a filmstrip, participating in a discussion, etc.).

N. On-Task: The student is appropriately engaged in carrying out an assigned non-subject matter task designed to *prepare* her or him for a learning and/or skill attempt (e.g., moving into squads, moving from the gymnasium to the playing field, reading prescription sheets at a drill station, etc.). This category includes all student managerial tasks undertaken to attain a state of learning readiness.

F. Off-Task: The student either is not engaged in the activity in which it is clear he or she should be engaged, or is engaged in an activity other than the one clearly advocated by the teacher (e.g., behavior disruptions, misusing equipment, fighting, etc.).

I.   Instruction of Peers: The student is teaching the subject matter to either an individual or a group of his or her peers. This category includes student performance of any of the three teacher instructional behaviors (e.g., verbal instruction—behavior 7, modeling—behavior 8, or physical guidance—behavior 9).

W.   Waiting: The student has completed a task and is awaiting the next instruction or opportunity to respond. A student waiting in line for a turn, waiting for the next teacher direction, waiting to get into a game from the sideline, waiting for the next activity to begin, and so on are all examples of this category.

Contextual Elements

T.   Transition: The structure of the education or sport setting changes from one form to another. This event should be recorded for the entire duration of the transition event to provide information on the length of transition and total evaluation time spent in transitions. Examples of this include student movement from skill station to skill station during a lesson, from skill practice to a lead-up game situation at the end of a practice session, and from warm-up activities to a skill practice activity.

P.   Preview: This category indicates that the lesson is in its introductory stage. The time period encompasses the initial portion of the class or practice experience. Elements that allow the class to attain a state of lesson body readiness are involved, which typically include taking roll, reviewing for students what has gone on in the previous lesson, initial teacher directed organizational statements, verbal encapsulations of what is to be encountered in the upcoming lesson, warm-up exercises, and so on. Ideally, this contextual phase should only take up the first 3 to 10 minutes of class time.

B.   Lesson Body: This category indicates that the lesson is in its main instructional phase. The time frame encompasses the middle portion of the class or practice period in which subject matter content instruction is central to the classroom focus. Station and/or drill work, lead-up games, teacher or pupil based instructional time, and so on typically make up this contextual event.

R.   Review: This category indicates that the lesson is in its closure stage. The time period encompasses the final minutes of the class or practice experience. Its elements typically include teacher-directed review of the major points of the lesson just encountered, tie-in statements with previous lessons or related subject matters, verbal encapsulations of what is to be encountered in the next class or practice meeting, final comments to individual students or groups, and so on. Ideally, this contextual phase should only take up the final 3 to 5 minutes of class time.

SOURCE: Adapted from selected category systems in Darst, Zakrajsek, and Mancini (1989) and taken in part from Hawkins, Sharpe, and Ray (1994)

illustrations contained in Tables 5.2 and 5.3, the actual numbers and letters used to collect data using the BEST software package are specified next to each behavior and event term to give the reader a sense of how each category system is organized for computer-based data collection. For a detailed discussion of how the category system in Table 5.2 was derived and used for implementation at both the static and sequential analysis levels, refer to Hawkins, Sharpe, and Ray (1994).

For the teacher education and education research example contained in Table 5.3, only the behavior and event terms are provided, as they are fairly traditional and can be found in a variety of behavior analysis descriptions in the education literature. This example was designed for use in evaluating elementary education teacher trainees in public school classroom settings. Only the terms are provided to illustrate in summary form how an all-inclusive category system might be constructed to serve evaluation needs when providing feedback information to teachers practicing in elementary education classroom settings. This category system is also contained in the software program described in the back of this text. This system is based in part on the work of Stallings, Needels, and Sparks (1987), which should be referred to for a more detailed discussion of both the definitions in this category system and how this observation system has been put to use.

EXAMPLES FROM SCHOOL PSYCHOLOGY

The school psychology category system examples contained in Tables 5.4 and 5.5 provide two category systems that have been used with success in research and development. The category system contained in Table 5.4 is provided in summary form only, as complete definitions and examples are readily available in the mainstream applied behavior analysis literature (e.g., Sharpe, Brown & Crider, 1995; Sharpe, Brown, & Foulk, 1999; Sharpe, Crider, Vyhlidal, & Brown, 1996). These references should also be consulted for examples of reporting static and sequential data in descriptive graphic form according to the Table 5.4 category system used for data collection. The first example provided in Table 5.4 has been used to document in static and sequential ways how educational treatments designed to improve the social skills of public school students have had an effect on the behaviors of students at risk. It is representative of an all-inclusive and overlapping category system

Table 5.3   Elementary Education Category System (ELED1) Summary Example

Teacher Behaviors	Student Behaviors
1. General Observation	S. Content Work
2. Specific Observation	seat activity
3. Encouragement	game activity
4. Verbal Instruction	board activity
information	L. Listening (passive)
concepts	Q. Questioning
questioning	R. Responding
6. General Praise	H. Helping
7. Content Specific Feedback	peers
8. Management	teachers
9. Reprimand	O. Organizing
0. Social Comment	P. Personal Needs
T. Off-Task	(library, sharpening
(inappropriate exit)	pencil, bathroom)
A. Secondary Activity	W. Waiting
(reading a story not related	F. Off-Task
to content, watching a film,	passive
playing a non-content game,	talking out
etc.)	disruptive
	X. Interpersonal

Context Events (Toggled Keys in ELED1)
I. Individual
G. Group
C. Whole Class
5. Instructional Aids

SOURCE: Adapted from Stallings, Needels, and Sparks (1987)

structure. In addition, student behaviors in the categories of positive social responses (e.g., following peer negative behaviors or taking a leadership role in modeling positive behaviors) and issue resolution (teacher assisted or teacher independent) in the time-based sequential context of student peer conflict were determined using this observation system structure. The category system illustrated in Table 5.4 is also representative of a socially based coding structure because of the inferences a coder must often make to determine the positive or negative nature of student social responses that are outside the strict physically based operational definitions in the category system.

Table 5.4   Positive Social Behavior Category System Summary

Teacher	*Student*
Teacher Observation	O. Organization
1. General Observation	
2. Positive Social Observation	
	S. Sport Engaged
Organization Directions	A. Teacher Attending
3. Teacher Directed	
4. Pupil Directed	W. Waiting
5. Teacher Model	
	F. Off-Task
6. Teacher Exit	
	Positive Social Response
Skill Content Feedback	R. Following Behavior
7. Verbal	L. Leadership Behavior
8. Higher Order	
	Issue Resolution
9. Positive Social Feedback	T. Teacher Assisted
	I. Teacher Independent
0. Interpersonal	
Context Events	
C. Conflict	
Grade Level	Activity Content
G1. First Grade	Recorded as
G3. Third Grade	Narrative Text
G6. Sixth Grade	

SOURCE: Sharpe, Brown, and Crider (1995)

The second school psychology example, contained in Table 5.5, is presented in more detail and is based on the common use by school psychologists of some form of structured observations in the classroom when assessing a student exhibiting a particular behavioral challenge or consulting about a student with a third party such as a parent (Rechsly & Wilson, 1996). Based on the appeal of applying generalized matching law theory (see Davison & McCarthy, 1988, McSweeney, Farmer, Dougan, & Whipple, 1986, and Myerson & Hale, 1988, for a thorough discussion of matching law) and a form of field systems theory termed *ecobehavioral analysis* in the school psychology literature (see

Greenwood, Carta, & Atwater, 1991, and Greenwood, Delquadri, Stanley, Terry, & Hall, 1985, for a detailed discussion of this) to the description and analysis of behavior-environment interactions in ecological context; this second example, which was developed and implemented by Shriver and Kramer (1997), provides insight into the complexity of interactions that a computer-driven observational effort may be capable of accurately describing and analyzing. The code is physically based and attempts to provide an inclusive and overlapping structure to the coding of all instances of all events that may conceivably occur in the education settings of interest. This coding structure is also amenable to static or sequential measurement. The teacher codes were developed to assist in determining what level of behavior coding specificity was required to examine possible interactions between teacher behavior and student behavior. Research efforts that used this coding system example found that more specific definitions of teacher behavior, and more specific delineations of similar behaviors, provided important information previously unrealized regarding effective and not-so-effective teacher-student interactions across a variety of settings and situations.

EXAMPLES FROM SPECIAL EDUCATION

Special education is one area of education that has provided a host of research and evaluation examples in which use of quantitative direct observation and the applied analysis of behavior have been the predominant methods of data collection and analysis. Tables 5.6 and 5.7 provide two representative illustrations of this. The category system in Table 5.6 provides an elegant contemporary illustration of an interbehavioral or sequentially based category system approach to the observation and evaluation of education settings in which moderate to severe mental delays are characteristic of the clientele. This category system example provides insight into how one might first construct a set of response classes that describe in a more general and inclusive way the interaction patterns that tend to occur between behavior-behavior and behavior-event relationships in the setting to be observed. In addition, this category system example provides a set of terms and definitions designed to document socially based participant perceptions, such as a constructive versus coercive environment, in a behavioral and primarily physically based way. For detailed examples

(Text continues on page 160)

Table 5.5   Matching Law-Based Ecobehavioral Observation System
                 Example

Task Structure	Student Behavior	Teacher Scheme
Opening	Reading Aloud	*Attentional Context*
Reading	Reading Silently	Group
Related Content	Writing	Target Student
Activity	Listening	Peer Student
Closure	Transition	No Attention
	Waiting	Off Camera
	Verbal Appropriate	
	Verbal Inappropriate	*Behavioral Context*
	Task Appropriate	Instruction
	Task Inappropriate	Listening
	Off Camera	Approval
		Disapproval
		Business
		Management
		Monitoring
		Other Talk
		Independent Work
		Off Camera

Operational Definitions

Task Structure

Opening: Opening is coded for when the students are engaged in
activities immediately on entering the classroom. Such activities include
removing and hanging up coats, setting up desks, pledge of allegiance, and
so on. The students may have assignments that they are expected to be
working on involving reading or writing. It is during this time that they give
lunch orders, the teacher may take roll call, and the day's activities are
planned and presented by the teacher to the students.

Reading: Reading is coded when the student's *primary task* is reading.
The student may be reading silently or out loud. The student may be reading
a reading primer or book, a library book, or any other material that involves
only reading (not writing on paper or in workbooks). The student may be
reading independently at his or her desk, in a small reading group, or with
the whole class. In addition, if the student reads for the class or a group
something he or she has written during the opening or the other reading
activity, then that is coded as reading as well.

Related Content Activity: Related content activity is coded for any and
all activities that occur during class time primarily devoted to reading *when
the student is engaging in activity that is not primarily reading.* Such activity may
include writing stories, drawing, working in a workbook or on a worksheet,

and other paper-and-pencil tasks that may involve reading but in which the primary activity is writing. This category is also coded when the students are listening to the teacher lecture or discuss lessons or presentations related to reading. Basically, everything not associated with Reading and Opening is coded in this category.

Closure: Closure is coded for activities that occur at the end of the reading period and for activities that are *not* related to the learning and/or teaching of reading skills. Such activities include students' transition to another academic period, cleaning up activities, getting and handing out snacks or materials, and so on. Closure is coded only when it is clear that the *majority* of the class is involved in closure activities.

Student Behavior

Reading Aloud: Reading aloud is coded when the student is observed looking at reading materials and is saying aloud what is written in the printed material.

Reading Silently: Reading silently is coded when the student is *looking at reading material,* such as a book, primer, notebook, workbook or worksheet, for at least 2 seconds, *and* his or her eye movements indicate that the student is scanning words, numbers, or letters. Rapid flipping of pages is coded Task Inappropriate and is not included in this category.

Writing: Writing is coded when the student is observed marking academic task materials such as a paper, a photocopy, or workbook pages with a pencil, pen, or crayon. Writing involves holding the writing instrument between thumb and forefinger and moving it in a manner likely to produce written numbers, letters, or words. Drawing pictures is not included in this category and is coded Task Appropriate or Task Inappropriate depending on whether or not the drawing follows the teacher's directions for the lesson.

Listening: Listening is coded when the student is looking at the teacher giving directions, commands, lecturing, or at another student who is asking or answering a question. Listening is also coded when two students are engaged in an activity together and the target student is looking at the peer or task as the peer talks. Listening is also coded when the target student is listening to another student or the teacher read aloud from a book or primer or worksheet. Even though the target student may appear to be following along reading silently, listening is still coded (and not Reading Silently).

Transition: Transition is coded when the student is required to change or get materials during and after an activity. For example, when a student fetches new materials or puts materials away, moves to a new location in the room (e.g., from a desk to a reading table), cleans up, gets into a line, and so on.

(Continued)

Table 5.5 Continued

Waiting: Waiting is coded during those times when the student has completed an assignment or transition and is awaiting instruction or direction regarding what to do next. Examples of this include a student standing in line, waiting for other students to quiet down while being quiet, sitting in desk and awaiting instructions, and so on. If instruction or direction has been given by the teacher and the student continues to wait and not follow that direction, then this behavior is coded as Task Inappropriate.

Verbal Appropriate: This is coded when the student is observed verbalizing about his or her academic subject materials, teacher instruction, or other appropriate topics related to the lesson. The student may be directing such talk at the teacher, another student, or him- or herself. For example, Jim asks Darlene "Which is larger on this page, seven or four?" Darlene answers, "Seven is larger, here, count seven fingers and then count four fingers." Jim then counts, "One, two, three, four. . . . " To code Verbal Appropriate, the talk does not have to be directly related to schoolwork, but it must be directly approved by the teacher in the context of the specified task.

Verbal Inappropriate: This category is coded when the student is observed talking aloud to a peer, teacher, or him- or herself about academic or nonacademic topics not related to the activity or task at hand and the student *does not* have teacher permission to be talking during that time. This category also includes verbal noises (e.g., grunts, laughing) that are *not* appropriate to the task or acceptable to the teacher.

Task Appropriate: This category is coded when the student is engaged in play behaviors or other activity (e.g., working on the bulletin board, drawing, etc.) approved by the teacher. Task Appropriate is coded whenever the student is behaving appropriately but the behavior cannot be coded in any of the other categories described above.

Task Inappropriate: This category is coded when the student is clearly engaged in tasks that do not have the approval of the teacher and are not related to the present task. Examples of such student behaviors include working on academic or nonacademic tasks that are not currently assigned, avoiding the assigned task by coloring rather than working on a problem, passive behaviors such as sleeping or daydreaming, and disruptive behaviors such as hitting or acting out inappropriately.

Off Camera: A common code across all three subcategories, this category is coded whenever the target student or teacher (depending on the subcategory) is off camera for more than 2 seconds.

Teacher Scheme: Attentional Context

A teacher giving *attention* or *attending* to students generally means that the teacher is speaking to, or behaving toward, a student or group of students such that the teacher is directly aware of student behavior. Such teacher behaviors may include teaching, listening, general talking, watching a student, touching a student, and so on.

Group: Group is coded whenever the teacher is observed attending to the class as a whole or to a group of three or more students (e.g., a reading group) to which the target student belongs.

Target Student: Target Student is coded when the teacher is observed attending specifically to one target student. This may occur on a one-to-one basis or in the context of the larger class. An illustration of the latter example is when the teacher's attention is on the whole class during class instruction but the teacher asks a target student a question. Such attention includes both verbal and nonverbal forms of attention (e.g., explaining a skill, observing a student perform a task, etc.).

Peer Student: Peer Student is coded when the teacher is observed specifically attending to a student who is not the target student. An example of this is the teacher monitoring a student who is paired with the target student in a reading activity.

No Attention: This category is coded when the teacher is observed not attending to any student or group defined in the previous three categories.

Off Camera: This category is coded whenever the teacher is off camera for more than 2 seconds.

Teacher Scheme: Behavioral Context

Instruction: Instruction is coded whenever the teacher is actively instructing or giving a lesson to a student or students. Teacher behaviors that may be coded Instruction include presenting information, asking questions, answering questions, writing on the blackboard, and so on as an explicit part of the current lesson's instruction (and not managerial assignments).

Listening: Listening is coded when the teacher is observed listening to a student presentation, reading aloud effort, recitation, question, and so on.

Approval: This category is coded when the teacher verbally or physically expresses approval to a student or students. This may take the form of praise, encouragement, appreciation, or satisfaction with student work, conduct, or general class performance. This teacher behavior is generally associated with teacher attempts to increase a particular student behavior. Examples of this include teacher behaviors such as repeating student answers with positive emphasis; gestures like clapping, smiling, winking, waving, patting a student on the back; statements like "I'm so pleased with your work" and "Good work, you can do it Jimmy"; and tangible rewards such as stickers and candy.

(Continued)

Table 5.5 Continued

Disapproval: This category is coded when the teacher expresses disapproval in the form of dislike, dismay, dissatisfaction, or disgust with a student or group's academic or nonacademic work, appearance, conduct, or performance. This category is generally associated with teacher attempts to decrease a student behavior. Examples of this teacher behavior include gestures such as taking things away, nodding back and forth, frowning or grimacing; punitive measures such as placing a student on time-out; and verbalizations such as "Jimmy, you never get those right" and "What is wrong with you?

Business Management: This category is coded when the teacher talks about class business, rules and regulations, daily schedules, the organization of future activities, and so on. All management activities, such as handing out papers, collecting lunch money, taking roll, and so on, are also included in this category. In addition, for Business Management to be coded, the teacher's attention must be directed at and not away from a student or group of students. For example, if the teacher is looking for materials in the closet and is not attending to students, then this category is not recorded.

Monitoring: This category is coded when the teacher is visually scanning the larger class in a general way or specifically observing a particular group of students or a particular student. To record this category, teacher observation must occur for longer than 2 seconds.

Other Talk: This category is coded when the teacher talks to students or a particular student about information unrelated to academic or general classroom activities. This category includes all interpersonal interactions, such as a teacher saying to a student, "I love your new dress" or "How did you do in the soccer game last night?"

Independent Work: This category is coded whenever the teacher engages in an activity that does not include any students in the classroom and the students are not being attended to in any way. Examples of this include the teacher reading or writing at her or his desk, looking in a cupboard of materials with her or his back to the class, and so on.

Off Camera: This category is coded whenever the teacher is off camera for more than 2 seconds.

SOURCE: Shriver and Kramer (1997)

of related research efforts that have been based on the category system represented in Table 5.6, refer to Sprague and Horner (1992, 1994).

Another example, contained in Table 5.7, provides a composite illustration of how direct observational methods have contributed to evaluation practices in special education settings. A quantitative direct

(Text continues on page 164)

Table 5.6   An Example of an Interaction Pattern Analysis With Terms and Definitions

Student Behavior Codes

Response Class	Behavior Code	Definition
Problem Behavior	– Major	Those behaviors that result in pain, property damage, or major disruption, and are judged by the teacher to be highly aversive
	– Minor	Those behaviors that do not result in pain, property damage, or major disruption. Minor problem behaviors will be rated by the teacher as mildly aversive
	– Non-compliance	Student does not engage in behavior (for 10 seconds) that meets the requirements of the preceding teacher request
Compliance	– With Minor Problem Behavior	Student engages in minor problem behavior but does comply with the current teacher request when it is his or her turn
	– Straight Compliance	Student responds or attempts to respond to the current teacher request within 10 seconds of the request. The response must meet or approximate the requirements of the request.
Agent-Action Request	– For Attention	Student verbal statement or gesture that indicates a conventional attempt to access attention or interaction from the teacher (e.g., "Look at me!")
	– For Tangible	Student verbal statement or gesture that indicates a conventional attempt to procure a desired item such as food or a toy (e.g., a student says "I want a cookie," which leads the teacher to an object)

(Continued)

Table 5.6 Continued

| No Response or Other | – No | No student response for 15 seconds following a teacher turn |
| | – Other | Any statement or gesture directed toward the teacher that does not meet the definition of any other student code |

Teacher Behavior Codes

Response Class	Behavior Code	Definition
Demand Request	– Initial Request	A verbal statement by the teacher to the student to perform a behavior or task. An initial request refers only to behavior demands that are not related to the previous request (e.g., a new instructional trial with new demand content)
Maintain Requests	– Repeat or Increase	A verbal statement or gesture by the teacher indicating a request that the student perform the same behavior or task stated in the initial request. The request must indicate the same or increased expectations (e.g., behavior, criterion, and time frame)
	– Correction	A statement or gesture by the teacher that indicates strong disapproval of student behavior. This includes "no" statements, threatening to remove privileges, and raising voice volume
Reduce or Remove Requests	– Decrease	A secondary verbal statement or gesture by the teacher, directed to the student, that is a modification of the initial request. This may include reducing the conditions or form of the request, providing prompts, reducing the criterion for completion, or changing the time frame

	– Reward and/or Praise	Any statement or gesture by the teacher that indicates approval of student behavior (e.g., praise, physical contact, smiles, positive statements, tangibles, etc.)
Other	– Response	Any statement or gesture by the teacher that does not meet criteria for any other code
	– No Response Ignore	No response by the teacher for at least 10 seconds following a student turn

Response String Definitions

Initial Request or String Start	(1)	A verbal statement by the teacher, directed to a student, to perform a task, a behavior, or an activity. The statement must indicate the behavior to be performed or the expected outcome of performing it
	(2)	The first student verbal statement or gesture that indicates a conventional attempt to access attention or interactions from the teacher (e.g., "Look at me!") after a response string end
	(3)	The first student verbal statement or gesture that indicates a conventional attempt to access a desired item of food, toys, or something else (e.g., saying "I want a cookie," thus leading the teacher to an object) after a response string end
Middle Turns		All interactions that occur between an initial request and the response string end
Response String End	(1)	When a student complies with a teacher request (i.e., escape)
	(2)	When a student obtains a tangible
	(3)	When the teacher provides positive attention and the student reduces or terminates the problem behavior (i.e., attention)
	(4)	Thirty seconds or more of no turns by either the teacher or the student
	(5)	When the teacher presents a request that differs in form or function from the preceding initial request

(Continued)

Table 5.6 Continued

Coding Interaction/Turn Intensity Hierarchy

A final strategy to using this category system to code teacher and special education student behavior, and behavior sequences (i.e., interactions or turns) is to code the most intense behavior performed during that turn.

Student Behaviors	Teacher Behaviors
1. Major Problem Behavior	1. Terminate String
2. Compliance With Minor Problem Behavior	2. Repeat/Increase Request
3. Minor Problem Behavior	3. Decrease Request
4. Tangible and Attention Requests	4. Reward
5. Noncompliance	5. Correction
6. Compliance	6. No Response/Ignore
7. Other Response	7. Other Response
8. No Response	

SOURCE: Jeff Sprague, University of Oregon

observation approach to research and evaluation in special education settings provides one means of fulfilling federal public law mandates that, for example, speak to the necessity of monitoring the daily performance of students with disabilities. As Johnson, Blackhurst, Maley, Bomba, Cox-Cruey, and Dell (1995) state, most observational tools developed for special education settings emphasize the objective and systematic collection of quantifiable measurable information, analysis of that information, and the direction and refinement of educational interventions based on that analysis. Direct observation and behavior analysis approaches to special education concerns have been proven effective in improving student academic performance (Fuchs & Fuchs, 1986) and have documented a corresponding *lack* of student improvement in the absence of this type of information (Utley, Zigmond, & Strain, 1987). According to Croll (1986), a method for assigning student and teacher actions to quantifiably measurable categories provides the potential for very useful descriptions and analyses of participant interactions in therapeutic settings. The category system terms and definitions examples listed in Table 5.7 are drawn from a compilation of special education efforts, and they provide important illustrations of how category systems may be developed for special education evaluation purposes (see Hunt, Alwell, Farron-Davis, & Goetz, 1996, and

Light, Collier, & Parnes, 1985a, 1985b, and 1985c, for a detailed discussion of term and definition development and related category system application use). In addition, the example provided in Table 5.7 illustrates in some detail many socially based parameters that can be incorporated into direct observation category systems to productive ends.

AN ILLUSTRATION FROM CLINICAL PSYCHOLOGY

Clinical psychology is another area in which much direct observational activity has been ongoing in relation to the study and evaluation of the various interactions in particular types of therapy sessions. The example contained in Table 5.8 provides insight into how a sequential or interbehavioral coding system in particular may yield valuable information on effective and not-so-effective communication patterns with clients in group settings. Most clinical work to date of this type has originated in medical center communities working with therapy groups with individuals who exhibit a range of common problems from psychotic language to substance abuse resulting in incarceration to schizophrenia to various other psychological challenges. Important to this example is the view that verbal behavior may be coded as a function of the time-based nature of interactive and interconnected responses rather than as a function of the independent and static characteristics of each isolated behavior or event. In this way, verbal interaction (or language) may be viewed as a dynamic sequence of interconnected events rather than as a disconnected set of verbal behavior characteristics, with the latter typifying the more isolated static view that a more traditional discrete behavior analysis might provide (see Bijou, Umbreit, Ghezzi, & Chao, 1986, Kantor, 1977, and Ray, Upson, & Henderson, 1977, for detailed discussions of this issue in relation to the analysis of verbal behavior). We recommend to the researcher that rather than stopping with a more traditional analysis of the number of times particular behaviors are emitted, her or his analysis with regard to this category system example should focus on the probability of any verbal behavior occurring as a function of its time-based proximity to another behavior within the coding system. Other sections provide illustrations of operational definitions for behaviors and environmental events that are similar to those presented in this example, so only a summary of terms is offered here.

(Text continues on page 169)

Table 5.7   Composite Illustration of Special Education Evaluation Codes

Parameter 1: Structure

Initiation:	Any verbal or active nonverbal behavior that engages or attempts to engage another person
Acknowledgment:	Any verbal or nonverbal behavior that appears to be in response to an initiation
Reciprocal Interaction:	An exchange that includes both initiation and acknowledgment behavior

Parameter 2: Function

Request:	When one partner is asking for objects, actions, or information from the other
Protest:	An indicated desire to avoid an undesired stimulus or to escape an ongoing stimulus
Comment:	When one partner is making a remark or providing information to the other
Assistance:	An interaction in which one partner is providing information or something else that helps the other partner accomplish some outcome
Greeting:	Any salutation that begins or ends an interaction

Parameter 3: Focus

Social:	An interaction whose major purpose is the interaction itself
Task-related:	An interaction in which an outcome is accomplished that goes beyond social contact

Parameter 4: Quality

Mismatch:	A reciprocal interaction in which the quality of one partner's communication is positive, and the other partner's communication is negative
Neutral:	A reciprocal exchange made with neither positive nor negative affect
Affirming:	An interactive exchange that is caring or loving
Complimentary:	An interactive exchange in which one partner praises or compliments the other
Sharing Pleasure:	When partners are jointly participating in a pleasurable activity or the reciprocal interaction itself is generating pleasure
Humorous:	An exchange in which one partner initiates a funny action or remark and the other partner responds appreciatively

| Displeased: | An exchange in which both partners express irritation, discontentment, indignation, and/or exasperation |
| Angry: | When both partners in the exchange express hostility, resentment, and/or animosity |

Parameter 5: Communication Turns

| Presence: | When two or more participants are involved in a verbal or nonverbal communication |
| Absence: | When two or more participants are not involved in a verbal or nonverbal communication act where one is clearly expected |

Parameter 6: Communication Function

Social Convention:	A greeting among participants
Request:	An exchange in which one partner is asking for an object or set of materials, additional information on a topic, clarification on information received, or attention from another participant
Provision:	An interaction in which one partner is providing information or clarification on a particular topic to the other
Imitation:	When what one partner does is in imitation of the other communication partner

Parameter 7: Mode of Communication

Communication Board:	When written signals are used to communicate
Vocalization:	Any form of verbal interaction
Nonverbal Gesture:	Any form of nonverbal communication

Parameter 8: Partner Identity

Paraprofessional

General Education Teacher

Special Education Teacher

Therapist/Related Services Personnel

Other Adult

Student Without Disabilities

Student With Disabilities

SOURCE: Ken Simpson, University of Illinois at Carbondale

Table 5.8   A Sequential Analysis Example of Therapy Interactions in a
Clinical Setting

Therapist to Client

1. Statement of Goals
2. Problem Knowledge/Description Statements
3. Problem Solution Statements
4. Problem Questioning
   Group
   Individual
5. Resistance Confrontation
6. Compliance Reinforcement
7. Client ReStatement
8. Interpersonal Statements
9. Problem Unrelated Statements
10. Nonresponse to Client Statement

Client to Therapist

1. Nonresponse to Therapist Statement
2. Resistance/Conflict Statement
3. Defensive Reaction
   Verbal
   Nonverbal
4. Guarded Reaction
   Verbal
   Nonverbal
5. Statement of Receptivity to Therapist Statement
6. Problem Knowledge Answer—Inappropriate
7. Problem Knowledge Answer—Appropriate
8. Unrelated Comments

Client to Client

1. Problem Related—Unsupportive
2. Problem Related—Supportive
3. Problem Unrelated—Unsupportive
4. Problem Unrelated—Supportive

Context

1. Group Therapy
2. Individual Therapy

SOURCE: Dennis Delprato, Western Michigan University

A SYSTEMS CODE FROM ETHOLOGY

Ethology, or the study of animal behavior in all of its forms and structures, is an area in the social sciences that has provided some pioneering work in the design and implementation of observational category systems, and in particular, in interbehavioral, sequential, and field systems theory in relation to those observational efforts. Roger Ray of Rollins College, for example, is a pioneer on both these counts (Ray, 1983; Ray & Delprato, 1989). Table 5.9 provides one illustration of how a set of terms and definitions may be constructed to observe animal interactions in controlled settings in inclusive and sequential ways (Astley et al., 1991). According to Astley and colleagues, "the ability to record and analyze ongoing social behavior among animals depends on the development of adequate measurement systems that lend themselves to mathematical analysis . . . the most commonly used approach is formal coding" (p. 173). The primary purpose of the coding system example included in Table 5.9 was to provide a data collection tool for enhancing understanding of social behavior in animals and the cardiovascular responses associated with those particular behaviors through statistical correlations among indices such as heart rate and body temperature and physical behavior. By correlating cardiovascular response with behavior, and by recording behavior occurrences in time-based sequence using this coding scheme, this example also attempts to overcome what some have criticized (see Johnston & Pennypacker, 1980) as the arbitrary nature of breaking up the natural time-based stream of behavior-behavior and behavior-environment interactions. Complete operational definitions, and the rationale for constructing those definitions, are laid out in explicit detail in Astley and colleagues (1991), thus only a summary of terms in the coding system is provided here.

Table 5.9   A Code to Integrate Animal Behavior and Cardiovascular
Response

Locomotion and Posture

1. Unidentifiable
2. Lie
3. Sit
4. Stand on 2 Legs
5. Stand on 3 or 4 Legs
6. Walk on 2 Legs
7. Walk on 3 or 4 Legs
8. Run
9. Climb or Jump
10. Hang
11. Lunge
12. Walk-Stand Sequence

Behavior

1. Unidentifiable

2. Feeding
   (a) Calm
   (b) Active
   (c) Excited
   (d) Anxious

3. Oral
   (a) Upright Drinking
   (b) Head Down Drinking
   (c) Licking Object
   (d) Biting Object

4. Grooming
   (a) Groomed
   (b) Groomed While Orienting to Environment
   (c) Presents for Grooming
   (d) Grooms Another

5. Maternal

6. Sexual
   (a) Approach Female
   (b) Mount With Thrusting
   (c) Copulation

    (d)   Toward Adolescent
    (e)   Approached by Male
    (f)   Present Hindquarters

 7. Submission
    (a)   Low Level
    (b)   Mid Level
    (c)   High Level, Retreat From Animal
    (d)   High Level, Retreat From Person
    (e)   Captured
    (f)   Present to Opposite Sex
    (g)   Present to Same Sex

 8. Aggression
    (a)   Low Level
    (b)   Mid Level
    (c)   High Level, Attack Animal
    (d)   High Level, Attack Person
    (e)   Fight
    (f)   Hindquarters, Same Sex

 9. Idle/Nonspecific
    (a)   Baseline Activity
    (b)   Extremely Active, Irritated, Upset

 10. Other
    (a)   Huddling
    (b)   Play
    (c)   Other

Environmental Setting

 1. Entrance Opened
 2. Food Brought Into Environment
 3. Food Delivered
 4. Food Removed From Environment
 5. Threat by Other
 6. Exit Opened

SOURCE: Astley et al. (1991). Reprinted by permission

NOTE

1.   These materials are available for free upon request from
Tom Sharpe
Department of Educational Leadership
College of Education
University of Nevada–Las Vegas
4505 Maryland Parkway
Box 453002
Las Vegas, NV, 89154-3002
Telephone: (702) 895-3634
E-mail: sharpe@unlv.edu

6

Reliability and Staff Training

What each man knows is, in an important sense, dependent upon his own individual experience: He knows what he has seen and heard, what he has read and what he has been told, and also what, from reliably interpreting these data, he has been able to infer.

— Russell (1948, pp. xi-xii)

After reading this chapter, you should be able to define the following terms and provide the information requested in the study guide below.

TERMS

Reliability
Accuracy
Consistency
Observer agreement
Data collector bias
Treatment fidelity or treatment
 integrity
Criterion standard
Staff training

Interobserver checks
Interobserver or Intraobserver
 agreement
Observer drift
Simple frequency
Point-by-point
Cohen's kappa
Pearson product-moment
 correlation

STUDY GUIDE

1. Discuss the three important purposes for conducting (a) reliability assessments with regard to the potential accuracy of data collection

and (b) treatment fidelity assessments with regard to the potential accuracy of treatment implementation.
2. Discuss the relationship among the terms *observer agreement, reliability,* and *accuracy* in relation to direct observation data collection activities.
3. Describe the three general steps recommended for implementing reliability and treatment fidelity procedures.
4. Provide a mathematical illustration of each of the three described reliability formulae, summarizing the relative benefits and drawbacks in using each formula.
5. Explain the two important procedural differences to consider when conducting a reliability analysis for treatment fidelity purposes, rather than for data collection accuracy purposes.
6. Discuss the benefits and drawbacks in using a Pearson product-moment correlation analysis to determine reliability.

A challenging issue for scientists engaged in direct observation approaches to applied settings, in which focus is on the recording of occurrences of multiple behaviors and events and their relationships with one another, is to convince those who read descriptions of their observational efforts that what was documented as observed actually occurred in accordance with their observational record. Even though we, as observers of particular situations, may be convinced by our data that certain things occurred and certain functional relationships exist among the behaviors and events recorded, it is necessary for us to use a set of procedures that will convince others that we recorded the same behaviors and events that would have been recorded if they had observed the same setting from which our data records were generated. This set of procedures is generally termed *reliability.* Locke (1992) wrote:

[The issue of reliability] confronts us with exactly what we are doing, as opposed to what we have come to imagine we are doing. It is a telling fact that teachers and researchers are surprised by some of the things they find in [their own] descriptive accounts. (p. 86)

This quote illustrates how important it is to provide a set of procedures designed to verify whether what is observed and recorded through the use of a particular observational category system is an accurate and reliable record of what actually occurred in the observational setting at the time the observations were recorded. When observations are conducted in a very controlled laboratory setting and only a few variables and related measures are focused on (such as temperature, heart rate, chemical amounts, etc.) with the use of particular measurement technologies (thermometers, physiological monitors, etc.), it is a fairly clear-cut decision whether data were observed and recorded with some degree of accuracy. In applied settings where multiple rapidly occurring behaviors and events are to be recorded, this is not the case. In this latter regard, procedures for convincing readers of experimental studies that implement direct observation methods for their data collection and analysis efforts that their data are indeed accurate representations of what occurred are necessary. This group of procedures is commonly called *reliability* procedures, and in the case where a determination of the accuracy of treatment implementation is called for, *treatment fidelity* or *treatment integrity* procedures.

The following provides an example of a situation that calls for the use of a such a procedure: An educational researcher is interested in the number of teacher feedback episodes provided in a classroom setting, and, relatedly, the number of correct subject matter practice trials that students perform as a function of increased teacher feedback. To increase the probability that the data collected on these two classroom behaviors are accurate, the researcher implements a set of reliability procedures over the course of the experiment. The researcher may also be interested in creating some form of instructional workshop for teachers designed to increase their use of certain types of feedback in their classroom settings. This workshop might consist of a variety of instructional procedures and of a prescribed amount of time per workshop and a certain number of workshops. To increase the probability that the workshop is implemented according to the specific procedures and descriptions that have been developed and reported by the educational researcher, the researcher would implement a set of reliability procedures to directly observe actual workshop implementation. In this way, the researcher can ensure that the workshop proceeds according to the specific procedures that were set up. In other words, the educational researcher is first ensuring the *fidelity or integrity of the treatment*—in this case, the workshop—implementation by collecting data to describe and support that the workshop was conducted according to the procedures and descriptions that were originally developed for it. A detailed accounting of how to go about implementing reliability and treatment fidelity procedures, and the importance and necessity of including these procedures in the reporting of observational research, is the subject of this chapter.

THE PURPOSES OF ASSESSMENT

Before we outline specific procedures for determining levels of reliability in data collection efforts and levels of accuracy in treatment implementation (i.e., treatment fidelity), we believe some important purposes for these procedures should be noted. First, it is important for the researcher to provide some form of information to demonstrate that data recorded using a particular category system is theoretically consistent. In the context of observational data collection, consistency involves two issues: (1) that if the same observer were to record data from the same observational setting (e.g., an archived videotape record) at different points in time, then that observer would come up with exactly the same data record for that same observational setting and (2) that if different observers were to record data from the same observational setting, then all of the observers would come up with identical data records. In other words, if data collectors are *consistent*, then it does not matter who collects the data or at what point in time, in relation to coming up with the same data record. Such consistency provides a level of confidence that the data collected are not dependent on variations in the interpretations of data collectors.

Another purpose of determining reliability and treatment fidelity issues involves the potential *bias of the data collector*; that is, each human being who is involved in the collection of direct observational data using a category system approach may bring to that data collection effort certain perspectives and biases that may act to alter the way certain behaviors and events are recorded. Implementing a set of reliability checks provides information designed to minimize argument that data may have conceivably been recorded as a function of an observer changing his or her interpretation of a particular behavior or event definition as a function of ongoing data recording efforts.

A third purpose of implementing reliability and treatment fidelity procedures in a direct observation study or evaluation activity is to provide a means of determining just how well each term in a particular category system used for data collection purposes has been defined. If behaviors and events have met the criteria of being objective, clear, and complete, and are hence operationally defined according to the definitional recommendations of Chapter 4, then the data outcome should not be affected by the person who collected the data. In other words, as the quality of behavior and event definitions increases in a particular category system, the ease with which different observers interpret a category system definition and record occurrences of certain behaviors and events in the same way as others, and in the same way over periods of time and different observational settings, should increase as well.

The general purpose of assessing for reliable data collection, and, relatedly, reliable implementation of a particular treatment (treatment fidelity), is to make sure that individuals or groups of professionals conducting direct observation activities are consistently accurate collectors of the type of information they collect and analyze. A variety of procedures are available to this end, and these procedures are considerably enhanced with regard to time and effort efficiency through the use of available computer-based assessment tools (refer, for example, to the software application capability description at the end of this text).

THE ISSUE OF DATA ACCURACY

In a discussion of a set of recommended procedures designed to ensure adequate reliability of data gathering practices, and adequate treatment fidelity, it is first important for us to distinguish between what is meant in the behavioral literature by the terms *observer agreement, reliability,* and *accuracy.* This is particularly the case in that much of the direct observation literature mixes and matches these terms to the point of methodological confusion. Generally, observer agreement procedures provide an indication of how closely two or more independent observers of the same behavior and event occurrences agree in their data recording when they are involved in collecting data on the presence or absence of the same occurrences in the same observational setting. According to Johnson and Bolstad (1973), the term *observer agreement* and the term *reliability* have been used interchangeably in much of the behavior analysis literature, although it remains important to understand the distinction between the two in a conceptual sense. The distinction is as follows: *observer agreement* is the extent to which two or more individuals agree on the presence or absence of behavior and event occurrences, whereas *reliability* is the consistency with which behavior and event occurrences will be recorded in the same way when they occur in the same way at different points in time. In other words, while two different observers may agree with one another in terms of their data records concerning the same observational situation at a particular point in time, those data records may not necessarily be reliable if each individual records in an inconsistent manner over time.

Another important term, *accuracy*, refers to whether or not a particular data record is actually representative of behavior and event occurrences as they actually occur within an observational setting of interest. Thus a data record is said to be accurate if it reflects what actually happened in the observational setting. Two independent observers may be reliably (and therefore consistently) collecting data on the same observational settings, but that does not necessarily mean that their data records are *accurately* reflecting what is actually occurring in those observational settings—both observers could conceivably be reliably and consistently wrong in their observations.

The challenge of a scientific activity devoted to the recording of directly observable events is to try to ensure that the data collected to describe a particular setting are accurate. Behavior analysis research efforts most often advocate the use of various agreement tests and related reliability procedures in an effort to increase the *probability* that the data collected for a particular research or evaluation purpose is accurate. Although data accuracy cannot be *ensured* in a pure sense through the use of these procedures, their use is designed to significantly increase the probability of accurate data recording efforts.

Kazdin (1982) lists the three important rationales for including procedures to ensure agreement in any research or evaluation enterprise involving the counting of behaviors and events. First, such procedures ensure a degree of consistency in the recording of similar types of information. Second, if independent observer agreement is ensured across data records, the potential for bias and changes in behavior and event occurrence interpretations across observers is minimized. Third, implementing agreement procedures provides a check for whether the behaviors and events to be observed are well defined. Conducting agreement checks among observers during the course of an experiment or evaluation activity is one way to ensure that different observers are interpreting behavior and event definitions and recording the occurrences of those behaviors and events in the same way. If these three rationales are met through the use of a variety of data reliability and treatment fidelity assessment procedures, then a data collector may be able to state with greater confidence (or increased probability) that the direct observation data reported using a particular category system is an accurate reflection of what actually occurred in a particular setting under observation.

A RECOMMENDED THREE-STEP RELIABILITY PROCESS

We recommend three specific steps to be included in any set of procedures designed to better ensure the reliability, and it is hoped, the resultant accuracy of direct observation data records. Although our discussion will refer primarily to ensuring the reliability of data to be collected, the same set of procedures is recommended to ensure that behaviorally defined treatments are implemented as intended (i.e., the issue of documenting relative treatment fidelity or treatment integrity). We believe that it is equally important to determine how reliably data were recorded within a particular experiment as to determine how accurately a particular treatment was implemented. In the former case, at issue is whether or not direct observation data are to be trusted as accurate descriptions of experimental situations. In the latter case, at issue is whether or not a treatment was implemented according to a set of stipulated experimental procedures, for, if not, the data in support of the relative effectiveness of that particular treatment may be an inaccurate reflection of treatment effects. It is with these thoughts in mind that we provide the following three-step set of recommendations for ensuring reliable and potentially accurate data records, and, relatedly, for ensuring accurate treatment implementation.

Step 1: Developing a Criterion Standard

First, we recommend the development of what we term a *criterion standard*. A criterion standard is simply a videotape record of situations similar to that of the experimental or evaluation setting to be observed for data recording purposes, which contain the same behaviors and events as in the category system to be used to guide data recording efforts. For example, a teacher educator interested in using a category system for evaluation and feedback and goal-setting experiences in practice teaching situations to be observed, would first make a videotape of similar practice teaching situations that exhibited multiple occurrences of all the same behaviors and events in the category system to be used for data collection purposes. When making the videotape record, it is important that the teacher educator make sure that all the behaviors and events in the category system to be used for evaluation purposes occurred with some frequency throughout that videotape record. Taking another example, if an ethologist was interested in studying the various interaction patterns of a particular species of baboons in the wild no correlation with our first example is intended here ☺), that ethologist would first make a videotape record of similar baboons in settings similar to the one to be observed, making sure that all behaviors and events of interest occurred frequently on the videotape record.

Once a videotape record containing examples of the behaviors and events to be observed is complete, the next step involves dividing up the videotape record into equal time segments using either a video-player time counter or a character generator that stamps time directly on the videotape record to signify the start and stop times of each segment. For example, if the teacher educator in our example prepared a 45-minute videotape record, he or she might next break up that record into nine 5-minute segments and record using the video-player's time counter the start and stop times of each segment.

Once a videotape record of behavior and event examples is made and segmented according to time units, two lead researchers (or evaluators, as the case may be) need to synchronize a data collection mechanism to the start times of each time-based segment on the videotape and collect a data record for each segment. Many software programs are available (again, refer to the software flyer included with this text) to facilitate the time-based synchronization among video player and computer-based data collection apparatus, and the related time-stamping of data records to be compared (this latter point is important, as will be seen later with regard to determining the reliability of recording time-based sequences of behavior-event occurrences). If researchers are not using amenable software synchronization programs or character generated time stamps on the video record, they can implement a procedure such as the starting of a 5-minute segment of interest, for example, on a videotape record (e.g., unpausing the videotape player at the same time the data collection application is turned on). Using our teacher educator illustration, each of the two lead observers would conduct an independent recording of each of the nine 5-minute segments, with each investigator conducting a respective and independent 5-minute data recording episode on the same day. In this teacher educator example, once the two lead teacher educators have completed the recording of all nine 5-minute segments on the videotape record, the data records from each time-segment should be compared across teacher educators using an appropriate reliability formula application. It is important to note here that whether researchers are using an amenable software application to implement a reliability comparison or performing these calculations by hand (something we do not recommend due to the time- and effort-intensive nature of the latter), a decision will need to be made regarding which formula among those included in this chapter's section, Reliability Formula Summaries, will be used (refer to this section for a discussion of the relative benefits and limitations of each formula to potentially be implemented). This step should be repeated using one of the recommended reliability formulae until the two teacher educators reach a minimum level of agreement across each of the nine 5-minute segment comparisons. Although a strict minimum statistical level of agreement is not rigorously stipulated in the literature—and this minimum level is a function in some degree of the number of codes in an observation system, the type of measures being used, and the related complexity of behavior and event occurrence in the setting under observation—a .85 minimum level of agreement is generally thought to be acceptable.

Once two lead researchers (or evaluators) consistently reach a minimum specified numerical agreement level for all of the videotape record segments, the data recording and comparing process just described should be undertaken again after a period of 2 to 3 weeks has elapsed. If the two lead researchers still consistently agree across all videotape record segments above a minimum specified level, then a final comparison step is conducted. This final step involves the comparison of each observer's first set of data records to each of their second matched set of data records. Using our teacher educator illustration, the first teacher educator compares the first 5-minute data record of the first set of nine to the first 5-minute data record of the second set of nine, and the second 5-minute data record to the second data record of the second set of nine, and so on until nine comparisons are made. The second teacher educator does the same. If each teacher educator agrees with his or her earlier assessments to a minimum specified agreement level for all nine comparisons across time, then the development of a criterion standard is complete. If this set of procedures is undertaken to completion, a set of data records will have been generated that correspond to specified time-based segments of a videotape record, and the data records will have been determined consistently reliable across two independent observers and determined consistently reliable over time within observers.

Observer 1: a1 a2 b1 b2 c1 c2 d1 d2

Observer 2: e1 e2 f1 f2 g1 g2 h1 h2

According to the illustration above, and continuing with our teacher educator example, a criterion standard is successfully produced if two teacher educators agree to a minimum specified level for comparisons a1-e1, b1-f1, and so on throughout the total number of observational segments contained on the videotape (commonly termed *interobserver agreement*) *and* agree to a minimum specified level for comparisons a1-a2, b1-b2, e1-e2, f1-f2, and so on throughout the first and second observations of the same segment conducted at different points in time for each respective observer (commonly termed *intraobserver agreement*). In all of these illustrated comparisons, agreement must be consistently above the minimum specified level across *all* of the time-based segments contained on the videotape record.

If, however, the two lead researchers do not consistently agree with their own previous assessments (in the second intraobserver agreement step), then the first interobserver comparison step must be undertaken again until the two lead observers return to consistent agreement with one another to a minimum specified level across all time-based segments. What we have found helpful in this instance, as this happens more often than not when one is initially developing a criterion standard, is for the two lead observers to slowly go through the videotape record together and talk over various disagreements and challenging behavior or event determinations. After this type of discussion, the two lead observers should make another effort to come to consistent and independent agreement with one another over all of the time-based segments contained on the videotape.

A less likely occurrence during this process is that two lead observers will consistently agree with one another (comparisons a-e, b-f, c-g, etc.), however, they will not consistently agree with their own assessments over time (comparisons a1-a2, b1-b2, etc.). This problem is commonly referred to as *observer drift* and is important to check for so as to ensure that it is avoided both in the development of a criterion standard and during the collection of actual data records for a particular experiment or evaluation project. If observer drift is occurring, then changes in interpretation of the behavior and event definitions are occurring with particular observers over time and will result in changes in the data records due to observer bias and interpretation rather than changes in the actual occurrences of the behaviors and events being observed and recorded. If this is the case during the development of a criterion standard, then we recommend that the lead observers first go through the entire videotape record together and discuss challenging behavior and event determinations and the instances in which observers have been changing their recording practices. After this type of discussion, a more rigorous agreement comparison procedure should be implemented to include (a) interobserver a-e, b-f, and so on comparisons; (b) intraobserver a1-a2, b1-b2, and so on comparisons; *and* the addition of (c) interobserver a1-e2, b2-f1, and so on comparisons across time. Using our teacher educator illustration, these three forms of comparisons should be undertaken according to the steps discussed until both lead observers have consistently agreed across all nine 5-minute videotape segments at the same point in time, at another, later same point in time, and with themselves and with each other across different points in time. If all three forms of comparisons are undertaken, and a minimum level of agreement is consistently reached within all three forms of comparison, then one can stipulate with a degree of confidence that the final data records that represent each time segment contained on the videotape record are accurate representations.

Although our discussion of the development of a criterion standard may seem daunting in terms of the time and effort invested, we feel that it is an important step to increasing the probability of accurate data records once an experimental or evaluation project is under way. Successful and rigorous completion of this criterion standard development step is crucial to ensuring the reliability and hoped-for accuracy of data records during an experimental or evaluation project, particularly if such a project is ongoing for long periods of time and involves multiple staff as direct observation data collectors. This is also a step most often overlooked when discussing and reporting behavior analytic data in the education and social science literatures. The importance of this step will become more apparent once the reader has thoroughly assimilated the nature of the second recommended general step of Training Staff According to the Criterion Standard that is described below. This is the step in which staff to be involved in actual data collection is trained according to the criterion standard that has been developed.

Step 2: Training Staff According to the Criterion Standard

Once a criterion standard has been developed for a particular set of research or evaluation projects, and includes a time-segmented video-tape record and a set of data records that correspond to those time segments, a next general step is to train a group of observers to conduct reliable and, it is hoped, accurate data collection efforts. This general procedure is commonly termed *staff training*. To do this, we recommend that the lead investigators who prepared the criterion standard first hold an informal discussion with all potential observers about the terms and definitions in the category system to be used, and that they use the criterion standard to show examples of what behavior and event occurrences tend to look like. Next, it is necessary for staff to be educated on the use and application of the actual data collection tool to be used (and we highly recommend an amenable software application for this set of procedures, such as that described at the end of this text)—until the observers to be trained are familiar with how to successfully operate the data collection applications to be implemented and, in the case of an independently prescribed reliability test, the reliability application as well. We think it should be noted here that use of computer-based software applications for data collection and compatible reliability analysis in which two data files are compared for similarity provides for an appealing and user-friendly means of having a data collection staff both learn required data collection techniques and conduct reliability tests among their respective data collection efforts and the data record criterion standard in an independent learning fashion.

Next, we recommend that all observers to be trained observe the segments specified in the videotape record in the criterion standard materials for the purpose of collecting data records (and, again, we recommend use of an amenable software-based reliability application for this). Using our teacher education example, this would involve a particular observer synchronizing the videotape record with the data collection apparatus and collecting data on the first 5-minute segment of the videotape record. Once this is accomplished, this observer would next tag both the first 5-minute criterion standard data record and the data record he or she just collected for the purpose of conducting a reliability assessment either by hand or with an amenable software application. After an observer has recorded and compared his or her data collection effort with the respective data record in the criterion standard materials, that observer should repeat this collection and comparison procedure with the second 5-minute videotape record segment, then a third segment, and so on. After three consecutive time-segment attempts on a particular day, if an observer meets a minimum specified level of agreement when comparing his or her data records to the records of the criterion standard on all three attempts, then that observer is, in our view, considered successfully trained. If a minimum specified level of agreement is not met on any one of the three attempts, then we recommend that that observer stop any further data collection attempts until the next day. In essence, we recommend that this three data collection attempts on consecutive time segments of the criterion videotape record procedure be repeated until an observer successfully meets a minimum specified agreement level on three consecutive 5-minute segment collection and comparison attempts.

Once observers have been successfully trained according to the specifications we have discussed, and assuming that these observers have a certain level of commitment and enthusiasm for the observation tasks to be conducted, lead observers should be confident in the initial reliability and potential accuracy of data collected by these trained observers. For large groups of professionals who plan to use the same category system for a similar group of observational tasks from year to year, we recommend that staff training be conducted for all observers on a yearly basis to ensure that all individuals within a group remain successfully trained. Although our initial recommended step of preparing a criterion standard is time consuming, once it is prepared this same criterion standard may be used to train a host of observers over a number of years. In other words, once a criterion standard has been successfully prepared, many observers may be trained for many research and evaluation projects in a relatively time-efficient manner, as long as each data collection task uses the same category system, and specified research and evaluation tasks are focused on the observation of the same types and classes of behavior and event occurrences.

Step 3: Implementing Interobserver Checks

Once a criterion standard has been prepared, and a staff of observers has been successfully trained, one remaining step to ensure the reliability and, it is hoped, accuracy of data records is necessary.

This step involves two trained observers independently collecting a data record on the same scheduled observational episode during the course of the actual experimental or evaluation activity. As Kazdin (1982) states, although there are no definitive rules for the number and timing of *interobserver checks*, it is generally recommended that such checks take place at least twice per experimental phase of an experiment, or if the researcher is conducting observations for evaluation purposes, at least once per month over the course of the experience. A few additional considerations are also important in relation to how often interobserver checks should be conducted. These include the number of observers involved with a particular project, the complexity of the observation system used in terms of number of categories, and how well two independent observers are agreeing with each other during a particular observation episode. If, for example, only a few observers are involved in using a fairly simple category system and they agree with one another at a high level with the first interobserver check, fewer interobserver checks would be necessary in the future. If, on the other hand, a large staff is involved in using a very complex observation system and is experiencing difficulty reaching a minimum specified interobserver agreement level, then interobserver agreement checks (and potentially regrouping the entire reliability activity through additional staff training) should occur more frequently.

In practice, to conduct interobserver checks two trained observers would first independently generate a data record from the same scheduled observation. Once this is accomplished, the data records of the two evaluators would be compared to provide a level of agreement. If agreement falls below a minimum specified level, then those observers should be retrained according to the staff training procedures discussed in Step 2 to bring one or both of these observers back to a minimum accepted level of agreement. After retraining, another interobserver check should be conducted with these same two observers to determine if their agreement levels have improved.

TREATMENT FIDELITY

What follows are some important considerations regarding researchers' determination of the relative reliability, and hence potential accuracy, of a particular treatment implementation when working in the area of experimental activities in relation to direct observation methods. We discuss this now, before proceeding to a sample of the most frequently used and accepted statistical formulae for conducting actual reliability comparisons, because of a few differences in how a treatment as procedurally defined and described is compared with direct observational records of how a treatment is actually implemented, in contrast to implementing a set of reliability procedures on data that are to be collected.

A first critical difference lies in the reliability step of developing a criterion standard. Instead of compiling a videotape record of representative behaviors and events, and a corresponding data record that matches the videotape representation; when dealing with treatment fidelity issues a first step of operationally defining in behavioral terms the specific measurable parameters of an intervention is required. When a researcher is interested in determining if a particular treatment designed for the benefit of a particular individual or group of clientele will be effective, a first step is to define that treatment using the characteristics of objective, clear, and complete with regard to the behavioral components of that treatment. Next, the specific number, duration, and order of use of each of the behaviors and events contained in that treatment must be clearly and explicitly defined. With these two steps accomplished (and in most published applied behavior analysis experiments, the treatment is explicitly defined during these two steps), an operationalized set of criteria are available that may be compared with data collected on actual implementation of the treatment in a particular setting.

A second difference relates to how, specifically, the operationalized descriptive account of a particular treatment should be compared with data generated in verification of acceptable levels of treatment fidelity. Generating a behavior-event record of the implementation of a particular treatment is fairly straightforward and may be conducted in the same manner that one would collect a data record for a particular situation (see Chapter 7 for a detailed discussion of this). Comparing this record to the operationalized treatment description, however, is somewhat different than doing a reliability comparison of two independent data records. A simple description using number, duration, rate, and percentage of observational time measures may be used to compare how closely the actual treatment implementation characteristics mirrored the operational description of the treatment. This method, however, is open to criticism as a simple intuitive eyeballing comparison may be open to qualitative interpretation concerning a judgment of an acceptable level of treatment fidelity. An alternative method is to have defined a treatment implementation specifically enough in terms of the number, duration, rate, and experimental percentages of time of each behavior and event included in the treatment, and to have also defined the treatment in terms of total length of occurrence, so that this treatment definition and a behavior-event data record of each treatment implementation may be compared using the statistical formulae described for use when conducting data record comparisons for reliability purposes. In this latter manner, a specific quantitative accounting of relative treatment fidelity may be ascertained. Lending additional rigor to the determination of relative levels of treatment fidelity within a particular experimental activity is the recording of behaviors and events contained in the treatment during nontreatment phases of the experiment to ensure that there is no occurrence of treatment components during phases of an experiment in which a treatment is withheld from a particular individual or group of clientele.

RELIABILITY FORMULA SUMMARIES

There are a number of statistical methods that can be used to determine reliability between two observational data records. Many of these methods have frequented the education and social science research literatures, and each has its particular advantages and disadvantages, which we will discuss in some detail. For each of the three recommended steps to determine a reliable data record in which a comparison between two observations is desired, the same formulae may be used. In addition, many behavior analysis texts provide a detailed conceptual and applied accounting of the mathematical equations and the relative benefits and drawbacks of each method when calculating levels of reliability. Thus only a brief summary is provided here of the statistical formulae that are most often used in the literature and are contained in readily available software programs to facilitate ease of use. For a more detailed discussion and a variety of more advanced examples and illustrations, refer to Bakeman and Gottman (1986, 1997), Cooper and colleagues (1987), Kazdin (1982), or any number of compatible textbooks in which statistical methodology is discussed in detail.

Simple Frequency

This method is one of the earliest represented forms of conducting agreement checks and is perhaps one of the easiest to perform, which provides a clear advantage in and of itself. Although it is most often used when only a number of occurrence or simple event count is utilized as a recording measure, it can also be used with intervals or durations of behavior if those time measurements are segmented into equally specified units amenable to counting. The *simple frequency* formula is as follows:

$$\frac{\text{Smaller Count Total}}{\text{Larger Count Total}} \times 100 = \text{Percent Agreement}$$

In essence, when two observers' data records are compared, the smaller behavior or event count from one observer is divided by the larger behavior or event count from the other observer. This number may then be multiplied by 100 to provide a percentage or reported as a decimal representation (i.e., 87% or .87). When using the simple frequency method of assessing agreement levels in two independent data records, a percentage of agreement may be reported for each individual behavior and event in the two data records according to the above formula and the numerical counts for each behavior and event in each of the two data records and/or an aggregate or total percentage across all behaviors and events in the data records may be reported.

Although this method of determining levels of agreement between data records is useful and appealing in its simplicity, and can provide a quick check to see if agreement falls in a relatively high or low percentage level, it has one major drawback. Comparing totals of numerical counts does not provide information related to agreement on the actual instances of each behavior or event as it actually occurred in time. For example, one observer may inappropriately record many noninstances of a particular behavior and not record some occurrences. The second observer may record occurrences of the same behavior accurately. In this case, one observer is recording inaccurately and the other is recording accurately. Although only one of the data records is accurate, they may have a very similar or identical total number of behavior occurrences and, hence, will be assessed as having a high level of agreement when using the simple frequency agreement method for comparison.

Point-by-Point

The second statistical formula we summarize is perhaps the most commonly accepted and utilized formula to date in the literature, and it is termed *point-by-point*. Again operating on a numerical count or statically segmented measure, this approach is an attempt to take into account whether there is agreement on each recorded occurrence of a particular behavior or event. The point-by-point formula consists of the following:

$$\frac{\text{Number of Agreements}}{\text{Number of Agreements} + \text{Number of Disagreements}} \times 100$$

$$= \text{Percent Agreement}$$

This formula first calculates the number of agreements that each observer agreed occurred for each behavior and event. This is conducted by using the smaller of the two agreement totals for a particular behavior or event as the number of agreements on that behavior or event. Next, this formula counts the number of times each observer disagreed on the occurrence of a behavior or event. This is done by taking the larger agreement total of one observer and subtracting from it the smaller agreement total of the other observer, for each behavior and event. The agreement number and the disagreement number are then plugged into the formula above and calculated. The outcome is a percentage of agreement and may be calculated for each separate behavior and event in each data record compared or for an aggregate total of all agreements and disagreements among all of the behaviors and events in a particular set of data records.

The point-by-point method of determining levels of agreement provides a distinct advantage over the simple frequency method because it allows a determination of agreement taking into account agreement on specific behavior and event occurrences and not simply the totaling of recorded occurrences. Two potential drawbacks to this method exist, however. First, agreements on nonoccurrences of behaviors and events are not included in the method, as inclusion of nonoccurrence information provides a danger of artificially inflating the agreement percentage. In other words, observers may more readily agree on nonoccurrences, and absences of a behavior or event may be more prevalent than occurrences in a particular data record. What is assumed most important to assessing agreement is the accurate recording of the occurrence of a behavior or event. If nonoccurrences were included in an agreement analysis, then a large number of nonoccurrences in relation to occurrences may mask the ability of observers to reliably and accurately make challenging discriminations of particular behavior and event occurrences.

A second potential drawback to the point-by-point method is that when behavior and event occurrences are high, agreement levels are typically artificially high. In other words, a certain level of agreement between observers will be calculated with this formula due simply to chance or random recording when the total number of behavior and event occurrences of interest are relatively high in number.

Cohen's Kappa

Although often criticized due to their inherent complexity, some more sophisticated statistical/correlational methods are available that have been developed in an attempt to more capably control for nonoccurrence and chance agreement when comparing data records (see the Issues in Interobserver Reliability special issue of the *Journal of Applied Behavior Analysis*, 1977, and Watkins & Pacheco, 2000, for a more detailed discussion of this). Although it is little used and reported in the experimental literature in the education and social sciences, we include *Cohen's* (1960, 1965) *kappa* in our software package because (a) this method is most often recommended when searching for a more sophisticated agreement statistic and (b) through the use of computer-based technology, more sophisticated methods of assessing agreement become much more time and labor efficient. Cohen's kappa is conducted using the following formulae:

$$\frac{\text{P-Agreements - P-Chance Agreements}}{1 - \text{P-Chance Agreements}}$$

$$= \text{Percent Agreement } (0.00\text{--}1.00)$$

In this first formula that describes completely the kappa measure, P-Agreements is calculated using the following:

$$\frac{\begin{array}{cc} \text{Number of Agreements} & + \text{ Number of Agreements} \\ \text{on Occurrences} & \text{on Nonoccurrences} \end{array}}{\text{Total Number of Agreements} + \text{Total Number of Disagreements}}$$

The P-Agreement formula is essentially the same as the point-by-point formula—except that it also takes into account agreements and disagreements on nonoccurrences of behaviors and events.

In the kappa formula, P-Chance Agreements is calculated using the following:

$$\frac{\left(\begin{array}{cc} \text{Number of} & \text{Number of} \\ \text{Occurrences} \times \text{Occurrences} \\ \text{(Observer 1} & \text{Observer 2)} \end{array}\right) + \left(\begin{array}{cc} \text{Number of} & \text{Number of} \\ \text{Nonocc.} \times \text{Nonocc.} \\ \text{(Observer 1} & \text{Observer 2)} \end{array}\right)}{\text{Total Number of Recording Intervals Squared}}$$

The specified advantages of using this formula (or those like it) is that it in theory takes into account agreement on nonoccurrences of behaviors and events and that it corrects to an extent for agreement due to random chance contained in observational recording episodes. A major drawback to this method of assessing agreement is that it is limited to the recording of the presence or absence of single behaviors within a specified time interval. In other words, to use this method with success, the method of observation must include segmenting the total observation period into equally spaced time segments and then limiting the observation process to the recording of the presence or absence of a single behavior within each specified time-segment. If multiple behaviors are to be recorded within the same specified time-segments, then a separate agreement analysis on each behavior or event of recording interest must be conducted if choosing an agreement measure such as Cohen's kappa. When recording the presence (or absence) of multiple behaviors and events in real time as they actually take place, this method of determining agreement between data records is considered by many to be far too time consuming and to potentially provide inappropriate agreement quotients.

Although we have incorporated one means to assessing agreement in our discussion that potentially takes into account non-occurrence and chance issues, the matter of providing a formula that definitively corrects for these artifacts *and* does not introduce new statistical concerns to the assessment method continues to be a topic of statistical debate. Although many complex statistical variations now exist in the literature in attempts to overcome nonoccurrence and chance issues, most experimental and evaluation projects interested in measuring agreement continue to rely on the point-by-point method until a definitive alternative is provided.

Pearson Product-Moment Correlation

One last statistical manipulation less often seen in the mainstream direct observation and behavior analysis literature is the use of a *Pearson product-moment correlation* to determine reliability in two independent data records. This method of assessing reliability also differs from the three just discussed, for instead of comparing data records from a particular observational session or day, the reliability over the entire length of a particular experiment or evaluation activity is determined. In the former three cases, reliability is assessed at a particular point in time and for a particular observational period, then these checks are typically reported in an experimental publication as a mean of all of the reliability checks and then a range with respect to the lowest and highest reliability score over the course of the experiment.

In using a Pearson r to compute reliability, a correlation coefficient is produced to reflect the relative agreement over all instances in an experimental or evaluative activity in which reliability was assessed. Similar to most statistical/correlational manipulations, the reliability number using this method can range from -1.00 to $+1.00$. A positive correlation number indicates a high level of correspondence (i.e., the data records of observers 1 and 2 that are being used for reliability comparisons tend to agree with one another) between the data records compared, and a negative correlation number indicates a low level of correspondence (i.e., the two data records used for reliability comparisons tend to disagree with one another or diverge in opposing directions). The formula used to compute Pearson r is as follows:

$$[\text{Number of Checks} \times \text{Sum of (Obs. 1 Scores} \times \text{Obs. 2 Scores)}]$$
$$- (\text{Sum of Obs. 1 Scores}) \times (\text{Sum of Obs. 2 Scores})$$

$$[\text{No. of Checks} \times \text{Sum of Obs. 1 Scores}^2 - (\text{Sum of Obs. 1 Scores})^2]$$
$$\times [\text{No. of Checks} \times \text{Sum of Obs. 2 Scores}^2 - (\text{Sum of Obs. 2 Scores})^2]$$

In this formula, the number of checks stands for the total number of times that two data records are compared for reliability purposes during the course of an entire experimental or evaluative activity. The scores of observers 1 and 2 are the actual scores in terms of a discrete measure (e.g., number count) of behavior and event occurrence used for the individual reliability comparison. From this formula an aggregate reliability indicator over the course of an entire experiment can be determined.

As with other formulae designed for reliability comparison purposes, there are some limitations in the use of Pearson r. First, Pearson r simply provides an indicator of covariation, or the degree to which the scores across two independent data collectors tend to produce similarly high or low counts of behavior and event occurrences. Use of this formula only indicates how two observers tend to move in similar directions from individual reliability assessment to reliability assessment. It does not provide information relative to specific agreement totals in each reliability comparison case. In an example where the amount of disagreement between two observers' data records was consistent across all reliability comparison checks for a particular experiment, then a Pearson r analysis would artificially inflate a determination of reliability—even though the two observers tended to not agree on each individual occurrence.

A second challenge relates to the potential for behavior and event occurrences to change dramatically in amount across different phases of an experiment. When this is the case, Pearson r analyses should be conducted separately on groups of reliability comparisons within each experimental phase so that the Pearson r indicators are not artificially inflated or deflated due to dramatic changes in the relative amount of behavior and event occurrence recordings contained in the data files to be compared as researchers move from experimental phase to experimental phase.

We think that a final set of general comments relevant to issues of reliability and treatment fidelity analysis is in order before we move on to Part III of this book, which details data recording tactics, experimental design types, and data analysis methods. Although we have provided a selection of methods for computing reliability in accordance with a set of recommended general procedures (i.e., the three-step process), it is ultimately up to the researcher to make the best match between the type of behavior and event data to be collected, the relative complexity of the observation system to be used, the measures of interest (e.g., static or sequential), and the character of behavior and event occurrences that should determine the match between particular reliability procedures and the statistical formula used for analysis. The range of sophistication and capability of each formula should also be weighed against the time and effort necessary to implement each formula for analysis and the level of accuracy necessary for reliable data determination. When determining measurement type in particular, it should be remembered that for all of the reliability formulae discussed, the measurement type—particularly if it was originally continuous (e.g., duration) or represented by a probability (e.g., sequence occurrence)—must be translated into discrete numerical counts to legitimately implement the formula of choice. Table 6.1 provides a summary of recommended procedures and statistical analyses.

In addition, one of the most pervasive challenges to the analysis of reliability is that a portion of the agreement between two independently coded data records could be due to chance. Although more sophisticated formulae such as Cohen's kappa are designed to overcome such challenges, they remain suspect at some levels and are designed for very specific and narrowly prescribed types of data records (for a sophisticated treatment of this issue, refer to Bakeman & Gottman, 1986, 1997).

Efforts to increase the confidence with which one can stipulate that data records are accurate representations of observational settings of interest, and that treatments have actually been implemented according to their operational descriptions, remain important and central features of direct observation and behavior analysis research and should be included in the published reporting of such activity. Thus the central purposes of conducting reliability and treatment fidelity assessments are (a) accurate observation, (b) consistency of observation across multiple observers, and (c) feedback on observation activity for those being trained in accuracy.

SUMMARY AND FOREGROUND FOR PART III

Part II of this text has provided a detailed set of guiding principles and specific procedures for developing a category system for use in

Table 6.1   Reliability and Treatment Fidelity Procedural Summary and
Accompanying Statistical Analyses

Purposes

Ensuring consistency of data recording
Avoiding data collector bias and ensuring data record accuracy
Ensuring operational character of category systems

Three-Step Process

1. Criterion standard development
2. Training staff according to the criterion standard
3. Implementing interobserver checks

Related procedure of ensuring treatment fidelity

Statistical Formulae

Simple frequency
Point-by-point
Cohen's kappa
Pearson product-moment correlation

research and evaluation activities. In addition, we have recommended reliability and staff training practices that are important and necessary, as well as a central focus of direct observation and applied behavior analysis methodology, for use when implementing the type of research activity described in this text. Chapter 5 has provided a selection of category systems that have been used in a variety of disciplines and that we feel are representative of contemporary category system construction (that include a field systems and sequential component to each system's structure and implementation). This concludes Part II of the text.

The chapters contained in Part III provide a detailed discussion of recommended procedures and practices for researchers engaged in the use of category systems constructed for the actual collection, analysis, and representation of direct observational data. Included are important issues of measurement, experimental validity, design types to control for validity threats and ensure the rigor of an experimental or evaluation activity, and a variety of mechanisms for static and sequential analysis of data collected through use of the category systems as described in this section.

Part III

Recording Tactics, Design Types, and Data Analyses

7

Approaches to Recording Direct Observational Data

Direct observation recording is the terminal event of a complex series that begins with defining the response class of interest, proceeds through direct observation, and culminates in creating a permanent record of the behavior(s) of interest . . . the quality of this scientific process cannot exceed the characteristics of that record.

— Johnston and Pennypacker (1980, p. 49)

After reading this chapter, you should be able to define the following terms and provide the information requested in the study guide.

TERMS

Number	Latency
Rate	Probability
Duration	Event recording
Percentage	Duration recording
Celeration	Time sampling
Cumulative record	Real time

STUDY GUIDE

1. List, define, and provide an example of each of the measurement options available to researchers engaged in direct observation research activity, which are listed in Table 7.1.

2. Discuss two important cautions for researchers when they limit measurement to a simple numerical count of behavior and event occurrence.
3. Explain the three distinct recording methods that can be used when collecting duration measures.
4. Discuss the critical difference between measures of duration and latency.
5. Explain the three types of probability (simple, conditional, and transitional) in relation to measurement options in this area.
6. Explain the meaning of the four sequential systems measures of rhythm, complexity, coherence, and velocity in an analysis of the time-based connections among behaviors and events in an observational setting.
7. Describe the various traditional data recording procedures, including the three types of time sampling (whole- and partial-interval and momentary time sampling), in relation to what is meant by recording in real time.
8. Define the term *discrete* in relation to pre-computer data recording techniques and in relation to the challenges that computer-based data recording in real-time overcomes.
9. Discuss the four steps to more complete description and analysis that should be applied by researchers who subscribe to systems and sequentially oriented thinking.

Placing emphasis on the quantifying of observable events in data collection activities necessitates that we use a set of procedures to make sure that when we are counting things we get it right. In other words, we want to make sure that the data record that describes an experimental or evaluation setting of interest is as accurate a reflection of what actually occurred as possible. Chapter 6 provided a detailed account of recommended reliability procedures to better ensure the consistency and accuracy of a data record. In this chapter, we provide a summary of the measurement types that have frequented direct observation and behavior analysis research and a description of the variety of ways in which data have been recorded. Thus we emphasize the potential importance and appeal of multiple measurement use and real-time recording practices to more inclusively and completely capture the full character of behavior-event occurrences in the settings to be observed and analyzed.

A wide variety of measurement types and related methods of collecting data according to a measurement type of interest have been used and reported in the direct observation literature. The majority of these measures and data collection methods relate specifically to the collection of data on behavior and event activity that can be directly observed due to the overt nature of the behavior and event occurrences of interest. In addition, and in relation to field systems and sequentially based contributions to direct observation methodology (and in particular those that are driven by computer-based data recording and analysis capabilities), some appealing alternative measurement types have been developed. Although some of these alternative measurement types are difficult to access and there is little empirical literature from which to draw examples and illustrations of their use, they are important to consider given their potential contribution to furthering understanding of complex interactive behavior-event situations.

MEASUREMENT OPTIONS

Table 7.1 provides an overview of measurement options for researchers interested in the quantitative recording of behavior and event occurrences in applied settings. Although this list does not include all of the wide variety of measurement options that have been used in the direct observation research literature, it does provide a representative sample. When choosing a measure or combination of measures to be used in a particular research or evaluation activity, it is important for researchers to consider the characteristics of the behaviors and events to be observed, as well as the static or sequential focus of the direct observation activity to be undertaken, which will become apparent in the following sections.

Once category systems have been developed and a staff is prepared for the collection of reliable and accurate data records, a final decision of measurement type should be made by researchers prior to actual data collection. This decision involves choosing a particular recording tactic (the subject of the following two recording procedures sections) and related data measure. Most traditional quantitative observation methods require choosing a set of procedures for actual collection of the data record and basing those procedures on the type of measure a researcher or evaluator is most interested in obtaining. Given the significantly enhanced capabilities of computer-based

Table 7.1   A Summary of Measurement Options

Event Records or Numerical Counts

This is a procedure in which the number of occurrences of a particular behavior or event are counted. This measure, which is often referred to as the *frequency of occurrence*, is the most rudimentary form of a discrete measure, indicating a specific characteristic of a behavior or event occurrence.

Rate of Occurrence

In this measure, *rate* refers to the average number of occurrences of a particular behavior or event during a specified standard time frame. For example, rate is determined by dividing the total number of behavior or event occurrences during an entire observational record by the number of standard time frames (e.g., if rate per minute is the focus of measurement interest, and a behavior occurred 29 times over the course of a 20-minute recording period, then the rate measure would be 1.45 or 29/20). This measure provides another form of recording the discrete characteristics of a behavior or event.

Duration Measure

This measure specifies the length of time that passes during the presence or existence of a particular behavior or event. In other words, duration is the extent of time that a behavior or event occurs. This measure may be taken as an individual duration for each behavior or event occurrence, as an average duration across all behavior occurrences of the same type within an observation session, or as an aggregate duration of all behavior occurrences within the same behavior category for the entire observational episode. Duration measures, while time based, are typically categorized as discrete measures because they provide another dimension of information related to the character of individual behaviors or events.

Percent of Experimental Time

This measure provides a ratio between the total amount of time elapsed during a complete observational recording episode, and the total amount of time (or aggregate duration) that a particular behavior or event was present within that observational episode (e.g., if the total observational time was 45 minutes and a particular event had a total aggregate duration of 19 inutes, then the percentage of experimental time for the event would be .42 or 19/45). This measure provides another discrete level to the characterization of particular behaviors and events operating within an observational setting.

Celeration

This measure provides a more complex accounting of the discrete characteristics of behaviors and events across observation episodes and is typically based on an accumulation of event record data over multiple observation sessions. *Celeration* is a change in the rate of responding over a specified time period, which indicates a trend over time specific to changes in rates of responding over specified periods of time. The concept of celeration was originated by Ogden Lindsley, who created the Standard Celeration Chart (SCC) for displaying any behavior or event recorded as long as time has been included as an element. The SCC uses responses per minute as its standard unit.

Cumulative Record

This measure provides an aggregate measure over time and extracted from simple numerical event records to represent behavior and event change. To calculate a cumulative record, the number of behavior or event occurrences for a first observation session are reported, then for each subsequent observation session, the number of behavior or event occurrences are totaled and added to the previous observation session total. In this manner, a generally increasing tally is provided across observation sessions.

Latency Measures

This measure records the amount of time that elapses between a particular behavior and event of interest (e.g., a teacher stimulus such as an instructional cue or a verbal question) and a particular succeeding behavior or event that is theoretically connected to the preceding event (e.g., a student return to appropriate skill practice or an answer to a question). This type of measure is time-based or sequential in character.

Probabilities

This class of measures constitutes the primary time-based measure included in a sequential analysis among particular behavior and event occurrences. Reported as a numerical indicator between 0.00 and 1.00, it provides a quantitative indication of the relative condition of occurrence among two or more specific behavior and event occurrences in time-based sequence.

Alternative Sequential Systems Measures

This set of measures, which includes rhythm, complexity, coherence, and velocity, provides quantitative description of how multiple behaviors and events within a particular data record operate according to a variety of combinations of the previous measurement categories to define the larger time-based system characteristics within which each particular behavior and event is operating.

recording tools like those referenced at the end of this text, however, these decisions have less impact than they did previously on the possible data outcomes of a particular research or evaluation project. This is due to the ability of computer-based recording tactics to develop an observational record that has been conceptually organized so as to enable the extraction of a wide variety of measures such as those listed in Table 7.1. In particular, if the researcher is organizing an observational record according to the start and stop times of each event occurrence, then it logically follows that most of the measures summarized can be extracted from data record information that includes when each behavior and event began and ended according to a time-based chronology. To visually construct how this might be accomplished, we suggest that while reading the following measurement type discussion, the reader return to the simple event matrix illustration provided toward the end of the section Differences in Assessment: Modeling an Interbehavioral Lens in Chapter 3 or view Figure 9.4 in Chapter 9. These two simple illustrations provide a sense of how organizing a data record according to the start and stop times of behavior and event occurrences of interest can facilitate the extraction of a wide variety of static and sequential measures. It is in this regard that the following sections summarize some of the more widely accepted, and some of the more recent innovations, in measurement related to direct observation activities.

Event Records or Numerical Counts

These first measures for behaviors and events in a particular data record provide a simple numerical tally or frequency of occurrence for a particular behavior or event that is present when recording observational data. This measure, the counting of the *number* of occurrences of a behavior or event of interest, provides a first level of description of the character of a particular behavior or event occurrence. It is necessarily limited to measuring discrete event occurrences that have a definite start and stop time of observed presence. This measure can be used to document either the occurrence of particular behaviors and events in isolation or the occurrence of particular behavior-event sequences as they occur in time. It is important to note here, as will be discussed in the following Duration Measures section, that using only an event record numerical count, as a measure for behavior and event occurrences in a particular experiment or evaluation activity, should be limited to measuring simple behaviors and events that have a consistent duration time (e.g., elapsed time of occurrence) when emitted. In addition, and when comparing data across observational episodes, using only numerical count data should be limited to measuring observational episodes or data records that are of equal length. If these two conditions are not met when using only event record numerical data for analysis, then a less than complete and related accurate representation of the character of the observational record may be produced—with consequently inaccurate results and conclusions coming from the analysis of that data record. Having noted these cautions, however, we can say that numerical count data records have proven a popular traditional measurement choice for most experimental and evaluation study focused on the amount of behavior occurrence in relation to efforts designed to either increase or decrease particular behavior or event occurrences.

Rate of Occurrence

This measure provides a next additional important element of descriptive capability in relation to the simple event record. Essentially, a *rate* of occurrence measure provides an average numerical count per standardized unit of time for a particular behavior or event of interest. This is an important measure when the total observation time elapsed across each observation setting to be compared is different in length. For example, if an investigator was interested in the number of questioning behaviors that a particular teacher used in his or her classroom and the potential impact of those questioning behaviors on student subject-matter-related responses, then that investigator might first tally up the number of questions asked in each class meeting. If the amount of time of each class meeting differed in any great degree, however, the number of questions asked might be influenced by the varying amount of total class time available to ask questions. In this regard, a rate measure would quantify question-asking behavior in terms of an average number of questions asked per time frame (e.g., in a 1-minute period, 5-minute period, etc.). If a rate measure were used in this data collection example, the number of questions asked would be standardized according to a specifically defined time period, and fluctuations in total amount of class time or total amount of observational time in each data record would not impact on the measure to potentially confound the reported experimental or evaluation results.

Duration Measures

Such measures provide an important indicator of how long a particular behavior or event lasts, and using a duration measure is a helpful addition to numerical counts in adding to the characterization of discrete or static occurrences of particular behaviors or events. A *duration* measure can also be recorded in three separate and distinct ways. The first relates to the length of time of each individual occurrence of a particular behavior or event of interest and is typically expressed using a measure of time that has elapsed (e.g., seconds, minutes, etc.). The second measurement type for duration requires taking an average, or reporting a mean, of all the durations for all of the occurrences of a particular behavior or event within a complete observational data record. A third way of recording duration lies in taking an aggregate, or total, duration of all occurrences of a particular behavior or event that has occurred in a complete observation record.

Using any or all of these duration measure types yields important additional information regarding the static characteristics of particular behavior and event occurrences. Another education illustration may prove helpful here. In the example of a classroom evaluator interested in Off-Task behaviors of particular students, numerical event record tallies would provide a sense of how often Off-Task behaviors occurred in a particular classroom setting. This is important information to a classroom teacher, for instances of Off-Task behaviors are something that a teacher would want to curtail. Without a sense of how long each Off-Task episode lasted, however, a complete description of Off-Task behavior may be lacking, particularly if each instance is of a different length. This latter form of information is the type that duration measures provide. For example, a student engaged in Off-Task behavior in a particular classroom setting for 1 or 2 minutes is very different from a student engaged in the same behavior for a much larger portion of the class period. In the same example, the case of a student engaged in one continuous episode of Off-Task behavior for 20 minutes during a particular class period, with that episode being the only one recorded, is very different from two or three students engaged in 12 to 15 Off-Task episodes that last only 10 or 20 seconds each. This example illustrates well, therefore, that oftentimes it is important to implement more than one measurement dimension when engaged in describing somewhat completely and with some degree of accuracy the particular characteristics of behavior and event occurrences of interest.

Percentage of Experimental Time

This measure is similar to the duration measures just discussed. *Percentage* of experimental time provides an amount of time that a particular behavior or event took up in relation to the total amount of observational time in a particular data record. In other words, a ratio is provided between the aggregate duration, or total time elapsed, for all occurrences of a particular behavior or event of interest within a data record and the total amount of time elapsed for the entire observational record. This measure provides another important dimension to the complete and accurate description of the discrete characteristics of behavior and event occurrences in a data record. Using our Off-Task example concerning the importance of duration measures, even if student Off-Task episodes are quantified by duration of each occurrence, average duration, and aggregate duration, a completely accurate comparison across observation episodes is not available unless those Off-Task episodes are described in terms of the total percentage of class time that they take up or the total percentage of the larger observational data record that represents each class time observation. This is a particularly important measure if the observational episodes to be compared differ in total length from episode to episode. For example, 10 minutes of total Off-Task time during a particular class period is much different in character depending on whether the total class period is 30 minutes, 1 hour, or 2 hours in length.

Celeration and Cumulative Records

These measures may also be helpful in describing the discrete characteristics of particular behavior and event occurrences, especially when a researcher or evaluator wants to determine the rate of acquisition of a particular skill over time, and they are therefore used when an observer is looking at trends across observational episodes arranged at periodic intervals. As Table 7.1 summarizes, *celeration* measures a change in the rate of responding over time. This measure first plots on a graph a rate measure for each observational episode in the order in which each observation was conducted. Once the episodes are plotted, a general trend is provided in relation to the relatively increasing or decreasing rate of occurrence for a particular behavior or event across multiple observation episodes. This trend may also be statistically represented by a mathematical equation that represents a line of best fit for the overall trend across observation sessions. Lindsley (1981) is considered the original developer of celeration charting as a measurement option, and recommends reference to a Standard Celeration Chart (SCC) that uses number per minute as the preferred measure of rate of behavior or event occurrence.

A *cumulative record* provides a more complex accounting of the discrete characteristics of behaviors and events across observation episodes and is typically based on an accumulation of numerical event record data and related graphing of numerical data over multiple observation sessions. Here, an example of calculation for this type of record may prove helpful. If a researcher is using a cumulative record measure to record the number of quizzes that students in a class complete to a certain predefined level of mastery, he or she would first tally and report the number of passed quizzes during the first observation session. The number of passed quizzes for each subsequent observation session is then totaled and added to the previous observation session total. In this manner, a generally increasing tally is provided across observation sessions. This measure and variations of it are most commonly referred to as a cumulative record. For a detailed accounting of celeration measures and the construction of a cumulative record, see Sulzer-Azaroff and Mayer's (1991) discussion, which includes detailed illustrations.

Latency Measure

A *latency* measure provides a time-based quantification of the time that elapses between a particular behavior or event occurrence of interest and a subsequent behavior or event that the original event may theoretically be functionally related to. Those being introduced to this measure sometimes find it difficult to distinguish from a duration measure. Essentially, duration specifies a total time that has elapsed for an occurrence of a particular behavior, whereas latency specifies a total amount of time that has elapsed from the termination of one behavior to the onset of another behavior of interest. Teacher questioning and student responding provide a nice example of when a latency measure may be important to include so as to ensure a complete and accurate description of not just the characteristics of each individual behavior included in an observational effort but the characteristic relationships in time among those behaviors and events as well. In this regard, a duration measure would record the amount of time it took a teacher to ask a question, or the total amount of elapsed time between the onset of the questioning behavior and the termination of the questioning behavior. A latency measure, on the other hand, would record the total amount of time that elapsed between the termination of the teacher's question and the onset of a student response, or the time that elapsed between the question being asked and a student's response.

Using a teacher questioning→student responding example, it is often important to determine the time-based sequential character among these two behaviors to determine issues such as (a) a student responding too soon and potentially incorrectly as a function of not listening to the complete question, (b) a student taking too long to respond indicating a lack of certainty about the appropriate response, and (c) the general relationship between a teacher's question type and his or her ability to elicit rapid and correct responses versus slow and incorrect answers from students. A case may be made for the importance of the researcher's including a measure of latency for behaviors when she or he is engaged in research and evaluation activities. Using our Off-Task recording example, of previous measurement sections, we note that an important dimension to the effective curtailing of Off-Task behavior clearly lays in making a determination of the relative time elapsed between the use of a particular teacher strategy designed to curtail particular Off-Task incidents and the actual cessation of that Off-Task activity. When using a latency measure, data related to the start and stop times of behavior and event occurrences are necessary to extracting this measure from a data record (refer again to the visual data record examples provided in Chapter 3 and Figure 9.4). This measure also provides a first level of focus as to the potential importance of not stopping a research or evaluation activity with measures of individual behavior characteristics alone but including a time-based sequential dimension to a behavior-event measurement strategy.

Probabilities

At one level of measurement, the term *probability* simply relates to a straight percentage among the number of times of occurrence for a particular behavior or event in relation to the total number of event occurrences for all behaviors and events in an observation record. A probability measure may also be used to compare the total duration of a particular behavior or event to the total length of time for the observation record in which that behavior is included. In this regard, the measurement term *probability* is similar to the percentage of experimental time measure previously discussed. When dealing with simple probability or a percentage in relation to time (e.g., duration), it is important to note that the category system in use must be exhaustive, or record something as occurring for the entire amount of elapsed observational time. If this is not taken into account in a data recording system, then inaccurate probability measurement may occur.

When using simple probabilities to represent number or time, a typical intent of the researcher is to provide information with regard to how total behavior and event use is allocated across the variety of behaviors and events in the observational system throughout a complete observational episode. This typical characterization of probability is similar to the percentage measure discussed previously. In this type of simple probability measure, or in the transitional or conditional probability measure type about to be discussed, the start and stop times of each behavior and event occurrence must be included in the observational record to enable the use of a probability measure. Again, the simple behavior and event matrix illustrations in Chapter 3 and in Figure 9.4 serve as examples of data records in which start and stop times for each behavior and event that is observed are recorded.

In the first case of simple probability, this measure provides a sense of how much a particular behavior or event occurred relative to the larger total set of behavior and event occurrences in a particular observation record. For example, if a researcher is interested in the simple probability of teacher questioning, he or she may first simply count up the number of occurrences of questioning behavior. Next, a count of the total of all teacher behaviors (e.g., other instructional behaviors, organizational and managerial behaviors, etc.) occurring in the same data record must be tallied. From these two numbers a ratio or simple probability may be ascertained by dividing the larger total into the questioning behavior total.

Another form of probability measure, and one we feel is most important to providing quantitative information to describe the time-based or sequential nature of particular behavior and event occurrences, is commonly termed a *transitional probability* (e.g., Bakeman & Gottman, 1986) or *conditional probability* (Ray & Delprato, 1989; Sharpe, 1997a). This type of probability makes numerically explicit the relative probability that a particular behavior or event either preceded or followed another specified behavior or event relatively more or less frequently than other possible preceding or following occurrences. This measure is akin to the descriptive and statistical illustrations provided in Chapter 3. Put another way, *simple probability* is simply the probability of a certain event occurring, whereas *conditional probability* is the probability of a certain event occurring given the occurrence of another particular event. Bakeman and Gottman (1986) further define a difference between the terms *conditional* and *transitional* as follows: The use of the term *conditional* simply designates a relationship to be quantified among events, whereas the term *transitional* takes on a Kantorian (see the discussion of the history and evolution of behavior analysis methods in Chapter 1) meaning to explicitly refer to the *time-based* relationship among particular behaviors and events. In the latter case, the probability numbers used to define a relationship in time among certain behaviors and events are further explained in terms of *lags*, or the relative proximity in sequence among certain behaviors and events of interest.

For example, the probability that a teacher provides some form of corrective verbal discipline immediately after an incident of student Off-Task behavior occurs in his or her classroom would be considered a lag-1 conditional probability. The probability that a teacher then moved on to the use of another behavior after corrective verbal discipline would be considered a lag-2 conditional probability, conditional to the original Off-Task target behavior. The transitional nature of the probability involves the specific time measures relative to the latency between the behaviors and events under conditional probability analysis. Conditional and transitional probabilities may also be analyzed according to certain events that precede a particular behavior or event of interest. In our Off-Task example, a researcher may be interested in the specific behaviors or events that immediately precede episodes of Off-Task behavior, so as to come to a conditional and transitional probability measurement of the kinds of specific behaviors and events that may tend to trigger incidents of unwanted Off-Task behaviors.

Researchers using this form of measure typically report it descriptively or statistically, as in the illustrations in Chapter 3. In addition, probability matrices may be constructed to represent the conditional and transitional probability between each behavior and event contained in an observational record and each and every other behavior and event (see Bakeman & Gottman, 1986, Sharpe & Hawkins, 1992a, 1992c, or the Preparing a Graph section in Chapter 9 of this text for a detailed discussion of respective statistical formulae, probability matrix illustrations, and graphic representation options). Essentially, a probability matrix first includes a list of every single behavior and event included in an observational system, represented along the horizontal and vertical axes of a graph paper type set of squares. Once the behaviors and events are listed along the vertical and horizontal axes, each box on the matrix is filled with the conditional probability that corresponds to the relationship among the occurrence of respective preceding and succeeding behaviors and events that correspond to vertical and horizontal axis indicators. For instance, looking at a particular behavior on the left vertical axis, and then scrolling across the graph paper to a corresponding behavior or event of interest on the top horizontal axis, provides a conditional probability of occurrence of the vertical axis behavior preceding the horizontal axis behavior. A similar matrix representation may be prepared to report the conditional probabilities of all events succeeding all other events within a particular observation system and for a particular observational data record by specifying the horizontal axis as succeeding behaviors.

Alternative Sequential Systems Measures

In our discussion of representative and often used measures of behavior and event occurrences with respect to the collection and reporting of direct observational data with a quantitative focus, a pattern of movement from the description of a variety of characteristics of particular discrete behavior and event occurrences to a description of the time-based connections among behaviors and events of particular interest should be apparent. In earlier chapters we have discussed this movement in relation to a historical methodological evolution in direct observation activities from the former to the latter focus. In this regard, the pioneering work of Skinner and Kantor has contributed important foundations in the respective areas of three-term contingency and functional relationship modeling and the importance of field systems and sequential analyses. The focus of the following chapters, in which we discuss methodology, is to show how a complete analysis of behavior and event occurrences should include both description and categorization of all of the behaviors and events necessary to complete an accurate analysis of a particular setting, to static measurement description of the characteristics of each and every behavior and event that has occurred in a setting of interest, and to an analysis of the time-based interrelationships of those behaviors and events under study. In addition, methods that allow time-based analyses to move from the relatively simple, dual behavior-event sequences to more complex sequences and the systemic character of multiple behavior and event interactions are important to consider. If this sort of more complete and inclusive analysis is made readily accessible through the use of amenable computer-based technologies (refer to the software description in Appendix B and on the flyer included with this book), then knowledge previously undiscovered regarding some of the time-based intricacies of complex interactive settings may be made available to the research and evaluation public. We therefore provide a summary of some alternative descriptive measurement language designed to communicate some sequential systems oriented data. Although alternative measurement language is not frequently seen in the mainstream observational literature as yet, the theoretical systems literature has provided a starting point for exploration of such language.

Ray and Delprato (1989) provide an excellent terminology resource in this regard, as does the education research body of work of Sharpe and his colleagues (see, e.g., Sharpe & Hawkins, 1992a). These references provide four basic terminology dimensions designed to describe a multi-event observational data record in systems-oriented ways. These term dimensions focus primarily on time-based relationships and on the larger character of behavior and event relationships as a system rather than as single behaviors or events described in relative isolation.

1. *Rhythm*. This term refers to regularly recurring temporal patterns of behaviors and events and the respective sequences that these events tend to operate within. The relative number or frequency and transitional probability of behavior-event sequences is a main focus of systems analysis. Thus rhythm involves the timing, regularity, and complexity with which behavior-event patterns are repeated over time.

2. *Complexity*. This term is used to describe and define a behavior-event system in terms of the number of different individual categories in a particular observation system and required for complete system description. In the category system examples provided in Chapter 5, it is easy to see that for some settings more terms and definitions are required for complete observation setting description than for others. We recommend adhering to the rules and procedures for category system development provided in Chapter 4 and developing category systems that are inclusive of all conceivable behaviors and events that will operate in the setting to be observed.

3. *Coherence*. This term describes the degree to which the behaviors and events operating in a particular observation setting are consistently related to one other. A typical measure of relative coherence is through the examination of a probability matrix as described previously. Coherence provides a descriptive capability with regard to the relative predictability, or conversely random nature, of behavior and

event occurrences in time-based sequence. Implicit in a transitional probability matrix are indications of the actual versus possible number of different behavior and event relationships. If one were to consider the number of sequence pairs that could have occurred (i.e., the total number of cells contained within a matrix) and compare this to the number that actually did occur (i.e., the number of cells that contain probability data), one might conclude that the number of pairs actually observed does not reflect all of the possible relations. Constructing a simple probability, or percentage, of the total number of cells versus the number containing data provides a quantification of the relative coherence of a particular observation record. The number of matrix cells containing entries compared with the total number of cells therefore reflects the probable reliability with which all of the behaviors and events in a particular data record are related to each other. In effect, coherence represents the degree of order and consistency in a setting. High probabilities of high frequency within few cells reflect a greater organizational coherence or predictability. Conversely, low probabilities of low frequency within many cells indicate less predictability.

4. *Velocity*. This measure provides an indication of the time-based rapidity with which behavior-event sequences tend to be emitted. This measure is similar to the rate measure discussed earlier; however, instead of providing a ratio of number of individual behavior or event occurrences according to a defined time standard, a ratio with a time standard is provided according to the observance of particular time-based behavior-event sequences. Using such a measure provides an indication of what we term the *velocity of sequential use*, or the rate at which behavior-event change occurs in an observation record.

From a discussion of the variety of measurement options that have been included in this section, it should be clear that the inclusion of a multiple measurement and sequential measurement focus when conducting direct observation activity is preferred for ensuring more complete and more accurate representations of the character of behavior and event occurrences. The advent of computer-based applications designed to facilitate a multiple measurement and sequential measurement focus as a function of engaging in direct observation activity warrants movement in the direction of computer-based direct observation methods for a wide variety of research and evaluation activities, particularly when multiple behaviors and events are occurring in complex interactive settings, and when multiple measures of those behaviors and events are helpful in gaining a greater understanding of the functional relationships among particular behaviors and events.

TRADITIONAL RECORDING METHODS

Most behavior analysis or systematic observation methodology texts provide a detailed procedural description of recording strategies popularized by researchers and evaluators alike. The most popular of these traditional strategies fall into two general areas, one specifying the type of measurement an observer is interested in, as we have just discussed, and the other specifying how the data may be collected in terms of the timing of actually observing and recording that data. As there exists considerable overlap among the two general areas of measurement type and recording strategy, we will discuss the latter with what we hope is not a too redundant mention of the former. The two most popular and traditional strategies specifying measurement type and related data recording methods are typically termed *event recording* and *duration recording* and are related to traditional direct observation data recording methods and pre–computer based tool data recording capabilities. Equally important strategies specific to the timing of conducting observations are typically termed *time sampling* strategies and include the most frequently used *whole-interval, partial interval,* and *momentary* time-sampling techniques. Utilizing these traditional data recording strategies has typically entailed the use of a coding sheet, a stopwatch, and a pencil, in which behaviors and events were recorded by hand and in which multiple personnel were often necessary to perform various recording tasks. Until recently, choosing among these three data gathering strategies was thought to be fundamental to any recording procedure that counted the presence or absence of behavior and environmental events in some way. Traditionally, it has also been important to detail the form and character of these data recording strategies in relation to the various benefits and challenges that each strategy provides to the reliable and accurate recording of certain types of quantitative information. In most respects, the choice of a recording tactic has been thought critical to the unit of measurement that a particular researcher or evaluator was interested in using, and critical to the chosen measurement method of reporting the data that were collected.

While researchers and evaluators in the education, social, and psychological sciences need to remain sensitive to the more traditional recording strategies that are discussed, and to their various advantages and limitations, the necessity of matching a particular data recording strategy to a particular observational measure or data reporting method does not exist when computer-based tools are used to record and analyze observational data. This is primarily due to the more capable and more inclusive nature of computer-based data recording methods with respect to measurement choices. Through such tool use and an appropriate data collection organizational structure (i.e., recording the specific start and stop times of each occurrence of each behavior and event of interest), one may include all measures that we have outlined in Table 7.1 during the data recording phase of an experiment or evaluation activity. This capability then allows, as a function of data analysis, the researcher to choose the measures and consequent data analyses that he or she wishes to report. This may also be accomplished with respect to the researcher's ability to record data in what we will discuss as *real time*. Nevertheless, we summarize in this section each of the more traditional, precomputer-based recording strategies to provide a foundation on which to discuss the potential appeal of a more inclusive data recording alternative termed *recording in real time*, which is based on the capabilities that computer-based recording tools provide.

Event Recording

The first of these traditional recording tactics, *event recording*, focuses on counting the number of behavior or event occurrences for a particular observational episode. With this method, focus is only on counting up the number of times each behavior and event in the category system occurs. This strategy is recommended in situations where the behaviors and events of interest occur with relatively high frequency and are of relatively short duration. If each observational session within a particular experiment or evaluation enterprise consists of about the same length of time, then the most appropriate measurement choice in reporting event record data is a simple numerical count. If observation sessions within a particular experiment vary in terms of length of time, then using a rate measure (see Table 7.1 and explanations of the table in the accompanying text) to report data may be a more appropriate choice. From the event recording of numerical counts, ratio data comparing particular behaviors and events, percentage data of one behavior or event relative to others, and celeration and cumulative record data (again, the relative amount of increase or decrease in behavior or event occurrences from observation period to observation period) may also be calculated and reported.

Duration Recording

This second traditional recording strategy focuses on the recording of how long particular behaviors and events tend to occur within particular observational episodes. When implementing a *duration recording* method, the individual durations of particular behaviors and events are recorded and information such as individual behavior and event durations, the longest and shortest duration for each behavior or event, average duration and ranges or standard deviations of durations for behavior and event occurrences within the same class of events, and length of time between behavior and event occurrences (i.e., latency) are the primary measurement focus. This tactic is recommended in situations where behaviors and events occur infrequently and in situations in which each occurrence tends to last for a long period of time relative to total observational time. Percentages of total observational time taken up by the occurrences of each behavior and event, and ratios among those percentages, may also be reported with this method.

Time Sampling

The next three categories of traditional data recording methods focus on how, exactly, a particular researcher or evaluator might go about actually documenting occurrences of particular behaviors or events of interest. This set of *time sampling* strategies provides various procedures in which the presence or absence of particular behaviors and events are recorded during specified time-intervals. These tactics require a decision as to when the data should be collected. With all time-sampling methods, each entire observational episode is first broken down into logically specified time segments. Once all of the episodes have been segmented, an observer can record the occurrence (or nonoccurrence) of behaviors and events of interest within each logically specified segment according to the strategies specified within a particular procedure. With *whole-interval* time sampling, an observer records within each specified time segment whether or not a specified behavior or event occurred for the entire time segment or interval period. With *partial-interval* time sampling, an observer records whetheror not a particular behavior or event occurred within each specified time segment, and she or he may also record the number of behavior occurrences or the percentage of that time segment in which a behavior or event occurred. In the third strategy, *momentary* time sampling, an observer records the occurrence or absence of a particular behavior or event only if it is occurring or absent at the precise point in time at which each specified time-segment ends.

Another education example may serve to illustrate these three time-sampling, or interval recording, tactics. If a teacher educator was interested in evaluating a particular instructional episode, for example, he or she might divide up a particular special education resource setting to be observed into logically specified 2-minute periods over the course of a 40-minute instructional session. If the observer's interest was in the behavior of appropriate student responding, he or she would record (a) using a whole-interval method, whether appropriate responding occurred at all during the course of each specified time segment, (b) using a partial-interval method, the number of appropriate responses observed within each 2-minute segment, and (c) using a momentary time-sampling method, whether the student was engaged in responding at the end of each 2-minute segment. These traditional methods provide additional measures of the number of intervals and percentage of intervals in which a behavior or event simply occurred or occurred at a desired level of occurrence. All of these time-sampling, or interval recording, tactics have typically been reserved for observations in which one or only a very few behaviors and events are to be recorded and in which time segments are typically connected with the presence or absence of a treatment or intervention designed to change behaviors and events of interest in some productive way—and at those particular points in time as defined by the segmenting of the larger observational episode. As the number of behaviors and events to be recorded increases, and the rapidity of potential behavior and event occurrences increases, these methods become less appropriate to the ends of complete and accurate quantitative description according to many of the measures outlined in Table 7.1.

Time-sampling procedures have been created in response to the challenge inherent in recording multiple measure information on multiple behaviors and events throughout an entire observational session. In each of these methods, time is provided between each logically specified time segment for data recording purposes. During these second time segments, or this down time, data is being recorded by hand and observations are not taking place. For example, an observer who is interested in recording the number of disruptive or self-injurious episodes of a particular special education student mainstreamed into a regular elementary education classroom would observe for the occurrence of those behaviors during each observational time segment, and would then record the occurrence, or number of occurrences, of those behaviors during each period of time devoted to the recording of information. The time-sampling methods described here provide an important way to determine if certain behaviors or events are occurring at certain specified points in time. One of the greatest drawbacks to these tactics, however, is that when observing behaviors and events that occur frequently and are of short duration when they do occur, the researcher may derive an inaccurate representation of an experimental or evaluation setting due to his or her having missed important information during each time segment devoted to the recording of behaviors and events. In other words, valuable information may be lost when the observer is devoting portions of an observational task to recording data rather than the actual observation of the setting of interest, particularly when that setting contains occurrences of multiple behaviors and events and when those behaviors and events occur often and are of short duration.

RECORDING IN REAL TIME

Although the traditional recording tactics just summarized have provided a wealth of useful and important information to a variety of education and social science concerns, there may be much more to be learned about interactive settings through a more inclusive means of observing behavior-behavior and behavior-environment interactions. More capable computer-based tools, for example, that include both static and sequential measurement capabilities, and those capable of recording the multiple occurrences of a broad variety of behavior and event types, can be of great advantage to those interested in direct observation with a behavior analysis focus. Such data recording capability should provide two important additions to quantitative direct observation efforts. First, more complete and inclusive description and analysis is made available. Once researchers are familiar with appropriate software applications, such as the one described at the end of this text, it becomes clear that computer-based tools will enable an observer to collect information on many more behaviors and events at the same time and to provide all of the measurement data listed in Table 7.1. The list that follows provides a summary of how each traditional recording procedure may provide certain measurement data, particularly when it is used in concert with amenable computer-based data recording tools.

1. *Event recording.* Numerical counts, and rates, ratios, and percentages among those behavior and event counts

2. *Duration recording.* Individual behavior and event occurrence lengths; mean, range, and standard deviations of occurrence lengths; shortest and longest length of occurrence; percentage of total observational time; and latency or length of time between behavior and event occurrences

3. *Time sampling.* Number and percentage of time segments in which a target behavior or event occurred, number and percentage of time segments in which a target behavior or event occurred at a minimum specified level, and number of specified time segments in which a behavior or event was respectively present or absent during the point of time-segment transition

Also, using computer-based data collection and analysis tools that include a field systems and sequential framework will enable observers to look at and analyze their data in new and innovative ways. Many times, for example, it may be necessary for an observer to examine several different measures (e.g., number, rate, percentage, ratio relationships, etc.) of the same behavior or event to come to a more complete understanding of the dynamics of a setting in which a complex variety of behavior-behavior and behavior-environment interactions are rapidly occurring. A multidimensional examination of the many individual characteristics of each behavior and event is important for a better understanding of how most sophisticated education and social science settings operate. In addition, however, the provision of a quantitative analysis of the patterns in time among behaviors and events as they actually occur over time is important for an explicit description and understanding of how certain behaviors and events tend to interact (see Hawkins, Sharpe, & Ray, 1994, Odom & Haring, 1994, and Sharpe, Hawkins, & Lounsbery, 1998, for detailed empirical examples of this measurement issue). In other words, it is important to a complete and thoroughgoing direct observation activity to describe and analyze the potential impact that certain behaviors and events have on certain others by describing and analyzing their relative proximity to one another in terms of their time of occurrence in a particular setting.

Most traditional and noncomputer-based behavior analysis and systematic observation methods have had a primary requirement that behaviors and events be defined in a discrete way with definitive start and stop times of occurrence. The term *discrete* in this context simply means that a definitive beginning and end time to each behavior and event being recorded is defined so as to be clear to those observing the occurrences of those events. The three major constraints of most earlier observational work that have attempted to operate within this definition have been that (a) we have had the capability to observe only a few behaviors or events at a time and have been forced to view all others operating within a setting of interest as external (or extraneous; see Kerlinger, 1986), (b) we have not had the tools to look at multiple behaviors and events in terms of explicit description and analysis of their time-based or temporal association with one another as they actually occur, and (c) we have often been forced to segment total observation periods into intervals with portions of the total observation period devoted to data recording management tasks rather than actual observation of the ongoing behavior and event occurrences in a setting of interest.

A *real time* recording tactic, made possible largely through the use of amenable computer-based data collection and analysis tools, is designed to overcome these three major constraints. First, using computer-based tools allows the recording of multiple behaviors and events by specifying each behavior or event to be recorded with a numerical or letter-based key on a computer keyboard. These alphanumeric specifications may be broken down further into finer and finer discriminations through the use of various numerical notations. In addition, a qualitative narrative notation may be used to further describe atypical or unique contextual variations of a behavior or event that falls within a particular category of an observation system but is not truly representative of the typical occurrence of that behavior or event as defined. Second, computer-based tool use enables observers to record the start and stop times of all behaviors and events, providing a time-based record of when those behaviors and events actually occurred throughout an observational period. From this type of information, complex statistical, correlational, and predictive mathematical formulae may be programmed to explicitly describe and analyze the many time-based associations among all behaviors and events occurring within a particular observation period and related data record. Third, and perhaps most important, using computer-based tools such as the BEST software referenced in the back of this text enables observers to collect their observations in real time without segmenting the total observation period and without including nonobservation time gaps in their observational strategies. Put simply, recording in real time simply means that an observer may record all of the behaviors and events of interest that are contained in a particular category system used for that observation at the time when they actually occur, and she or he will not have to devote any of the observation period to data organization tasks to the point of stopping actual observation and related data recording activities.

Recording in real time is the recording of behaviors and events as they naturally occur for the entire specified observation period—without taking any time out for data recording or other nonobservational tasks. A computer-based data record of this might look something like the following:

Alphanumeric Event, Start Time, Stop Time, Notation

1, 00023, 00028, 0
3, 00026, 00049, 0
8, 00050, 00123, 0
C, 00087, 00137, 0
1, 00138, 00152, 1
and so on

The first column indicates a behavior or event of interest as signified by a number or letter on a computer keyboard, the second and third columns indicate the start and stop times (typically in seconds) of each occurrence of each behavior or event, and the fourth column indicates numerical separations of certain behaviors or events (e.g., multiple levels of questioning with questioning behavior designated by a "1") or the option of including narrative fieldnotes for that particular behavior or event occurrence (not shown here). Once an observer becomes familiar with computer-based tool applications, recording in real time will involve simply pressing and holding different keys on a keyboard, pressing and holding multiple keys if certain behaviors and events occur at the same time or overlap, and recording multiple data files from a videotape record of the observation period, to be merged and time-ordered later using amenable data organization support software applications if the number of behaviors and events to be recorded and the complexity of their occurrence warrant it.

We have borrowed from Ray (Ray & Delprato, 1989), Lichtenstein's (1983) interbehavioral and sequential behavior descriptions, and real time observation recording implemented according to the interbehavioral and field systems theoretical framework founded by Kantor, to provide the following four steps to a more complete and inclusive description and analysis of complex interactive settings of interest. Though license in interpretation has been taken here, these steps include linguistic description, topographic representation, symbolic illustration, and algorithmic modeling. *Linguistic description* involves the design and implementation of a set of terms and definitions, or a category system, commonly understood by a particular group of observers and from which meaningful descriptive-analytic interpretations of particular settings stem. *Topographic representation* involves the ways in which observations based on those linguistic descriptions are quantitatively represented, including the many measurement forms detailed in Table 7.1 and the many ways of representing the data in graphic and tabular formats summarized in Chapter 9. *Symbolic illustration* includes the ways in which one can further elaborate on and therefore contextualize originally developed topographic representations through qualitative and narrative means. Finally, *algorithmic modeling* involves the ways in which one can use statistical, correlational, and predictive mathematical equations to demonstrate the time-based transactional probability relationships among the behaviors and events contained within a particular linguistic description, as well as related efforts to simulate behavior-behavior and behavior-event occurrences given situations similar to those that have been observed and may therefore occur at some future point in time.

In summary, through the use of a computer-based real time approach to data recording, we can combine the appealing features of each of the more traditional recording tactics with all of the various traditionally recommended reporting measures, *and* include the four elements of sequential or time-based measures and richer contextual narratives just discussed into one preferred method.

8

Constructing an Appropriate Research Design

All we think we know from the conducting of "good" science, we have attained through the appropriate matching of our research questions with the method of data collection and a related research design type.

— Unknown

After reading this chapter, you should be able to define the following terms and provide the information requested in the study guide below.

TERMS

Internal validity	Treatment
External validity	Maintenance
Generalization	Multiple baseline
Replication	Stability
ABAB designs	Reversal
Baseline	Probe design

STUDY GUIDE

1. Discuss the specific forms that internal and external validity concerns may take in relation to the common terms provided in Table 8.1 and to a variety of experimental and descriptive direct observational activities.

2. Explain and illustrate the two different definitions of *generalization* that are used in the behavior analysis literature.
3. List and discuss the six main features of experimental designs that are necessary to articulating with confidence that observational data point to a functional relationship between certain behaviors and events.
4. Explain the descriptive and predictive functions of a baseline phase with regard to the importance of the use of repeated measures and of establishing data stability or pattern within this phase.
5. List and illustrate a variety of design types (e.g., ABAB design variations, multiple treatment, multiple baseline, changing criterion, etc.) in relation to how each controls for particular competing internal validity explanations for data changes across experimental phases.
6. List and discuss some of the guiding assumptions necessary to a multiple baseline design.
7. Describe the important summary considerations to be taken into account when developing a design structure for research or evaluation purposes.

The previous portions of this text have discussed in some detail the history and evolution of direct observation and behavior analysis as an appealing research method worthy of consideration when studying complex interactive settings. In addition, detailed information with respect to the construction of category systems to guide observational research, and with respect to important reliability issues designed to ensure the accuracy of the data collected, have been provided. This chapter extends the previous chapter's articulation of measurement issues by providing a discussion of (a) recommended research design types for the researcher organizing the structure of an experimental or evaluation activity and (b) the context of the measurement options and data collection methods information provided in Chapter 7. The construction of an experimental organizational structure—in other words, the design of just when observational data will be collected and when a particular experimental treatment or evaluation activity will be administered—is the next important step for the reseaarcher involved in direct observation research activity. This is an important next step whether you are a researcher in a laboratory setting; an applied scientist working in postsecondary education, psychology, or social science programs; or an applied professional interested in scientifically supported diagnoses of what is occurring in a particular professional situation.

Whether the researcher is involved in a research project or an evaluation activity, it is important for us to discuss the many types of factors, known as potential threats to experimental validity, that she or he should consider when structuring a direct observation activity. The main objective of considering an experimental or reasonably scientific and systematic descriptive design structure is to provide a systematic approach to the examination of data collected, so that valid and legitimate explanations of measured changes in particular behaviors and events can be made and alternative explanations for those changes, which involve factors outside of the experimental or evaluative relationship, are either controlled for or ruled out. It is in this regard that we begin this chapter with a discussion of the main validity issues of concern to the researcher who is attempting to describe or experiment with particular settings of interest.

VALIDITY ISSUES

Before we consider actual design type options, a discussion of experimental validity is in order. When structuring an experimental or descriptive situation, the researcher's intent is to rule out potential alternative explanations of the behavior and event relationship of interest and to provide a structured argument in support of the behavior and event relationships that have been discovered. This is true whether the researcher is involved in formal manipulation of behaviors and events in a situation for experimental purposes or in systematic description of the possible behavior and event relationships in a certain situation to understand how to potentially make that situation more effective or therapeutic for its participants. Two categories of validity are typically used to describe and discuss the potential threats to, or alternative explanations for, a particular experiment or evaluation activity, and they operate on the premise that a primary objective of the researcher involved in direct observation activities is to determine functional or causal relationships among particular behaviors and events of interest.

It should also be remembered from discussions contained in earlier chapters that a determination of "cause" between particular behaviors and events of interest is a difficult enterprise. Again, correlating the respective presence or absence of two events with one another does not necessarily mean that there is a causal relationship, nor does simply disproving the null hypothesis contained in a statistical manipulation. We agree with Thomas and Nelson (1996) on this account that cause and effect is most appropriately viewed as a probability or potential functional relationship among behaviors and events of interest, with determination established only by the application of logical and structured analysis of data contained within a well-designed set of data collection and analysis procedures. The logical analysis process involves the preparation of a structured argument for a particular behavior-event relationship, and within that argument the ruling out of potential alternative explanations for the character of the changes over time of those behaviors and events. The primary objective of developing an organizational structure for the collection of descriptive data and the potential introduction of various experimental treatments, or the development of a data collection and analysis design type, is to meet the requirements of an effective argument. Contained within the development of an appropriate design type are the steps of participant selection, treatment definition, measurement choice, design type organization, and experimental control issues in relation to the appropriate interpretation and analysis of the data to be collected. It is in this last regard that a discussion of validity issues is important.

There are two general categories of validity, which are termed *internal validity* and *external validity* and are generally defined as follows:

1. *Internal validity.* This type of validity refers to the extent to which a particular data collection and analysis activity, by way of its organizational structure, can rule out alternative explanations of the character of and change in behaviors and events over the course of that activity.

2. *External validity.* This type of validity refers to the extent to which the results of a particular data collection and analysis activity can be generalized to other participants and settings that were not directly involved in the activity but are similar in character to the primary observational situation. The point of external validity assessment is to make possible an argument that the same character and change seen in the behaviors and events observed in the primary setting might be seen in other similar situations. This is typically verified in behavior analysis methods by *replication,* or the repeating of the same experiment in a different situation and with different study participants to

determine if the same outcomes would occur as a function of treatment exposure.

Complete control of an observational situation, to the point where the researcher has complete confidence in his or her ability to meet both validity concerns, is difficult to impossible in research and evaluation activity in complex interactive settings. A more realistic approach might be for researchers and evaluators to be familiar with a variety of potential validity issues, and armed with these issues to design their direct observational efforts so that the validity issues we summarize may be met with a degree of confidence. If validity assessment is engaged in to the point of a confidence level that we recommend, a strong case may be made for the functional behavior-event relationships that are documented through a particular direct observation data collection and analysis activity.

Table 8.1 lists the validity concerns originally categorized by Campbell and Stanley (1963) as they have been interpreted by a wide variety of research methods textbooks. Discussion of a variety of validity issues is necessary because it illustrates the importance of attending to careful design of a direct observation data collection and analysis activity. This is particularly the case when the researcher's intent is to make some form of predictive conclusion in relation to the potential functional relationships among certain behavior and event occurrences. This is true whether the researcher is engaged in very structured experimental research where certain treatments are being introduced, withdrawn, and manipulated according to rigorous experimental procedures or is engaged in systematic description of a variety of behaviors and events in a particular professional setting of interest to learn how to proceed for greater effectiveness and/or therapeutic value. The focus of the argument with regard to any experimental or evaluation enterprise involves whether the behavior and event changes are due to certain data supported behavior-event relationships or to relationships cited in alternative explanations.

Beginning with the history and the maturation threats to internal validity, Table 8.1 presents in a relatively straightforward manner the importance of attending to careful design structure when conducting direct observational activity. When the researcher is conducting field-based direct observational activities to determine the possible functional relationships that may exist among certain behaviors and events, it is important for her or him to rule out other possible explanations

Table 8.1   Summary of Validity Issues Categorized by Internal and
External Types

Internal Validity Types

1. **History:** Outside events that occur during an experiment that are not a
   part of the defined treatment or experimental relationship situation but
   could have an impact on the character or changes in behaviors and
   events measured during an experiment
2. **Maturation:** Processes internal to the participants in an experiment that
   could impact on the character or changes seen in particular behaviors
   and events, and processes that occur as a function of the passing of time
3. **Testing:** Any change in behaviors and events measured in an
   experiment that may be attributable to the repeated measurement
   of hose behaviors and events
4. **Instrumentation:** Any change that may take place in the instrument
   used to measure behaviors and events over the course of time
5. **Statistical regression:** Any change in the measure of behaviors and
   events over time that might be due to a reversion of those measures
   toward an average measure, instead of an initial more extreme measure
6. **Selection bias:** Any differences in behavior and event measures across
   experimental participants or experimental groups that may be due to
   how those participants or groups were selected or assigned
7. **Experimental mortality:** Any attrition of experimental participants that
   as a result alters the outcome of the experimental results
8. **Treatment diffusion:** Any exposure of an individual experimental
   participant, or group of participants, to a particular treatment that
   according to the experimental structure the individual or group was
   not supposed to be exposed to or familiar with
9. **Expectancy:** When certain experimental participants or groups perform
   differently on a particular behavior or event measure due to the data
   collector's expectation that those particular participants or groups will
   perform relatively better or worse

External Validity Types

1. **Reactive or interactive effects of testing:** The extent to which
   experimental participants are aware that they are being measured and
   that their behavior is changed due to this awareness
2. **Reactions to experimental arrangements:** The extent to which
   experimental participants are aware that they are involved in an
   experimental situation and therefore change their behavior as a
   function of knowledge of experimental involvement
3. **Interaction of participant selection and the experimental treatment:**
   The extent to which experimental pretest intervention makes
   experimental participants aware that they will be measured and
   they alter their behavior accordingly

---

4. **Multiple treatment interference**: When multiple treatments are used in a particular experiment, the extent to which exposure to one treatment alters the character of behaviors and events during another treatment condition

5. **Generality across participants, settings, responses, and time**: A general category that speaks to the extent that the results of a particular experiment may be legitimately claimed for other arguably similar participants, settings, behavior response classes, and different points in time not directly involved in the experiment that was conducted

NOTE: Table constructed in large part from Campbell and Stanley (1963) and related interpretations provided by Kazdin (1982) and Thomas and Nelson (1996).

that are either due to outside influences such as changes in family or professional settings, lifestyle patterns, outside educational influences, or a range of sudden life-altering events or due to changes in the development and growth patterns of the participants under observation during the course of that observational activity. Testing, instrumentation, and statistical regression types of internal validity are also important to consider, particularly due to the importance that the direct observation and behavior analysis methods covered in this text place on ensuring the reliability and accuracy of data collection efforts over time (see Chapters 4 and 6 for a more detailed discussion of these issues). The repeated exposure of subjects to being observed, changes in the form and character of the category system used for observation, and changes in the ways in which particular observers may interpret the use of a category system over time are all examples of validity concerns that may inappropriately impact the form and character of behavior and event occurrences during an observational enterprise. In relation specifically to the issue of statistical regression, the researcher should carefully consider the initial measures of particular behaviors and events so as to avoid an inappropriate comparison among changes in behavior and event measures over time due to an extreme score during initial measurement rather than to the effect of a particular treatment on that behavioral measure over time.

Our statistical regression discussion is also related to the issue of selection bias. Taking an education illustration, a particular researcher may be interested in the impact of a particular reading instruction treatment on a variety of third graders who initially exhibit a range of reading proficiency skills. If these third graders are initially grouped according to skill level and a reading proficiency behavior score is initially assigned, two internal validity concerns may arise. The first concern, related to statistical regression, is about the potential for the highly skilled readers to score relatively high on a second reading proficiency test, but not as high as their original scores, and for the less skilled readers to score a bit higher than their original low scores due to the tendency for the readers to score more toward a theoretical mean of all high and low skilled readers and not to readers' exposure to an effective reading proficiency instructional procedure. The second concern, related to selection bias, is about selecting certain participants for the reading instruction experiment who may, for some reason other than exposure to the reading instruction (e.g., participants were relatively high skilled in reading proficiency to begin with), show improved reading scores over the course of the experiment.

It is also important for the researcher conducting a direct observation of the potential relationships among behaviors and events to ensure that the participants being observed will remain present in the observational setting for the duration of the observation activity (see the last group of internal validity concerns in Table 8.1) so that complete and representative data can be collected. In addition, care needs to be exercised to ensure that only the participants who are meant to receive a particular treatment are exposed to that treatment, and that those exposed do not have any preconceived behavioral expectations as a function of knowing that they will be exposed to a particular treatment. In all of these internal validity respects, great care should be exercised in the organization and structuring of a particular experimental or evaluation activity, given some of the important foundational tenets of behavior analysis. Remember that one of the guiding principles of conducting direct observational activities that include an applied behavior analysis component is focused on the importance of determining those behavior-event relationships that may be most therapeutic for particular clients in particular settings. In this respect, it is of utmost importance that a researcher or evaluator engaged in this type of work give careful consideration to all internal validity issues, so that a strong case may be made that the types of treatments being administered and/or descriptive relationships being concluded are, indeed, functionally related to the behavior and event changes documented and not due to some other competing reason. If great care is not taken in this respect, and the latter case is true, then a particular treatment or behavior-event relationships that the researcher has argued would be of value for a particular client or group of clientele actually may not be effective or, in the worst case, may have a deleterious effect.

Although generality is often de-emphasized in direct observation activities due to a primary focus on providing as therapeutic a situation as possible for a particular set of clientele under a specific set of circumstances, it is nonetheless important for us to touch on some common external validity issues to ensure that the reader has at least some familiarity with them. These issues are important to the researcher who is organizing and structuring multiple experiments along a common area of interest, for the primary activity that behavior analysis researchers are engaged in to attain *generality*, or the potential for effective use of a treatment beyond the primary experimental setting in which it was documented as effective, is replicating the same observational situation again and again with careful manipulation of certain situational characteristics so that over long periods of time and through the use of multiple setting data sources, legitimate generalization of a particular treatment or behavior-event relationship may be claimed with a degree of confidence.

There is much overlap between the threats to internal validity just discussed and the character of potential threats to external validity listed in Table 8.1. What we are discussing here is not so much a difference in type of validity issue as it is a difference in the effect of an existing validity issue (i.e., whether observed relationships are attributable to the specific behavior-event situations analyzed and concluded about or to other explanations and whether those relationships are generalizable to other situations). Again, external validity is concerned with the ability to *generalize*, or with how the behavior-event relationships documented in a particular observation activity may be said to apply to other similar individuals and situations outside of the primary observational setting.

There exist two general definitions of *generalization* in the behavior analysis literature that are important to mention. The first definition is provided by Stokes and Baer (1977) and stipulates that generalization is present when the occurrence of a particular behavior or event is present during nontraining conditions that have been set up for that behavior or event. A second and more rigorous definition of generalization is offered by Hake and Olvera (1978) and stipulates that generalization of behaviors and events only occurs when it is maintained and used by the reciprocal and internalized contingencies of the behavior-event interaction itself and no longer by any external reinforcing behaviors that were present when the behavior or event in question was originally trained. In other words, and in relation to this latter definition, generalization is only said to have occurred when a certain individual uses a particular behavior or event as a function of his or her appropriate choice to do so and also in the absence of any behavior or event training or externally reinforcing conditions similar to those that were in place during the original education in effective use of the behavior in question.

Therefore it is important for the researcher who is organizing and structuring a particular direct observation activity to consider the potential impact of unique or atypical effects of measuring behaviors, the arrangement of observational conditions, and participant selection processes that may limit the findings of a particular observational activity to only that particular setting or a very narrow range of similar settings. In addition, it is important for the researcher to specifically describe and keep separate different treatment conditions contained in the same observation activity so that their potential influence on one another will be avoided (in terms of altering in inappropriate ways the behavior and event measures of interest during the observation activity). In this latter regard, the importance of conducting checks for treatment fidelity and treatment integrity, as discussed in some detail in Chapter 6, is readily apparent. Finally, researchers must give careful consideration to organizing and reporting the results of a particular observation activity—in terms of clear and complete descriptions of participant and setting characterizations, the range of behavior and event classes used to measure change in the setting under observation, and the time frame for all observations and the related treatments that may be included—so that readers of reported results may make careful judgments concerning the relative potential effectiveness of a particular behavior-event relationship to other similar situations and settings.

THE SIMPLEST CASE: AN ABAB DESIGN

Having armed the reader with familiarity with some important validity issues related to the design of a direct observation activity, it is now appropriate for us to discuss some of the design types that frequently appear in the behavior analysis literature. Our design type discussion includes designs that are common to reporting observational behavior-event data that have used traditional discrete measures of behavior and designs that use sequential measures to report behavior-event occurrences. The design types discussed in this section include a range of designs—from what may be considered pre-experimental designs because of their minimal accounting or control for the variety of internal validity issues contained in Table 8.1 to rigorous experimental designs that attempt to account for all of the internal validity issues just described.

A Pre-experimental Case

At its most simplistic level, it is not unreasonable to think of the methods described in this book in terms of nonexperimental activities. For example, a wide variety of professionals who practice in applied educational and clinical settings, and have limited ability to formally manipulate their settings in experimental ways, may still benefit from direct observation approaches to the description and analysis of behavior and event practices of interest. As a function of daily educational and clinical practice, many professionals are naturally undertaking some form of systematic observation of their situations in ongoing efforts to improve the effectiveness of those situations. In these situations, no formal experimental intervention is possible or even required. The aim of observation is primarily descriptive, using conventional thinking over behavior and event occurrences to manipulate future practice toward increased effectiveness. In these types of cases, the primary interest is on baseline data, or the "A" phase of an experimental design, which involves a complete description of what is actually occurring in a particular situation in the absence of an intended treatment. A treatment or manipulation of behaviors and events may be proposed or may naturally occur at certain points in time, which is known as the "B" phase of an experimental design. However, due to a variety of cost and personnel constraints, it may not be feasible to implement a formal ABAB or other recommended experimental type design manipulation. In this simplest of design-type cases, professional practitioners tend to use this design type to observe when things are going relatively effectively and continue with their professional activities, or they observe when things are going relatively ineffectively and make a professional practice (i.e., treatment) change. In this regard, and although simple AB-type direct observation situations are fraught with internal and external validity issues, we begin with this pre-experimental type design discussion to connect the methodology's importance to a variety of potential professional practitioner users. Clearly, the multi-event data collection and analysis procedures described in this book are not restricted to use in formal experimental methodology activities. In fact, the methods are extremely valuable to anyone interested in the direct quantitative observation of behaviors and events. The form and sophistication of the methods presented here is more a function of personnel and resource capability than it is of professional interest. We believe that it is also important to mention, however, that we discuss all design types with the caution that the full-fledged experimental designs to be discussed next are preferrably used when such use is feasible due to their ability to argue favorably for the control of many validity concerns.

The Simplest Experimental Case

Although a variety of simple case study designs exist in the methodological literature, and have historically appeared with some frequency in the applied research literature, we begin our current discussion with the simplest example of an experimental design that attempts to account for some internal validity concerns, the ABAB design. Most pre-experimental case study designs only provide for an experimental phase where a particular treatment is present for certain participants or groups for a certain period of time, and many of these types of designs do not provide a strong basis for comparison with a no-treatment condition, thus, they lend little support for ruling out major threats to the internal validity issues contained in Table 8.1. For this reason, we thought it best to begin an experimental design discussion with the simplest form of design type that endeavors to provide some validity control. In any design worthy of researchers' consideration, a few important main features should be present as follows:

1. the collection of objective measurement information that has been assessed to a minimum acceptable level of reliability

2. the assessment of the character and change of behaviors and events of interest over a period of time

3. the reliance on an initially stable level of behavior and event performance prior to any treatment or intervention occurrence, which typically is called a baseline phase (or "A" phase) in the behavior analysis literature

4. the multiple comparison of periods of time in which no treatment is in evidence with periods of time in which a specified treatment is in evidence

5. the use of treatment fidelity assessment to ensure the reliable and accurate implementation of a specified intervention

6. the use of objectively prescribed rules of governance for interpreting data results across treatment and no-treatment conditions

If all of these conditions are addressed, then researchers and professional evaluators should be able to stipulate with confidence, as a result of data gathering and interpretation efforts, that (a) a limited to nonexistent set of potential factors could have explained the character of the behaviors and events contained in a particular observational activity other than the functional relationships specified as data supported and (b) through experimental replication activities the behavior-event data documented in a particular situation may be extended to a variety of similar situations not under direct experimental scrutiny. A graphic illustration of an *ABAB design* is presented in Figure 8.1 to help the reader understand experimental design types.

The simplest case of a behavior analysis design constructed to take into account some of the internal validity concerns listed in Table 8.1, the ABAB design, does so by using a comparison of measurement on the same behaviors or events across a set of experimental conditions in which a particular treatment is not present (i.e., the A phase) to a set of experimental conditions in which a treatment is present (i.e., the B phase). Fundamental to this design type, and that of all the others that we will present for discussion, is the requirement that repeated measures of the same behaviors and events be taken over a specified period of time, usually specified in a number of days, weeks, months, or even years. The requirement of a repeated measurement component is direct observation and behavior analysis research is important in the following way: Repeated measures during an initial experimental phase in which a particular treatment is not present provide important information on the particular pattern of behavior and event occurrences that are the focus of an experiment. This particular pattern can be stable, steadily increasing, steadily decreasing, or cyclical, but the important element to this first design element is that there exists a pattern in the data that can be described in comparison to other experimental phases in which a particular treatment is implemented. This type of pretreatment

Figure 8.1   An ABAB design illustration representing number of correct and
incorrect responses and percentage of instructional
sessions spent on task

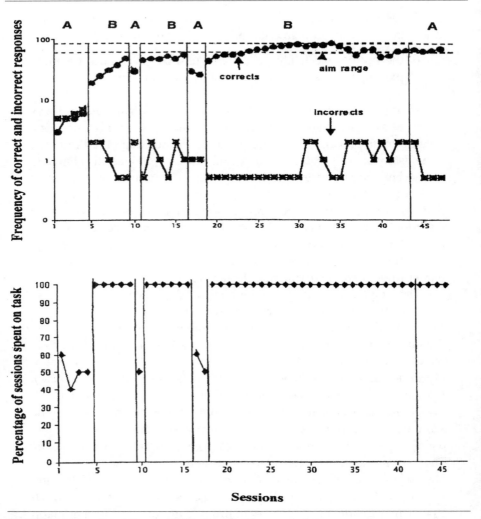

SOURCE: McDowell and Keenan (2001). Reprinted by permission

information is important to the consideration of potential internal
validity concerns, for it provides an objective representation of the performance of particular behaviors and events of interest in the absence
of any intervention. Once a particular treatment is administered by an

investigator, or shows up naturally without formal manipulation, data may be used to describe any changes in the same behavior and event measures used to describe the pretreatment or *baseline* condition just discussed—changes that can be documented by comparing the two experimental conditions of *no-treatment* and *treatment*. This first experimental phase, typically called a *baseline* and represented by an A,[1] has three functions (Kazdin, 1982).

The general purpose of a baseline phase is to provide information concerning behavior and event characteristics prior to the presence of what it is hoped will be a therapeutic intervention. The first type of information is considered descriptive, in that it provides objective information in relation to the current character of certain behaviors and events of interest and highlights in measurable ways a particular behavioral problem or challenge. The second type of information is considered predictive, in that if the baseline data provide a stable or repetitive pattern, then from this data a prediction may be made concerning how the data may continue in character in the absence of the introduction of a particular treatment. This second type of information allows for a comparison to be made across experimental phases for the purpose of making determinations of potential functional relationships among certain behaviors and events of interest.

Figure 8.1 provides an illustration of comparing a baseline set of behavior measures to a treatment phase set of behavior measures in simple ABAB design type format. In this illustration, McDowell and Keenan (2001) used two traditional measures of number of occurrence (what they term *frequency*) and percentage of sessions to record attention deficit hyperactivity disorder (ADHD) learner response characteristics during a letter acquisition task. Their data included the number of correct and incorrect responses to a letter acquisition task and the percentage of acquisition sessions in which the learner remained on-task. Although a simple rule of thumb in relation to applied behavior analysis design types is that a minimum of two baseline and two treatment phases must be included in an experimental design, this illustration provides four baseline and three treatment phases, further increasing the rigor of this ABAB design illustration. The logic of requiring a minimum of two of each experimental condition in a particular experiment goes something like this: If only one baseline and only one experimental phase were implemented for a particular investigation, then even if a stable or cyclical pattern existed for the data in each experimental phase, this pattern could conceivably be due to a variety of internal validity concerns (like those listed in Table 8.1). However, if two baseline and two experimental phases are included in a particular study and conducted at different points in time, and similar experimental phases exhibit similar data patterns, then a case may be made for the functional relationship between a particular set of experimental conditions (i.e., presence or absence of a set of behaviors constituting an experimental treatment) and the measurement character of particular behaviors and events of interest.

In Figure 8.1, it is clear that a stable pattern of percentage of on-task letter task acquisition sessions for the represented ADHD learner exists within the first baseline condition and across all baseline conditions. It should also be noted that the first baseline condition contains multiple data points in evidence of a stable baseline character for the percentage measure. It is important here to emphasize that data measures must be conducted at regular intervals over time until some form of regularly occurring data pattern emerges in the initial baseline data gathering condition of an experiment. Typically, stability of a data pattern in a baseline may be acquired with three to five data points; however, ensuring stability may require many more points. The most important issue is one of continuing to collect baseline data over multiple observation sessions until some form of stable data pattern emerges. Without this, comparisons across experimental phases cannot be legitimately made.

In the upper panel of Figure 8.1, a slowly increasing but also predictable data pattern is evident in the first baseline condition for the number of occurrences of both correct and incorrect learning task responses. This latter baseline illustration demonstrates an alternative data pattern (i.e., a slow increase) that can also be used as a legitimate baseline indicator of the character of the behavior measure in question, in that although the data pattern is not stable (i.e., a generally flat line from point to point), a consistent and hence predictable pattern is in evidence (i.e., a slow consistent increase from data point to data point).

From the baseline data represented in Figure 8.1, a clear comparison of particular data changes from baseline condition to treatment condition may be made, with resultant conclusions reached about the relationship between the introduction of a particular treatment, in this case a particular form of instruction on letter acquisition skills, and the changes in the behavior and event measures used to document changes due to treatment implementation. When similar measurement characteristics (e.g., the same percentage measure characteristics across all treatment phases of Figure 8.1), and consistent patterns in those measurement characteristics (e.g., a generally increasing number of occurrence trend from treatment phase to treatment phase and within each treatment phase in Figure 8.1) exist within multiple similar phases of an experiment, we may stipulate with greater confidence that the functional relationships between a treatment and the character of the behavior and event measures used is a legitimate relationship and not due to some other circumstances and involving internal validity concerns. For a thorough discussion of the specific ways and related rules and procedures with which graphed observational data should be analyzed, refer to the Visual Inspection section of Chapter 9.

Although the simple design case just illustrated provides an introduction to the ways in which a set of experimental conditions may be organized and structured, the ABAB design is not without its limitations. Although the design in Figure 8.1, as well as the following design types, may be used to report the wide variety of discrete and sequential measurement types summarized in Chapter 7's Measurement Options section, it does not illustrate how to further rule out competing internal validity concern explanations for the changes in behavior and event measures reported in an experiment. For example, although the effects of a particular treatment may be made clear by an ABAB design simply by switching back and forth repeatedly from baseline to treatment to baseline conditions, those effects could still be due to potentially competing internal validity concern rationales. Thus cyclical patterns in participant history that match the timing of the B phases of an experiment could have resulted in changes in the character of the behavior and event measures, providing an inaccurate functional relationship analysis among treatment and measure. A variety of testing, instrumentation, statistical regression, and selection biases could also conceivably be of impact when the researcher is using a simple ABAB design. In these respects, additional design types that are structured to help rule out potentially competing internal validity explanations should be explored. This is important when the researcher is deciding how to structure and organize an experiment, for the following two questions must be answered when conducting direct observational research with a behavior analysis component.

1. Do the data representations in particular treatment phases of an experiment differ enough from the data representations in the preceding baseline phases to warrant a conclusion that a particular treatment had an effect on the data measure?

2. Does the particular design type organized and used to conduct an experiment provide arguments that rule out potentially competing internal validity concerns?

Variations on the Simple ABAB Case

In an effort to provide greater experimental control within the standard ABAB experimental design, a variety of variations have been proposed and, relatedly, seen in the published literature. These include the alternative ordering of baseline and treatment phases, deciding on the number of particular phases to include, manipulation of the number and type of different treatments included in the experiment, and determination of the number and character of the participants and settings to be observed. In addition, variations have included the way in which reversing from a treatment condition to another baseline condition occurs in cases where it may be inappropriate to the therapeutic value of a particular client to simply withdraw a treatment condition that is of great help to that client.

Regarding ordering baseline and treatment phases, it is often the case for researchers involved in direct observation activities in a variety of education and therapeutic situations that the particular set of behaviors and events that comprise a treatment already exists naturally in the setting of interest. For example, a particular teacher in a classroom situation may be engaged in the use of a certain set of appealing instructional strategies that warrant objective and measured documentation using behavior analysis techniques. In this case, the treatment has been ongoing and is a natural component of the setting to be documented and studied. This type of documentation experiment would necessarily start with a B phase. Also, there are many cases where a particular researcher or clinician may want to provide a set of practices designed to increase the use of a set of behaviors where there has been no evidence of behavior occurrence prior to the onset of the treatment to be used. In this case, an extended initial baseline phase for the recording of –0 occurrences of a particular set of behaviors or events may not be necessary.

In the case where a BABA type of design structure is to be implemented, and returning to our education illustration just provided, it may also not be in the most therapeutic or best interests of a particular set of clientele (in this case, students) to completely withdraw the treatment due to ethical or professional effectiveness concerns (e.g., if a particular instructional treatment that was perceived to be relatively effective were to be withdrawn to simply demonstrate experimental control, a disastrous return to ineffective levels of instruction may ensue, with a variety of deleterious effects on the students served). In this case, a variety of alternatives to strict return to a baseline phase are available and relate to many of the experimental procedures listed in the Specific Procedures section of Table 2.1 in Chapter 2. For example, and related to the DRO procedure defined in Table 2.1, instead of a simple withdrawal to a strict baseline condition, the baseline phase immediately after a particular treatment phase could consist of the reinforcing of a variety of behaviors—except the one that was reinforced during the just preceding treatment phase of the experiment.

In addition, a variety of behavioral consequences could be administered noncontingently in a following baseline phase of an experiment. Using our education illustration theme, a teacher could in an experimental phase be involved in providing positive verbal reinforcement to students who are practicing a skill correctly. In the following baseline phase, the teacher could continue to provide positive verbal reinforcement to students, however, not connect it to particular correct skill practice trials but simply deliver the reinforcing verbalizations in a more general way (i.e., noncontingently).

In relation to the number of experimental phases, a general rule of thumb is to provide a minimum of two phases each for each type of experimental phase to be included in an experiment, akin to the simple ABAB or BABA variation case. Oftentimes when a researcher is conducting experiments over longer periods of time, the addition of more phases to increase experimental rigor is warranted (e.g., ABABABA or some variation thereof). Important to the addition of multiple phases of an experiment is also the potential addition of a maintenance phase or a generalization phase. A *maintenance* phase is defined as an extended baseline phase at the end of an experiment in which the experimental treatment is totally withdrawn for an extended period. This phase is provided to make a determination of whether the behavior and event changes that occurred as a function of the introduction of a particular treatment may be well maintained in the absence of continued treatment. In many cases, one of the most important discoveries to document (and particularly with regard to educational treatments) is whether or not certain desirable behaviors and events are used in appropriate situations by particular clientele in the experimental setting long after the procedures used to change those behaviors and events in desirable ways have been withdrawn. Relatedly, a generalization phase of an experiment is used to document the existence of continued use (or in some experimental cases nonuse) of certain behaviors and events in situations similar to, but other than, the original setting in which the original experimental observations took place and in the complete absence of the original treatment conditions in the original experimental setting.

The simple ABMaintenance design illustrated in Figure 8.2 is a design option using an extended maintenance phase. In this experiment, Parker and Sharpe (1995) studied the long-term effects of teaching varsity basketball team leaders the use and nonuse of a variety of peer-interaction behaviors, and also the consequent effects of this on other varsity team members. In Figure 8.2, a baseline phase was first conducted to provide a case for the stable character of target behavior use, an intervention phase was next implemented to train team leaders on use and nonuse of a selection of target behaviors, followed by an extended maintenance phase to determine the long-range use and nonuse of those target behaviors in the experimental situation in the absence of the educational treatment.

As can be seen in Figure 8.2, important information can be made available by the inclusion of a long-range maintenance phase at the end of an experimental design, for in this case the use of trained behaviors continued well beyond exposure to the treatment phase (i.e., the teaching of those behaviors to particular clientele).

An important illustration of adding a generalization phase to an experiment is provided in Figures 8.4 and 8.5 in the multiple baseline design explanation section that follows. In a study conducted by Sharpe, Brown, and Crider (1995), emphasis was on the teaching of particular positive social behaviors with elementary education students in a physical activity setting, and on studying the potential generalization effects of that teaching in other education settings that both differed from the primary experimental setting in many ways and did not include the treatment contained within the primary experimental setting. In this set of design illustrations, experimental phases were designed to collect direct observation data on the same measures used in the primary treatment phase setting in situations where (a) the same study participants were observed, (b) the treatment conditions were never present, and (c) the setting arrangements for the generalization phase were substantially different from those in the primary treatment setting.

A final consideration in relation to variations on the simple ABAB design case concerns adding multiple treatments to the design type. This is most typically referred to by the use of additional letters to indicate multiple separate and distinct treatment phases (e.g., an ABACA

Figure 8.2   Basketball team leader and team member target behavior change
examples as a function of a simple ABMaintenance design

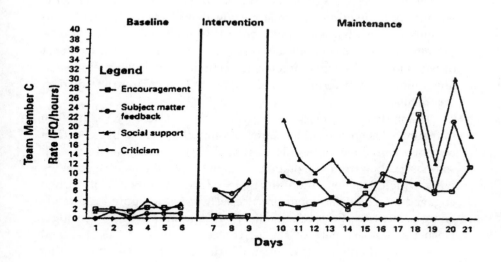

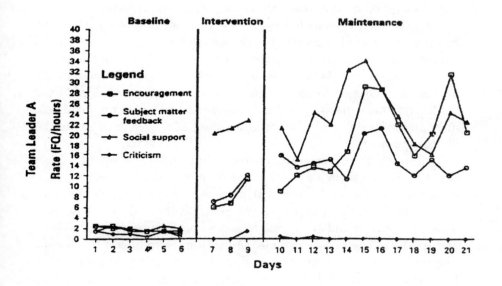

SOURCE: Parker and Sharpe (1995). Reprinted by permission

or ABCDE design) and of the A designation to indicate baseline phases of the experiment. Inclusion of separate treatments within a particular experimental design is often recommended when an observer either is attempting to determine the relative effectiveness of a variety of components within a treatment package or is trying to determine the relative effectiveness of separate and distinct treatments on a particular set of behaviors and events targeted for change. Figure 8.3 provides an illustration of an experiment conducted with two separate and distinct treatments.

The study by Sharpe, Spies, Newman, and Spickelmier-Vallin (1996) in Figure 8.3 is an education example comparing the relative effectiveness of a verbal feedback only treatment (T1) to verbal feedback with self-observation from videotape treatment (T2) on the relative accuracy with which teachers monitor their educational behaviors when engaged in actual classroom practices. The data in Figure 8.3 provide an agreement coefficient (i.e., reliability) determined by comparing a teacher's best estimate of the percentage of time the teacher and students spent on an 11 teacher and 8 student category system coding scheme for each observed class period to a behavior and event data record collected on that observed class period. The agreement coefficients were then represented over time as a function of the various baseline and treatment conditions organized for the experiment. As the data in Figure 8.3 show, a comparison may be made between the baseline conditions in which no education treatment was provided to increase the self-monitoring accuracy of the practicing teacher participants and the various treatment conditions that were provided to increase the level of self-monitoring accuracy of the teachers involved in the experiment.

Although these variations on the simple ABAB design provide some additional methods for the control of the internal validity concerns listed in Table 8.1, some challenges exist that beg the discussion of yet additional design options. For example, if a return to baseline levels of behavior and event measures does not occur with the second and third baseline phases of an experiment reported after a treatment phase has taken place, then a case cannot be convincingly argued for the changes in target behaviors and events shown by the first treatment phase being due to the introduction of a treatment condition. Another possible explanation is that although a treatment may have been responsible for changing the character of the measures of the target behaviors, over time other internal validity factors may have come into play that continued the behavior change influence. In either of these

Figure 8.3   The level of self-monitoring accuracy agreement across teacher monitoring and behavior data records for teachers receiving two feedback treatment types.

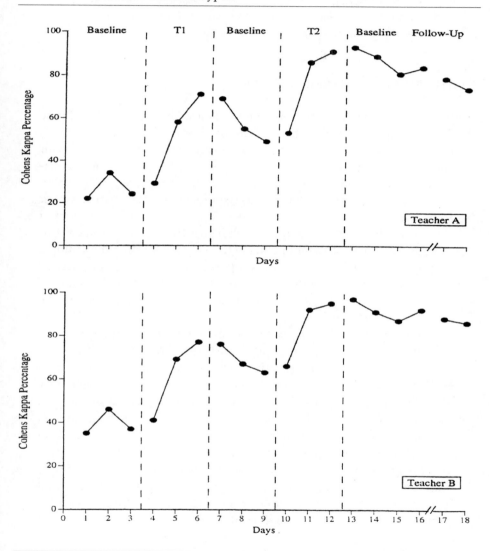

SOURCE: Sharpe, Spies, Newman, and Spickelmier-Vallin (1996). Reprinted by permission

cases, there may be an explanation, other than the desired one between treatment and target behavior measure, for the behavior and event changes reported. In the case of the use of multiple treatments over time, as in Figure 8.3, an argument may be made for potential interaction effects among treatments or the delayed effects of one treatment as the experiment moves from treatment condition to treatment condition, and not the individual effects of each treatment, as potential causes for documented behavior change.

THE MULTIPLE BASELINE DESIGN

In answer to the many concerns mentioned with respect to the simple ABAB design and its variations, a *multiple baseline* design has become a predominant design of choice for the researcher structuring a behavior analysis experiment. In this design type, multiple participants or settings are included in the experiment and each is represented by a separate graph. An initial baseline is first conducted for each participant or setting represented in each separate graph, and then the treatment of interest is introduced to and/or withdrawn from each participant or setting at distinctly different points in time. By juxtaposing the multiple graphs above one another in the preparation of a data graph, participants or settings in a nontreatment baseline condition can be compared at the same point in time with participants or settings receiving the designated treatment.

Figures 8.4 and 8.5 illustrate a multiple baseline design type used in a study by Sharpe, Brown, and Crider (1995) that was conducted to determine the effects of a positive social skills training procedure on both discrete and sequentially based target behaviors of elementary school students. The positive social skills training procedure was also monitored for potential effects on these same target behaviors in education settings other than the primary physical activity-based social skills training setting. As can be seen from Figure 8.4, three separate and distinct experimental settings were monitored and the treatment was administered at different points in time for two of the settings, and a continuous baseline was provided for in the third setting. Figure 8.5 provides a data illustration of the same first two student groups in the original two experimental settings and monitored in different classroom situations to determine if there were any treatment generalization effects. Discrete and sequentially based measures of the number of student conflicts and off-task behaviors and number of positive leadership and issue resolution behaviors in the sequential context of student conflict were recorded to determine the effects of the positive social instructional treatment.

Figure 8.4   Multiple baseline intervention data on numbers of student conflicts, leadership behaviors, issue resolutions, and off-task behaviors in gymnasium settings

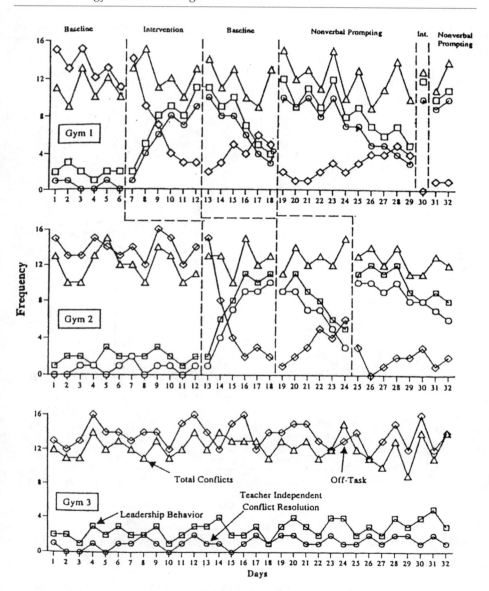

SOURCE: Sharpe, Brown, and Crider (1995). Reprinted by permission

Figure 8.5   Multiple baseline generalization data on numbers of student conflicts, leadership behaviors, issue resolutions, and off-task behaviors in regular education settings

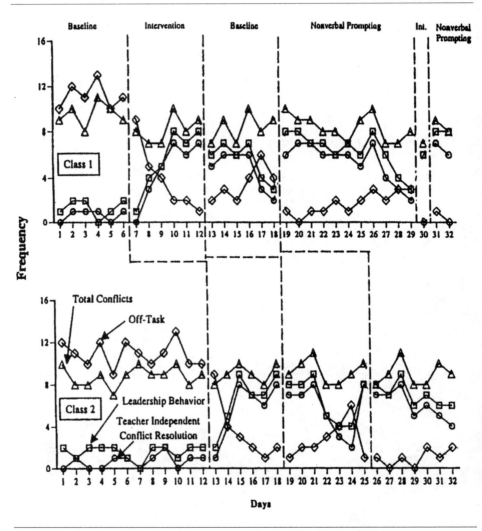

SOURCE: Sharpe, Brown, and Crider (1995). Reprinted by permission

A few guiding assumptions are important to the use of a multiple baseline design. First, a case must be made for the similarity and, hence, for the appropriate comparison across each participant or setting that has been designated for comparison in each graph. If such a case is not made, then unwarranted comparisons will be made across participants operating in respective treatment and baseline conditions—with resulting internal validity concerns. Next, a consistent, or *stable*, data pattern in each participant or setting baseline to be compared must be established for the descriptive and predictive purposes previously discussed as important to the establishment of an initial baseline. Finally, each baseline for each participant or setting to be compared must exhibit similar characteristics. These assumptions legitimate comparison across participants or settings.

If these assumptions are met and a multiple baseline design is implemented, the data representations provide an important design structure for arguing that many, if not all, of the internal validity threats listed in Table 8.1 are taken into account when making treatment to behavior measure relationship claims. This is the case, for a multiple baseline design demonstrates that a particular treatment has an effect only during those times that it is present for certain participants or situations, and it also demonstrates that those effects demonstrated in a treatment phase of the experiment for currently exposed participants or settings *are not* in effect at the same points in time for those other participants or settings not currently exposed to the treatment. Viewing the multiple baseline data representations in Figures 8.4 and 8.5, for example, provides a strong argument that the changes in the respective social skill measures are due to the social skills training procedures, in that positive data changes are evident in all treatment phases for all settings represented and are consistently not in evidence for those settings in which treatment procedures are absent at those same points in treatment implementation time. In other words, although a variety of internal validity factors, such as history, maturation, testing, and instrumentation concerns, may have had an effect on the data at some point in time, it is difficult to make a case that these validity factors would manifest themselves in a pattern over the course of the experiment that exactly coincided with the staggered treatment implementation pattern across different participants or settings.

As with the simple ABAB design case, there are some variations of the multiple baseline design that are worthy of mention. Again, researchers and evaluators armed with different design types, and some variations on these main design types, are in a position to organize and construct an experiment so as to control for a variety of potential internal validity challenges. A first level of variation, alluded to in our original discussion, involves the researcher's decision whether to compare individual participants or settings in the construction of the multiple baseline for comparison across graphs. This decision is largely a function of the particular focus of an experiment and the unit of behavior or event measure in relation to that focus. For example, if an education researcher was interested in the effects of certain disciplinary practices on the incidence of off-task student behavior in some general sense, then designing a multiple baseline experiment according to a class-by-class comparison and totaling the number and percentage of class time for off-task behavior for each classroom setting might be most appropriate. If, on the other hand, this same education researcher was interested in the variable effects of a particular discipline strategy on particular students who exhibited the same types of off-task behavior, then a comparison of the incidence and percentage of time devoted to those incidents across individual students (or experimental participants) within a multiple baseline framework might be more appropriate.

In these respects, considerations of how to organize a multiple baseline design across a particular set of similar or distinctly different situations, settings, or even time frames may be warranted, depending on the particular focus of an experimental activity. In addition, the researcher must take into account the number of baselines to be used and the related timing of those baselines. As we demonstrated in our previous ABAB design type discussion, the adding of baseline phases and additional treatment phases adds to the rigor of the experiment. Finally, the researcher must consider when it may be best to provide only partial withdrawal of a treatment during a baseline phase of an experiment and when an initial baseline is not necessary or feasible. It is important to the construction of a design type that baseline and treatment phases be appropriately matched with the questions to be answered and with the internal validity issues that may challenge an analysis of an experiment's results.

A last important point with respect to the multiple baseline design, and one that has already been mentioned but is worthy of reinforcing again, is the importance of (a) showing that changes in the target behavior and event measures only occur as a function of introduction of a treatment phase to the experiment *and* (b) demonstrating a case for legitimate comparison across settings or participants due to the similarity of baseline characteristics across those multiple settings or participants. In these respects, experimental caution must be exercised by researchers to ensure that each setting or participant to be compared is independent and distinct from each and every other setting or participant. If this case cannot be made, then the potential for behavior and event change due to interaction among those settings or participants to be compared is present, with potentially inaccurate conclusions ultimately drawn with respect to treatment effect relationships.

ADDITIONAL DESIGN OPTIONS

There are a wide variety of possible combinations of design types that can be used in the organization and structuring of an experiment. Some additional design types that frequently appear in the literature, not so much because they control internal validity concerns as because they are structured to document particular behavior-event relationships, should be included in our design discussion.

One such design type is commonly termed a *changing criterion* design. Organized according to a variety of ABAB or multiple baseline variations, the central feature of this design is the specification of a well-defined behavior or event criterion to be reached at certain phases of the experiment. For example, many at-risk or deleterious health behavior management procedures use a changing criterion design component. For example, if a health educator were interested in reducing the amount of alcohol consumption in a targeted population of college students, then he or she might first collect a representative sample of those college students and record the number of alcoholic drinks they consumed each week. Once a consistent pattern was established as a baseline, this health educator might set up a gradually and progressively reduced criterion of a maximum number of alcoholic drinks that may be consumed in the first week following baseline, the second week, the third week, and so on down to a recommended maximum number of consumed drinks allowable in a particular week. If study participants were successful in limiting to this gradually reduced maximum number, then an extended maintenance phase might be introduced to the experiment to determine the long-range effects of a changing criterion design on changing alcoholic drink consumption behavior. In reporting this type of behavior, a changing criterion design typically uses the same type of graphic data representation used here in previous design illustrations, with the important addition of a horizontal line in each phase indicating the specified criterion to be met in relation to the actual data.

Another design variation worthy of some additional elaboration concerns the study of multiple treatments. As in Figure 8.3, a particular researcher may be interested in how multiple separate and distinct treatments may impact on a particular behavior change need (e.g., multiple forms of discipline on a pervasive off-task or disruptive behavior in a classroom setting), or she or he may be interested in how particular components of a treatment package may have a variable effect on targeted behaviors or events (e.g., the separate effects of instructional components, such as verbal, live modeling, and video-based corrective feedback, on the successful execution of a particular complex skill performance). When these types of multiple treatment questions are the focus of an investigation, some important considerations are necessary if the researcher is to avoid the possibility of alternative internal validity explanations of a treatment effect. One common design type within the multiple treatment approach is to provide data on multiple situations or participants that are documented as legitimate comparisons, and then to *reverse* the treatment order across those situations or participants in systematic ways. In the Sharpe and colleagues (1996) study that was partially represented in Figure 8.3, a more rigorous design comparing the effects of multiple treatments might be to provide the following:

Participant 1: Baseline, T1, Baseline, T2, Baseline, T1+T2
Participant 2: Baseline, T2, Baseline, T1, Baseline, T1+T2
Participant 3: Baseline, T1, Baseline --------------------→
Participant 4: Baseline, T2, Baseline --------------------→
Participant 5: Baseline, T1+T2, Baseline-----------------→
Participant 6: Baseline, T1+T2, Baseline, T1, Baseline, T2
Participant 7: Baseline, T1+T2, Baseline, T2, Baseline, T1
Participant 8: Baseline -------------------------------→
And so on

Alternatively, and hypothetically, a multiple treatment design structure might take the form of the following:

Participant 1: ABACADAE
Participant 2: ACADAEAB
Participant 3: ADAEABAC
Participant 4: AEABACAD

Or the following:

Participant 1: A B A BC A BCD A
Participant 2: A BC A BCD A B A
Participant 3: A BCD A B A BC A
Participant 4: A BCD A -----------------------------→

Participant 5: A BC A -------------------------------→
Participant 6: A B A --------------------------------→
Participant 7: A C A --------------------------------→
Participant 8: A D A--------------------------------→

In this manner, or through the use of variations on the design structures provided, a rigorous design structure may be developed that specifies different treatment effect comparisons across arguably similar experiment participants and that provides for some of the necessary baseline to treatment phase comparisons specified as important in the respective ABAB and multiple baseline discussions. In addition, important treatment order and treatment combination comparisons are provided through these types of design structure manipulations to guard against potential treatment interaction, delays in treatment effects, or treatment order artifacts that could provide alternative explanations for changes in behavior and event measures other than exposure to certain treatments and combinations thereof.

DESIGN CHOICE SUMMARY

Infused throughout discussion of some of the research design structures that have frequently appeared in the literature, and that have been developed to overcome a variety of internal validity challenges, is the message that there exists no one design structure best suited in a general experimental sense. Clearly, careful consideration of the organization and structure of a research design to be used to report the findings of a direct observation or behavior analysis research or evaluation activity must be undertaken by the researcher dealing with a variety of potential competing explanations for the characteristic changes in data measures other than the primary explanation of treatment effect or naturally occurring behavior-event relationship. In addition, the relationship among the types of questions considered within a particular research or evaluation activity, the measurement type choices to be made among a variety of discrete and sequential options, and how the data should ultimately be represented impact on the choice of experimental design structure.

In this chapter, we have attempted to provide the reader with familiarity with many of the internal (and, although they are de-emphasized in behavior analysis methods, the related external) validity concerns that may arise when a researcher is organizing a research or evaluation activity. We have also given the reader familiarity with some of the more prevalent and accepted design structures available to the researcher who is reporting research and evaluation activities. What remains is the informed matching of the research and evaluation questions and intentions of a particular direct observation activity with how that activity may be structured from a design perspective. In this regard, the items to be taken into consideration include:

1. determining the unit of analysis to be used (e.g., individual participant behaviors, aggregate setting behaviors, etc.)

2. determining a measurement type and unit in relation to the unit of analysis and the related design structure to be chosen (e.g., choosing among a variety of discrete and sequential measures)

3. establishing baseline conditions

4. deciding on the number of each type of experimental phase to include (e.g., baseline, treatment, partial treatment, maintenance, generalization, etc.)

5. determining the length, order, and timing of experimental phases

6. specifying the type of design characteristics to be used (e.g., simple ABAB, multiple baseline, changing criterion, multiple treatment, etc.)

7. determining the order of treatment, if multiple treatments are to be studied, and the timing of those treatments across settings or participants

When considering these points, the researcher engaged in the organizational and structural tasks of developing an appropriate design type for a particular direct observation activity should also endeavor to create flexibility in combining design types and related measurement types. This will enable the researcher to (a) describe and analyze in more inclusive ways particular behavior and event phenomena of interest and (b) control for as many internal validity challenges as can be feasibly accounted for.

Finally, it is also important for the researcher to consider taking a field systems and sequential view when organizing a design structure.

This is particularly worthwhile with direct observation efforts in applied settings where multiple participants are exhibiting multiple behaviors within a changing environment. For example, it may be important to document behaviors and events that are not focused on directly in terms of measuring the effects of a particular treatment but that may either have an influence on the primary experimental measures or be influenced by the intended treatment. In these cases, a more inclusive behavior and event recording procedure is necessary to implement a *probe design* to track these types of behaviors and events. A more inclusive view is also important when organizing a design in which a complex treatment package is gradually introduced or withdrawn in a sequential or partial manner.

This chapter has provided a general framework of examples and illustrations for the researcher to consider when she or he is organizing and structuring a design type. The next important discussion in relation to the actual collection of data involves how the researcher may go about analyzing direct observational data and which specific visual inspection and statistical techniques should be used when analyzing respective discrete and sequential data forms. What will be seen in Chapter 9, as well as what we have hoped to provide in this chapter discussion, is the strength of behavior analysis designs in terms of their flexibility and related opportunity for inductive improvisation as the data collection process unfolds.

NOTE

1. We do not know why A is used to refer to a baseline experimental condition and B is used to refer to a treatment condition, and this labeling does confuse some of those who are new to behavior analysis methods and design types, but nonetheless we must all hold to these traditional design descriptors so that existing literature may be interpreted appropriately.

9

Analyzing Observational Data

When each measure of behavior is plotted on a graph immediately after the observational period, the investigator has ongoing access to a complete record of the subject's behavior. Instead of waiting until the investigation or teaching program is complete, behavior change is evaluated continuously, allowing treatment and experimental decisions to be responsive to the subject's performance.

— Heward (cited in Cooper, Heron, & Heward, 1987, p. 108)

After reading this chapter, you should be able to define the following terms and provide the information requested in the study guide.

TERMS

Experimental criterion
Therapeutic criterion
Social validation
Mean
Level

Trend
Latency
Parametric
Split-middle technique
Conditional probability

STUDY GUIDE

1. Explain what is meant by *social validation,* list the types of procedures that are typically involved in it, and describe the potential benefits of adding this procedure to a direct observation activity.

2. List and provide an illustration of the eight main characteristics necessary to effective behavior graph construction.
3. Discuss some of the major benefits to the visual analysis of data through its presentation on a graph versus other potential methods of data reporting.
4. Explain and illustrate the four primary visual inspection techniques in the two categories of magnitude of change and rate of change.
5. Discuss the three main challenges concerning the use of visual inspection of data graphs as the main data analysis form.
6. Explain the three primary challenges to the use of statistical analyses as a complement to visual analysis of data graphs.
7. Explain and graphically illustrate the split-middle analysis technique.
8. Referring to this chapter's discussion and the mathematical materials in Appendix A, explain the concept of quantifying time-based behavior and event relationships using conditional probability formulae.
9. Illustrate a variety of graphic representations of sequential data.

Chapter 9 provides a detailed discussion of the specific rules and procedures for analyzing observational data during and after its collection, and categorizes these rules and procedures to some extent by whether the measures to be implemented are discrete (i.e., characteristics of behaviors and events themselves) or sequential (i.e., characteristics of the time-based relationships among particular behaviors and events). We begin our discussion with some of the more traditional procedures used when analyzing the graphic representations of data discussed in Chapter 8's design section, and with why visual inspection of data graphs may be a preferred technique when engaged in applied research and evaluation activities. We then provide an overview of some suggested statistical techniques in relation to visual inspection procedures and accompany this overview with some cautions about using statistical procedures when conducting direct observation activities with small groups of subjects. A detailed section on the variety of techniques available to represent, analyze, and statistically model sequential data is included last to provide some important and appealing ways for the researcher to analyze time-based behavior and event relationships of interest.

In general, there exist two traditionally defined categories of evaluating a data record, and hence, evaluating a particular educational or therapeutic setting of interest. The first category has commonly been termed an *experimental criterion* and focuses specifically on whether or not a particular treatment or set of target behaviors and events of interest has had an effect on certain other behaviors and events focused on for potential change. In this first category, the use of visual inspection of data graphs, select recommended statistical procedures, and a variety of sequential data analysis approaches are used to make such determinations.

The second category for evaluating a particular setting of interest has commonly been termed a *therapeutic criterion* and focuses on whether the effects of a particular treatment or set of behavior-event relationships can be defined as having had a positive effect on the lives of the participants involved in the observation activity, both in the immediate observational setting and beyond (Kazdin, 1982). This second type of evaluation is inherently more subjective and is where the appeal of combining behavior analysis methods of the direct observation of quantitative dimensions of behaviors and events with qualitative narrative and self-report methods has seen increasing activity (see, e.g., recent studies such as Okyere, Heron, & Goddard, 1997, and Sharpe, Lounsbery, Golden, & Deibler, 1999). Adding qualitative methods of data collection and reporting is most often, again, termed *social validation* in the behavior analysis literature. Through the use of implementing a series of questions to study participants, social validation activities often provide important information with respect to (a) whether or not study participants viewed a particular educational or evaluation activity as having been of benefit, (b) their relative receptivity for being involved in the study situation at some future point in time, and (c) their relative disposition for the use of a particular set of study procedures in some future instance. Although this type of qualitative participant response information is not a direct measure of documented behavior and event relationships, or of the change in those relationships as a function of an observational situation, it can be important to the more effective structuring of behaviorally based treatments in the future so as to ensure greater receptivity and understanding. Conducted prior to, during, and/or after an observational activity, social validation data gathering attempts to answer important questions such as (a) Are the objectives that I desire as a function of an observational activity shared by the observational participants and/or the larger community from which those participants were selected? (b) Are the treatments that I have implemented well received by the observational participants and potentially well received by a larger community? and (c) Are the data results from my observational activity likely to convince others to use the treatments that I have developed? (Bailey & Burch, 2002).

PREPARING A GRAPH

The predominant form of data analysis for the researcher engaged in behavior analysis activities, and when using an experimental criterion, is the visual inspection of quantitative behavior and event data from a graph such as those illustrated in Chapter 8. Before we elaborate on the specific rules and procedures that should be adhered to when conducting a visual analysis, we want to summarize graph construction for those new to the recommended preparation techniques. There are a variety of visual structural and organizational forms for graph preparation available in the reported direct observation literature, to which the *Journal of Applied Behavior Analysis* and the *Journal for the Experimental Analysis of Behavior* provide a definitive and readily understandable guide (see the example of preparation guidelines in Figure 9.1). In addition, a variety of computer programs are now available that have been designed to make the graph preparation process relatively easy and much more feasible when dealing with multiple behaviors and events, with multiple measures of those events, and with adding some basic statistical information to a graph (such as mean and standard deviation lines, lines of best fit, etc.) when analyzing graphic data. One of the appealing features of the BEST software (Sharpe & Koperwas, 2000) described at the close of this text, for example, is the inclusion of a sophisticated graph construction program that enables with relative ease and the click of a mouse the ordering of multiple observation sessions to be represented across the horizontal axis of a graph, the immediate presentation of behaviors of choice across data records, the selection of measures of choice for those behaviors represented on a graph, statistical support manipulation options on the behaviors represented, and includes a scrolling mechanism for the representation of all behaviors and events in a data record for the purpose of initial data comparison within and across phases.

As the opening quotation for this chapter suggests, behavior change is an ongoing and dynamic process and so too must be the mechanism for representing the character of behaviors and events of interest to ensure continuous and close contact with those changes. According to Cooper and colleagues (1987), "The data produced throughout a scientific study of behavior are the means for that contact; they form

Figure 9.1   Printed guidelines for the preparation of behavior graphs

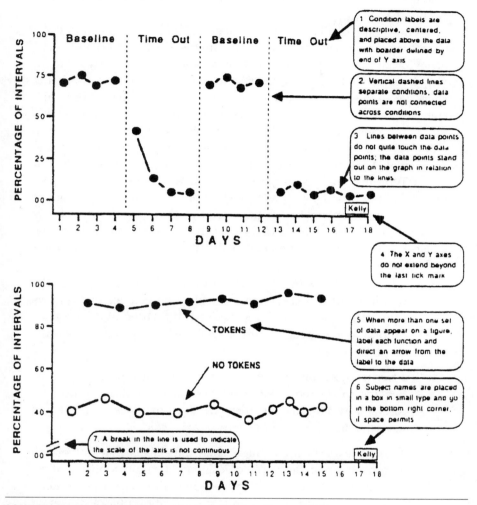

SOURCE: *Journal of Applied Behavior Analysis.* Reprinted by permission

the basis on which every important decision is made—to continue with the present procedure, to try something new, or to reinstitute a previous condition" (p. 107). It is in these regards that the importance of visual inspection of graphic representations of behavior and event data comes into play. If behavior and event data are represented visually, and an appropriate format is chosen to represent those data to demonstrate the important discrete and sequential characteristics of behavior and event relationships of interest, then the important functional relationships that exist within a particular data set may be made readily apparent and easily diagnosed.

A line graph similar to that contained in Figure 9.1 is the most common form of graphic representation in the direct observation and behavior analysis literature. In simple geometric terms, a two-dimensional representation using Cartesian coordinates demonstrates the character of the behavior and event relationships of interest. Both discrete and sequentially based data may be readily represented using this format, although some appealing alternative visual forms are available that are specific to the reporting of sequential data (refer to the Sequential Analyses section that follows for representative illustrations). Typically, this type of graph is designed to show changes in particular behaviors and events as a function of the presence or absence of particular treatments, whether these are overtly imposed or naturally occurring in a particular setting. All of the necessary elements to the construction of such a graph are contained in Figure 9.1. They include

1. a horizontal axis that provides a time-based dimension for the unfolding of an experiment or evaluation activity that follows (typically labeled and represented by observation sessions unfolding in a specified time increment such as minutes, hours, days, weeks, etc.)

2. a vertical axis that shows the measurement type used for the behaviors to be represented (if this measurement type is not represented by a 0-100 scale, then two diagonal lines are presented to designate a break in the vertical axis scale)

3. a set of experimental phase condition labels that are placed across the top of the graph to designate the type of phases of the experiment over time, which are akin to the baseline, treatment, withdrawal, maintenance, and generalization phases discussed in Chapter 8

4. a series of vertical dashed lines to designate phase changes (the lines designating actual data points should not be connected across these vertical dotted phase lines)

5. a set of specific points designated by dots, triangles, squares, and so on—symbols that signify actual data measures for a particular time period that corresponds with the horizontal axis

and that are connected by a line to signify the ongoing character of that data measure over time (each data point represents the quantitative measure of the behavior or event represented at the point in time designated by the horizontal axis. In the event of missing or uncollected data points for a particular time period or breaks in the time period on the horizontal axis, the double diagonal lines mentioned in element 2 above should be used to signify a break on the horizontal axis, and the data points on either side of the break should not be connected by a line).

6. a set of data measure terms connected by an arrow to a particular data line to specify just what type of behavior or event that each data line represents

7. experimental or evaluation participant names provided within a rectangle in the lower right corner of each graph to specify the particular client or setting for which the data represented within the graph were collected

8. a figure title that provides additional explanation of the graphic data record and is typically located just under the graph with a numerical figure heading highlight

Although there exist a host of variations on the traditional graphic display provided in Figure 9.1, our initial example provides insight into the most often used form of visual representation for analyzing the discrete characteristics of behaviors and events of interest. Some important variations include the use of (a) multiple data line paths to facilitate the comparison of multiple behaviors and events across the same measurement type, (b) multiple measurement scaling, typically represented on opposing vertical axes on either side of a graph to juxtapose two different measurement types for the same behavior or event, (c) multiple experimental participants on one graph to show differences across participants on the same measure, (d) bar graphs to demonstrate a more interpretable visual for some data forms, and (e) cumulative records for those data measurement forms discussed in some detail in Chapter 7.

Some additional comments on the construction of a data graph are in order. With regard to vertical axis scaling, it is important for the researcher to mark off the measurement system in equal intervals beginning with –0. It is also important to represent the complete range of the scale (e.g., from –0 to 100 when dealing with a percentage measure) and/or to provide a consistent measurement range across all of the graphs in the same data analysis reporting so as to avoid incorrect conclusions on the part of the data analyst. For example, if the researcher is plotting the number of off-task occurrences for each of five students across five separate data graphs, then the vertical axis for each graph should contain the same measurement range. The horizontal axis should also be represented by equal units, typically time based, across its axis. In addition, if there are breaks in the equally spaced time-based stream according to the data plotted, then two angled hash marks should be placed in between the two data point markers on the horizontal axis to indicate the breaks.

Like Heward (Cooper et al., 1987), we recommend that graphs be prepared in one color, preferably black, with a minimum of eye-catching visual artwork, for this only tends to detract from the primary focus of analyzing behavior and event changes according to the data plotted. Clearly, the preparation of a data graph requires adherence to specific technical skills to (a) present a data record as it was collected and as it actually occurred in a particular setting and (b) avoid any visual artifact in preparation that may either distract from data analysis or distort an appropriate data analysis.

Some major benefits to providing visual graphic representations of behavior and event data include the following: First, as a function of graphically plotting the data collected during those collection efforts, an ongoing and fairly immediate record is provided that can be used as a guide for making experimental and evaluation decisions during the course of an experiment. Second, and relatedly, a graphic analysis of data feature provides, during the course of an experiment, for an element of inductive flexibility. In other words, as interesting findings become apparent in the data record as a function of graphic display and during the course of an observational activity, the structure of the observational design, the type of measures used, the timing of various treatment implementations and withdrawals, and the types of settings and participants studied may be manipulated accordingly.

Another important feature of using visual inspection of graphs as a primary analysis technique is its user-friendly nature and related ease of interpretation by both the scientific and lay professional communities. Unlike a variety of traditional statistical analysis techniques and large group comparison methodologies, visual analyses provide an easy to understand and striking analysis of important functional relationships. Finally, and in relation to its user-friendly character, visual inspection of graphs provides a more conservative approach to making a case for a behavior-event relationship of interest. The logic goes something like this: Many relationships determined significant through the use of a traditionally accepted statistical technique may only be discernable through that technique and not show up on a graphic representation of the data. If such a relationship can only be supported through a particular statistical technique and is potentially not discernable through visual evaluation, then the relationship in question might not be discernable by the professional or lay viewer of the setting in which the relationship is documented as present. If the relationship is not discernable to the naked eye, then it may be a challenging activity to entice a particular group of clientele to use a particular treatment or complex set of behavior-event relationships, particularly if it is time or labor intensive and no discernable effects may be seen with the naked eye, either on a graph or in a setting designed for treatment use. In relation to this last point, graphic representation of behavior-event data provides an appealing means of providing feedback and goal setting during an evaluation activity, especially given the clear ease of use and ready assimilation of data reports that can be managed by a variety of clientele when that data are prepared in graphic form.

VISUAL INSPECTION

Once a graph is prepared, it is necessary for the researcher to have a set of consistent procedures to use in analyzing the data represented on the graph. This set of procedures is designed to determine if the experimental criterion has been met. In other words, a set of procedures must be followed that is consistent within and across each experimental report that employs visual inspection of behavior data graphs, to determine if a relationship among particular behaviors and events can be scientifically supported. Typically, a behavior relationship is supported if a case can be made that the character of the data in a consequent phase looks substantially different than they would have if the new set of circumstances contained in that consequent observational phase would not have been implemented. Graphic representation is also designed to allow scientific judgment as to whether the requirements of the experimental design type have been met in relation to treatment implementation.

Also, as discussed in the previous section, it can be argued that the relatively unrefined and insensitive character (Kazdin, 1982) of visual inspection of behavior graph techniques is a benefit to direct observation activities rather than a potential drawback. Because the procedures for determining behavior and event relationships from visual inspection are somewhat unsophisticated, large changes must be demonstrated in a graphic representation to demonstrate a behavior relationship. Weaker and potentially significant results that may be determined by a statistical manipulation will often go undetected using visual inspection. This advantage is quite appropriate to most applied research and evaluation activities that deal with the description, prediction, and control of behavior in complex interactive settings, for it (a) encourages researchers to discover and implement only very effective behavior change treatments as demonstrated by visual inspection and (b) is a powerful tool for advocating the use of those treatments on the part of other professionals and a variety of clientele through graphic representation of noticeable and appealing behavior-event relationships.

There are two main categories of visual inspection, commonly termed *magnitude,* or amount of change, and *rate,* or the speed with which change occurs. These two categories must be analyzed within and across experimental phases to determine if a change in a particular set of behaviors and events has occurred as a function of a particular treatment or as a function of a particular set of other behaviors and events presenting themselves in a particular setting. Within these two general categories there exist two subcategories that are important to making a determination of the relative and respective magnitude and rate of behavior change over the course of a particular graphic data representation.

Magnitude of Change

The two subcategories used to determine the magnitude of change over the course of a graphic data representation include *mean* and *level* determinations. The graph preparation guidelines contained in Figure 9.1 provide a straightforward illustration to discuss just how the magnitude of change should be determined from a graph. First, the term *mean* is used to describe the average of all the data measures within one experimental phase as compared to the average of all the data measures within the next or another experimental phase as represented on a graph. In Figure 9.1, the mean percentage of intervals for the first baseline in the upper graph is 74.0 (or 74 + 75 + 73 + 74/4 = 74.0), and the mean percentage of intervals for the first treatment (or Time Out) phase of the experiment is 16.25 (or 39 + 15 + 5 + 6 = 16.25). It is relatively clear that 74.0 differs in great degree from 16.25. A magnitude of change or amount of change can, therefore, be stipulated as having occurred from the initial baseline to the first treatment phase based on the graphic representation. In addition, it is easy to see that most professional groups, and indeed most clientele served, in educational and therapeutic situations may easily make a judgment that a substantial mean change occurred across phases. When reporting this type of data in an article, a typical process would be for the researcher to discuss the actual means across phases and then report the highest and lowest single data point within each phase as an indication of the measurement range within that experimental phase (e.g., $M = 74.0$, range 75 to 73).

A general visual inspection guide to analyzing for amount of change across phases using a mean indicator is to first determine the mean or average measure within an experimental phase and then draw a horizontal line on the graph and inside that phase. If in the next phase, or another phase to be compared, the data points all lie above or below the line drawn in the first phase, then a reasonable case may be made for an experimental effect across phases. In some cases, as we will discuss in our treatment of recommended rate analyses, an observational phase may be broken up into equally spaced segments and mean change comparisons across each segment and within the same phase may be conducted. This may be accomplished in the same manner as when the researcher conducts mean comparisons across phases.

The next indicator of magnitude or amount of change is termed *level*. This amount of change determination is provided by taking the last data point measure within a particular phase and comparing it to the first data point measure contained within the next phase. In other words, a level change determination is made by comparing the difference between the two data points that surround a particular vertical dotted line on a graph that indicates a phase change in the experiment. For example, the last data point in the first treatment (Time Out) phase in the upper graph contained in Figure 9.1 is 8. The first data point in the following baseline phase is 74. When comparing the measurement 8 to the measurement 74, a clear case can be made for a substantial level change difference across these two experimental phases. This visual inspection technique is often highlighted on a graph by drawing a short horizontal line through each of the data points used in making a level determination, and then providing a vertical double-headed arrow that stretches from each data point to data point horizontal line with the amount of difference contained within the vertical line at its midpoint (in this case, the number 68). This measure provides another indication of the amount of change in a behavior or event measure as a function of a different set of circumstances as indicated by an experimental phase change. Although both a mean and a level change are evident across the four experimental phases of the upper graph contained in Figure 9.1, this need not be the case, particularly if there is great variability in the data within each phase or if there exists a generally or slowly increasing or decreasing trend in the data patterns within each phase. As such, a determination of the rate or speed with which behavior or event change occurs within and across phases is necessary.

Rate of Change

The two subcategories used to determine the rate, or speed of change over the course of a graphic data representation, are *trend* and *latency* determinations. The first indicator, *trend*, provides information related to general increases or decreases in the direction of the data from data point to data point, within and across experimental phases. This type of information is an important addition to visual inspection, for in many cases mean and level indicators across experimental phases may indicate a lack of behavior change, however, the direction or trend of the data within each phase may be markedly different, hence indicating an important behavior or event change over time that would not be uncovered using amount of change indicators alone. A first level of trend analysis is visual and describes the general direction of the data within a particular experimental phase and any important trend changes that occur either within or across experimental phases. A second level of trend analysis is statistically based and is described in the following Some Recommendations Regarding Statistical Analyses section. The data contained in Figure 8.3 in Chapter 8 provide an important example of a trend analysis. In Figure 8.3, the level of agreement data show no level change across experimental phases, and a limited mean change from phase to phase, unless one is comparing the first baseline to the final baseline or follow-up phase of the graphic representation. Important to a trend analysis, however, is the positive increasing trend demonstrated in the T1 phase for both graphs in contrast to (a) the stable character of the data (i.e., no trend) in the first baseline phase and (b) the decreasing trend in the second baseline when treatment T1 was withdrawn. In this regard, adding an analysis of data trends provides important information in relation to substantial data changes based on changes in experimental conditions over time. It is important to demonstrating substantial behavior change using a trend analysis for the researcher to demonstrate a trend change (e.g., no trend to trend or trend to no trend) or reversal of trend (e.g., positive to negative or negative to positive trend) across phases in the preferred case or a substantially increased or decreased trend across phases in the absence of a trend reversal.

The second indicator of rate or speed of potential behavior change, termed *latency*, provides a sense of how quickly the character of particular behavior or event measures changes. Figure 8.2 in Chapter 8 illustrates this. Latency of change describes in specific terms just how long it took, in terms of the number of data points, for any visual change in a particular behavior or event to occur. When viewing the intervention versus consequent maintenance phase of the upper graph in Figure 8.2, a case may be made, for example, for a small mean and level change in the reported social support and subject matter feedback data. Important to the additional documentation of potential treatment effects for these data are the latencies of change across phases. Looking at the graph across the observation session days in the maintenance phase of the experiment, a case may be made for a latent positive increase in both behavior measures when compared to the mean behavior levels represented in the preceding intervention phase of the experiment. In this regard, a case may be made through visual inspection for the latent or late onset of positive behavior changes in the rates of use for both subject matter feedback and social support, even though initial level changes were not present and mean changes across phases were minor.

Latency of change also speaks to another factor that should be taken into account by the researcher reporting data changes through the use of visual inspection. As can be easily seen by the latent data change illustration contained in Figure 8.2, the number of data points that are included in a particular experimental phase can have an important effect on the interpretation of the results of an experiment. For example, if the experiment represented by Figure 8.2 would have been concluded with observation day 17, a very different results interpretation, namely limited effect of treatment, would have been necessarily concluded. As a general rule of thumb, each experimental phase reported on a behavior graph should extend until there is clearly a lack of variability, or a cyclical variability, in the data represented. This determination can take as few as 3 to 5 data points, as shown in the initial baseline data representations of Figure 8.3 and the first intervention data phase of Figure 8.2, or as many as 12 to 16 data points, as shown by the maintenance phase of the upper graph in Figure 8.2. When using only a few data points to demonstrate baseline stability, or when demonstrating a substantial change in a behavior measure across phases, the type of measure and potential behavior-event interactions that could conceivably impact on targeted behavior change should be carefully considered. When the researcher is engaged in direct observation activities in complex interactive settings, increasing the number of data points contained within a particular observational phase will increase the level of confidence that the genuine character of certain behaviors and events as a function of particular situations and behavior-event interactions is well represented.

The four types of visual inspection discussed, and sensitivity to the relative variability in the data, provide a foundation of traditional visual inspection techniques when interpreting behavior graphs. Clearly, changes in mean, level, trend, and latency; and changes in the variability of the data record within and across phases, involve an interpretation process in which each interpretation component overlaps to some degree with the others. In this regard, it is often necessary to implement all of the visual inspection techniques discussed to ensure a complete evaluation of a data record that is graphically represented. When substantial visual effects are easily viewed in the data, a strong case may be made for a particular behavior-event relationship (depending on appropriate design construction to rule out a variety of internal validity challenges), and the need for potentially inappropriate statistical analysis support is minimized. In the case where behavior changes are not so substantial, some concerns related to visual inspection may arise. For example, the visual inspection methods just discussed have sometimes been criticized for their subjective nature when the researcher is reporting weaker behavior changes. In other words, the question arises of how reliably multiple independent evaluators of a particular data graph may come to the same conclusions when using the same visual inspection techniques. A variety of studies have shown that when weaker behavior change effects are reported, a panel of independent practiced behavior analysts tend to disagree over how the results should be articulated in relation to whether or not to advocate for a particular behavior changes as having occurred (see, e.g., DeProspero & Cohen, 1979). In addition, and although visual inspection is viewed as a benefit to the demonstration of only substantial and very effective behavior change relationships, overlooking weaker behavior-event relationships can have some unwanted outcomes. For example, a particular behavior-event relationship that is initially documented as weak, or is very latent in demonstration, may be discarded by a particular researcher. Such a course could then lead to the lack of important future discoveries and the consequent lack of inclusion of a potentially important component to the science of behavior change. Finally, the very nature of behavior analysis design and related visual inspection requires a degree of stability in data patterns to allow for legitimate comparisons across experimental phases. When data records are extremely variable, a visual inspection method of data analysis is quite challenging. Therefore, a summary of cautions related to the use of statistical analysis procedures with direct observational data records, and some consequent statistical analysis procedure recommendations, are provided as an alternative to or as additional support for graphic data records that exhibit some of the challenges just mentioned.

THE CHALLENGE OF STATISTICAL ANALYSES

Some important challenges and assumptions need reiteration and clarification here to ensure that readers have a clear understanding of just what may be made available by complementing visual inspection of a graphed data record with a particular statistical analysis procedure. Once these challenges and assumptions have been reviewed here, those readers interested in using additional statistical support should proceed with caution for the reasons detailed below. The first caution, as explained in Part I of this text, concerns the fact that although most statistical procedures provide a mathematical analysis of whether particular changes in targeted behaviors and events can be explained by chance or random occurrence, and a statistical manipulation will provide data to support that a change has occurred, the statistical data may not provide any evidence that a change is due to a particular set of behavior-event circumstances or a particular treatment. This caution, which is primary in behavior analysis methods, applies to the oftentimes overemphasis on the use of statistical manipulations in the research literature to make claims about functional or causal relationships of interest when there may be weak or little support for those relationships.

A second important caution relates to the potential violation of the assumptions of most traditional statistical tests when researchers implement them with typical direct observation data. *Parametric* statistical manipulations (e.g., t or F tests) make the three assumptions of (a) a normal distribution of population characteristics on which data measures are taken, (b) a normal distribution of sample characteristics drawn from the larger population on which data measures are taken, and (c) independence of observations. Most direct observation data collected over time and through repeated measures of the same setting directly violate these three assumptions, making parametric statistical support of visual data interpretations inappropriate.

With respect to population and sample characteristics, most statistical tests require a certain minimum number of observed participants in a study for the statistical test to be legitimately employed. The very limited number, and oftentimes single subject, of observed participants in most behavior analysis activity provides an additional lack of compatibility with the use of statistical analyses as additional support for a potential functional or causal behavior-event relationship. There do exist a variety of nonparametric statistical techniques that do not require conformance to the aforementioned assumptions, however, and that could potentially be legitimately used in support. In addition, tests for autocorrelation or serial dependency among adjacent and nonadjacent data points in a behavior data record can be used to determine relative independence of a data set. For a more complete treatment of these issues, a number of excellent parametric and nonparametric statistical analysis texts exist, and we recommend in particular relation to behavior analysis designs the Cook and Campbell (1979) *Quasi-Experimentation* text, as it provides an excellent statistical resource complement. For a thorough treatment of the range of parametric statistical techniques, we recommend that the reader consult Keppel (1982) or Thomas and Nelson (1996).

SOME RECOMMENDATIONS REGARDING STATISTICAL ANALYSES

The reader should keep in mind the aforementioned statistical challenges as we move on to providing some cautious recommendations in Table 9.1.

Table 9.1   Summary of Selected Statistics for Use With Direct
Observational Data

Tests and Requirements

t and F tests

1. These tests are especially well suited for depicting change from one experimental phase to another in which data paths do not demonstrate serial dependency or autocorrelations.
2. The tests evaluate whether or not a significant difference exists across data means for experimental phases.
3. The tests are applied to experimental phase data means.
4. Their special requirements include an equal number of data points to be included within each phase mean calculation for comparison purposes—evidence of a lack of serial dependency among data points must be provided to support t or F test use. (Jones, Vaught, & Weinrott, 1977)

Time-Series Techniques

1. These analysis techniques are especially well suited for detecting change from one phase to another when the data path for a particular participant or setting is determined to be serially dependent or when autocorrelations exist among data points within a particular experimental phase.
2. They evaluate whether or not there exists a significant change in the level or trend between two adjacent experimental phases (but separate t tests are used to compare for changes in level and trend. The t tests take into account the degree of serial dependency as reflected in autocorrelation).
3. The special requirements of time-series techniques include several data points or observations, typically more than 50, to determine the precise time-series analysis model that best fits and resultantly characterizes the data path. (Cook & Campbell, 1979; Hartmann et al., 1980)

Split-Middle Techniques

1. These analysis techniques are especially well suited for the examination of trend comparisons across experimental phases.
2. They evaluate the rate of change in behavior over the course of different experimental phases through the use of plotting linear trend lines and statistically comparing the differing slopes of those lines.
3. The statistical evaluation includes the projecting of linear trend lines of baseline data into an intervention phase. A binomial statistical test is then applied to determine whether or not the number of data points in the intervention phase fall above or below the projected line of the baseline.

(Continued)

Table 9.1 Continued

---

4. The special requirements of split-middle techniques include the need for several observations within two or more separate experimental phases to compute trend lines for comparison purposes. Observations within each experimental phase also need to be equally spaced in terms of timing of observations. (White, 1971, 1972)

NOTE: Taken in part from Kazdin (1982), pages 246-247, and reprinted by permission.

One simple choice, given adherence to the assumptions of the statistical test, would be to implement a *t* or *F* test to compare mean data across phases. Alternatively, an analysis of variance might be computed to determine significant differences across multiple ABAC and so on phases. These tests may conceivably be appropriate if tests for serial dependency and autocorrelation among data points within each phase are negative and if multiple participants are observed within each experimental condition.

A variety of time series statistical analyses is another option for demonstrating substantial changes in behavior and event measures over time as one compares data paths across multiple observation sessions and multiple experimental conditions. This set of statistical techniques tests whether or not a significant difference exists in data path trends across experimental phases versus a line of best prediction of the initial phase data if it would have extended into consequent experimental phases. This approach is somewhat limiting, however, in that a large number of data points are necessary to avoid violation of the assumptions of the statistical test. An alternative statistical method designed to predict lines of progress in behavior data records across experimental phases has been termed an *ordinary least squares linear regression equation* (see Cook & Campbell, 1979). Although this method may appear mathematically daunting to novice statisticians, it does provide a reliable mechanism for predicting and comparing data paths across experimental phases.

One popular statistical technique that has frequently appeared in the behavior analysis experimental literature is commonly termed a *split-middle* technique. Developed by White (1971, 1972), it provides a simple four-step statistical method for determining data trends when the vertical axis is separated by equal intervals. The steps include

1. dividing the data points within a particular phase into two equal parts—if there are an equal number of data points then

the dividing line falls in between two central points, if there are an odd number, then the dividing line falls on the middle data point

2. finding a *mid-rate* and a *mid-date* within each data section and plotting their respective crossings—the mid-rate is found by counting upward or downward across the data points in a subsection to the halfway mark, the mid-date is found by counting left or right to the halfway mark in the data subsection, and the intersection of the mid-rate and the mid-date is then plotted for each subsection of the data

3. drawing a line of best fit through each mid-rate and mid-date intersection point

4. counting the number of data points that fall both above and below the line of best fit drawn in step 3—if the number is not equal then a shifting of the line up or down, but keeping its slope, is implemented. (This line provides a split-middle trend line from which a mathematical equation of its slope may be computed. Mathematical slope equations across experimental phases may then be compared statistically for significant differences in trend.)

The statistical manipulations summarized here, and discussed in greater detail in the cited references, are provided as a representative guide. As statistical inference methods continue to develop and evolve, a variety of applications and related procedures will continue to be made available in the literature. Our intent is to provide only an introduction coupled with some cautionary words and to focus primarily on the descriptive and predictive techniques that comprise a central core to direct observation and behavior analysis methods. To culminate our discussion of analysis techniques with respect to quantitative observational data, we next provide a substantial section on the analysis of sequential data forms.

SEQUENTIAL ANALYSES

Up to this point, this chapter has focused primarily on some of the more commonly used traditional data analysis techniques that are recommended for use when the researcher is representing and analyzing behavior and event data. The techniques discussed so far have appeared in the literature primarily when researchers have reported data measures concerning a variety of discrete characteristics of behavior, and when they have reported those measures over time as a function of over treatment or as a function of the presence of a set of naturally occurring behaviors and events that present themselves across systematically defined observational phases. Operating on the assumption that successful argument for the inclusion of the sequential measurement and analysis of behaviors and events in interactive settings has been made (refer to Chapters 1 through 4 and Chapters 6 and 7 for discussion of these issues), we now embark on a detailed discussion of the ways in which sequential data may be represented and analyzed.

As the reader will remember from our discussion in the Illustrations From Education section of Chapter 3, the most straightforward form of representing data sequentially is to simply order the occurrence of certain events as they naturally precede and follow certain other events. Once this is accomplished (and collecting data using computer program methods really helps the researcher to collect a more inclusive and sophisticated sequential data record; see The Implications of Computer Technology section in Chapter 3), the researcher's analysis focus is on the specific characteristics of the sequential connection, or transaction, among particular behaviors and events of interest rather than on the characteristics of each behavior or event as an isolated occurrence or entity. This type of analysis is rooted in the interbehavioral theory of Kantor (see The Foundations of Field Systems and Sequential Analysis section in Chapter 2 for a thorough discussion of this). When analyzing behaviors and events sequentially, our recommendation is that first each behavior and event operating within a particular situation be discretely described in more inclusive and systems oriented terms and that then the interdependency across time, or sequential transactions among behavior-event occurrences, be explicitly quantified for a complete understanding of behavior-event relationships. In other words, first sequential analysis efforts should focus on more inclusive documenting of all of the behaviors and events that are present or operating within a particular situation by recording multiple measures of multiple occurrences of multiple behaviors. Then efforts should focus on numerical indicators of the form and character of the time-based relationships among those behaviors and events, typically expressed using a *conditional probability* coefficient. In this latter regard, Altmann (1965) and later Bakeman and Gottman (1986,

1997) and Gottman and Roy (1990) have laid an important mathematical foundation (see Appendix A: Sequential Analysis Formulae for a summary).

To this point in our analysis discussion, we have focused on the ways in which the discrete characteristics of particular behaviors and events may be represented and consequently analyzed. Clearly, the discrete character of each behavior or event in a particular data record is important information, with this type of information typically displayed in a table listing each behavior and event and multiple measurement data for each of those events as a precursor to a sequential analysis (see Hawkins, Sharpe, & Ray, 1994, or Sharpe & Hawkins, 1992a, for a representative illustration of this). Four data representation and related analysis techniques are generally available to the researcher representing the sequential characteristics of a behavior-event data record. We summarize these techniques in following sections. All of the techniques are based on a mathematical determination of the probability with which certain behaviors or events follow certain other behaviors and events in time, as illustrated in the discussion in the Illustrations From Education section in Chapter 3. This is accomplished by computing a conditional probability coefficient for the time-based connection among two or more events. To do this, one must first record the occurrence of a particular behavior or event (or behavior-event cluster) of interest, and then record the occurrence of other behaviors and events of interest that occur around that targeted behavior or event within a specified time from the occurrence of that targeted behavior. Once this information is gathered, a comparison is made of the number of time-based occurrences of surrounding events to a larger base rate of all of the possible surrounding behavior or event occurrences. The base rate is calculated by adding up the total number of occurrences of all of the behaviors and events in the data set that occurred in the specified time frame around the primary behavior or event of interest. A mathematical conditional probability formula is used to determine the probability with which certain behaviors and events tend to precede or follow certain other events as a function of the larger base rate of total possibilities. A second mathematical formula is also used to determine the relative meaningfulness of the conditional probability data arrived at through the primary conditional probability equation. Appendix A provides an illustrative mathematical summary of the equations used for determining conditional probabilities and for determining the relative meaningfulness of those conditional probabilities.

Once the actual conditional probability coefficients for particular time-based behavior-event relationships are determined, the researcher must choose among the variety of methods available for data representation and related analysis. Representation options include simple tree structure representations, probability matrices, a variety of descriptive graph forms, and the construction of a conditional probability table. Each of these options is summarized in the following sections, with appropriate references provided for those readers interested in greater analysis and related mathematical model detail.

Tree Structure Representations

This first general form of sequential data representation involves what has been commonly termed *kinematic analysis,* or tree structure representations, in the sequential analysis literature (Ray & Delprato, 1989). Kinematic analysis provides a visual model of how many of the behavior and event sequences of potential interest, or how a potential functional behavior-event relationship, may be described as sequentially related within a particular data record. Typically, data representation takes the form of a table that lists behavior-event sequences of interest in a particular data record, followed by a listing of how often each sequence occurred and a related conditional probability of occurrence with respect to all possible sequence occurrences in that particular data record. Behavior-event sequences may be manipulated for listing according to the length of the sequence, minimum number of occurrences or a minimum conditional probability of occurrence, or according to particular target behaviors and events in which a variety of surrounding sequential relationships are the focus of analysis. Figure 9.2, which provides an example of this first form of kinematic analysis, was taken from a listing of dual behavior-event chains in a research monograph designed to uncover some of the important differences among effective and not-so-effective practicing teachers (Hawkins & Sharpe, 1992).

Alternative forms of kinematic analysis include the representing of behavior-event sequences in a sequential tree structure type of format or in a parameterized sequence format, like the respective examples shown in Figure 9.3. For illustration purposes, figures from the teacher education research work of Hawkins and Sharpe (1992) are again used, with the numbers in Figure 9.3 indicating a variety of potentially effective instructional behaviors. Using these representation forms, sequential patterns among particular behaviors or events, and what

Figure 9.2   A tabular illustration of behavior-event sequence chain listing format

Expert Dual Chains	Frequency/ Probability	Expert Dual Chains	Frequency/ Probability
12 → 17	(16/.16)		
19	(25/.26)	24 → 17	(19/.20)
26	(18/.19)	19	(11/.11)
31	(14/.14)	21	(22/.23)
	.75	26	(12/.12)
		31	(17/.17)
17 → 17	(25/.09)		.83
19	(38/.14)		
21	(32/.10)	26 → 17	(59/.18)
26	(70/.25)	19	(31/.09)
31	(47/.21)	26	(41/.12)
	.75	31	(84/.25)
			.64
19 → 17	(36/.18)		
21	(18/.09)	31 → 17	(59/.17)
26	(30/.15)	19	(37/.10)
31	(41/.21)	21	(33/.09)
	.63	26	(80/.23)
			.59
21 → 17	(27/.17)		
24	(24/.15)		
26	(27/.17)		
31	(38/.24)		
	.73		

SOURCE: Sharpe and Hawkins(1992a). Reprinted by permission

types of behaviors tend to precede or follow that behavior or event of interest, may be represented for analysis. In addition, many potentially repetitive behavior-event sequences and many important time-based functional relationships may be articulated as a function of a particular direct observation analysis.

Figure 9.3   Alternative sequential tree structure or kinematic analysis data
representation samples

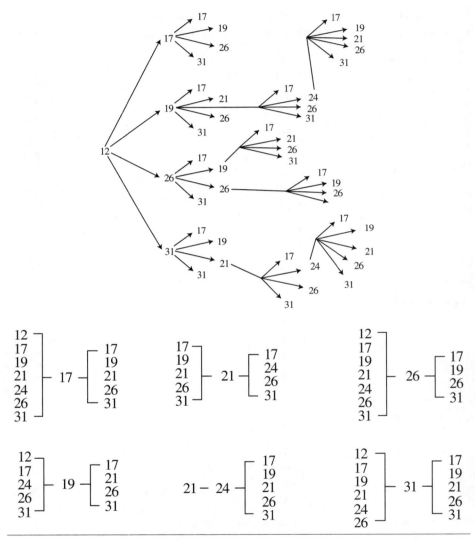

SOURCE: Sharpe and Hawkins (1992a). Reprinted by permission

Prior to moving to other forms of sequential data representation
and analysis, we should mention a few cautionary limitations of this
type of sequential data representation form and the nature of its use as
an analysis technique. First, sequential tree structures and related

kinematic analysis representations are purely descriptive. Although ease of production and representation is greatly facilitated through computer-generated data collection and consequent sequential analysis techniques, these data representations are designed to gather an initial sense of the time-based sequential character of a particular data record. As such, they are designed to provide an initial description of the potential time-based relationships among behaviors and events that may exist in a particular data record that has been gathered to describe a particular observational setting. Researchers should exercise caution when presenting these data representations to avoid making any strong claims with regard to potential functional relationships among certain behavior-event sequence configurations and to avoid making any strong claims with regard to behavior-event prediction and control. Second, these data representation techniques are limited to the viewing and somewhat conjectural analysis of behavior-event sequences that exist in one data record that has been generated from one observational episode. In this second regard, this type of descriptive viewing is limited to the form and character of behavior-event sequences that have occurred in one situation only. Other forms of data representation and related analysis are required to make any sequential data comparisons and potential sequential behavior-event change or relationship determinations over multiple data records and, hence, over longer periods of time (e.g., observational activity involving multiple observational episodes and design phases).

Probability Matrices

A second form of visual representation of behavior-event sequences, and another form of kinematic analysis, lies in the construction of a probability matrix. A specific set of construction steps is contained in Appendix A, and is therefore only summarized here. This option for representing sequential data is based on representing all the behaviors and events in a particular data record on both the horizontal axis and the vertical axis of a matrix, akin to listing each behavior and event across the top and left side of a piece of graph paper. Once this has been done, it becomes possible to do a numerical count (or frequency) and a conditional probability (see the Illustrations From Education section in Chapter 3 and Appendix A for a complete discussion of conditional probabilities in relation to a sequential analysis) for each behavior-event sequence with a length of two as designated by the corresponding box in the matrix is provided within each matrix cell, typically with the vertical axis behaviors defined as the predecessor and the horizontal axis behaviors defined as the successor in each behavior chain. Such a matrix, once constructed, reports the number of occurrences and the conditional probability (i.e., probability in relation to all other sequences of two behaviors and events in a data record that have the same preceding behavior) for each behavior-event sequence of two in length, in which the onset of each recorded behavior or event either immediately preceded or succeeded the onset of all other behaviors and events in the data record.

Usually the vertical left axis of a matrix designates preceding behaviors and events, and the top horizontal axis of a matrix designates succeeding behaviors and events. A probability matrix is developed according to the start times of occurrences of each behavior and event, to allow for the sequential study of an overlapping behavior-event data record. The total or aggregate number of occurrence data for each individual behavior or event should be reported in the last, or right-most, vertical column of the matrix, and the total number of individual conditional probabilities for each behavior and event row should add up to 1.00 for a total conditional probability of occurrence. Although this type of visual sequential data representation contains the same inherent challenges as the sequential tree structures, or kinematic analysis examples, contained in the prior section (e.g., descriptive limitation and single observation analysis), a matrix representation provides for a somewhat more systematic and inclusive sequential data representation, for it (a) contains all behaviors and events that exist in a particular data record and (b) facilitates a systematic numerical occurrence and conditional probability comparison across the inclusive variety of dual behavior-event sequences that occurred within a particular observation episode. Those interested in more detailed matrix data representation illustrations should consult Hawkins and Sharpe (1992), Ray and Delprato 1989), or Sharpe and Hawkins (1992a).

Conditional Probability Table

Another form of visual representation of behavior-event sequences, and one that provides perhaps the greatest flexibility of reporting, is the conditional probability table. In this format, a specific listing of behavior-event sequences of interest, the relative length (i.e., number of behaviors or events in a sequence) of each behavior-event sequence, and the corresponding number of occurrences and conditional probabilities of each particular sequence is reported in tabular format. This option for representing sequential data is provided to give the researcher flexibility in reporting the character of behavior-event sequences of interest and to provide additional information in relation to the character of the preceding and succeeding behaviors and events in a particular sequence in terms of timing of occurrence. In other words, oftentimes a researcher will be interested not just in the immediately preceding or succeeding behaviors and events that surround a particular target behavior or event of interest but in the timing of when a particular behavior or event may occur before or after another event, regardless of the relative immediacy of that behavior or event. This is important information, for example, when studying the relative lag time or immediacy with which certain clientele may respond to a particular stimulus or stimulus package. An education research and evaluation example in which this type of sequential data representation is important is the direct observation and recording of a variety of types of teacher questioning and student answers to each type of question and questioning incident, *and* the length of time between question and response—in the context of other teacher and student behavior occurrences that may be ongoing in a classroom setting. Clearly, this type of sequential data reporting is also limited in character in its descriptive nature and in its ability to analyze data within one observational episode and corresponding data record.

Descriptive Graphs

Graphic representation of sequential data provides a variety of options, of which some more popular forms will be illustrated separately and discussed in some detail here. Some of these forms of sequential data representation and analysis also provide an important set of across observation analyses of sequential data that use many of the visual inspection techniques discussed in the preceding Visual Inspection section, lending greater rigor to sequential data reporting and analysis activities.

The first form of graphic representation of sequential data we will be discussing provides an important means of viewing potential behavior-event sequential relationships that have occurred within a particular data record. Limited to one observation session, and purely descriptive in character, this graphic representation form provides a general view of the number of occurrences, and relative length of occurrence, for each behavior or event occurrence in the data record. Figure 9.4 provides an illustration of this representation form.

Figure 9.4   A sequential analysis graph illustration depicting the number of occurrence and duration of select behaviors and events across time

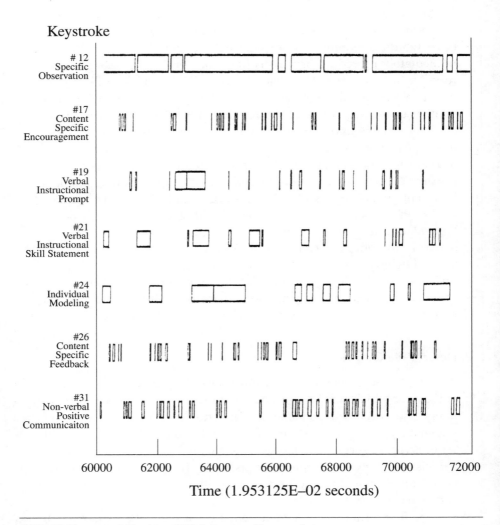

SOURCE: Sharpe and Hawkins (1992a). Reprinted by permission

In Figure 9.4, behaviors and events of interest are listed on the left vertical axis of the graph. A time-based metric is used for the horizontal axis to represent when in the data record certain behavior and event occurrences began and ended (e.g., the start and stop time stamps discussed in Appendix A). In Figure 9.4, both the alphanumeric indicator and actual behavior term are represented on the vertical axis, and time is represented in microseconds over an approximate 4-minute duration taken from a data record on a practicing teacher. From this illustration, it is clear that the number of each behavior occurrence may be counted according to the number of rectangular boxes in the horizontal line for each behavior listed on the vertical axis. The length of the rectangle signifies the relative length or duration of each behavior occurrence and can be quantitatively determined from viewing the corresponding time metric on the horizontal axis. Software programs like the one described at the end of this text are of immense help in facilitating graphic representations such as that in Figure 9.4, for behavior and event specifications on the vertical axis may be made with a click of a key, and time parameters may also be easily expanded and collapsed according to the researcher's analysis needs.

The greatest appeal of this type of graph representation is that it enables one to view in a general way how certain behaviors and events tend to occur in time-based sequence with one another. Although specifically quantified conditional probabilities of particular sequential behavior$\leftarrow\rightarrow$event relationships are not represented, an important means to the visual representation of multiple potential sequential relationships among multiple behaviors and events as they actually occurred in number and in duration in a particular data record may be made available for general inspection. Although this graphic data form is limited in the same way as our preceding sequential tree structure and matrix data representation examples (i.e., descriptive capability and single observation episode analysis), it does provide a uniquely important visual description of the time-based location and extent of multiple behaviors and events of interest that are operating in a particular observation setting.

With few historical exceptions (e.g., Henton & Iverson, 1978), until the advent of a sequential lens conceptualization with respect to observational data analysis, coupled with an amenable computer-based data graphing capability, such a data representation technique has been largely unavailable. By the repeated graphic juxtaposing, viewing, and interpreting process using this graphic representation form, a fairly detailed and inclusive sequential view of particular observation episodes conducted within a larger experimental activity may be made available.

Once a researcher has conducted a fairly complete sequential analysis of the behavior-event relationships in one particular data record and a corresponding observational episode, through the use of the sequential data reporting and analysis techniques discussed to this point, we recommend a few graphic representation forms for sequential data to analyze potential sequential data changes across observational episodes and related design phases of a particular direct observation activity. A rather simple graph procedure has already been illustrated in Figure 3.2 in Chapter 3. In the Chapter 3 illustration, a measure of the number of a teacher's Instructional Opportunities (IO) is represented in traditional behavior graph format according to the preparation guidelines outlined in Figure 9.1. Then, the number of Appropriate Instructional Actions (AIA) is represented on the graph. The discussion in the article from which this graph was reprinted makes it clear that the general number of AIA is a function of recording whether or not this type of teacher behavior occurred in the direct time-based context of IO occurrences. Although using this type of descriptive graph representation format does not explicitly represent which AIA occurrences happened as a function of which specific IO occurrences, and explicit quantitative coefficients for the conditional probabilities of each of those specific relationships are not reported, a general sense of the relative number of times an AIA occurred in time-based sequence with IO occurrences is represented across observation sessions and related experimental phases. As we articulated in detail in the Illustrations From Education section in Chapter 3, this form of graphic representation of sequential data provides (a) a general descriptive accounting of behavior-event sequences of interest and (b) an element of prediction and control of information with respect to the design and analysis procedures outlined in earlier sections of this chapter; however, it is specific to the representation of sequential data analysis interests.

Another, and similar, illustration to that provided in Figure 3.2 is contained in Figure 9.5. Taken from earlier education research efforts by Sharpe, Hawkins, and Ray (1995), the data graph in Figure 9.5 plots the actual conditional probability of occurrence for specific known effective teacher behavior-event sequences of interest across experimental conditions and across treatment and control groups. If conditional probability data are extracted from individual observation sessions for particular behavior-event sequences of interest, and then these data are plotted on a traditional behavior graph according to the recommended graph preparation guidelines in Figure 9.1, a set of accepted visual inspection and related statistical manipulation procedures may be used to analyze sequential data occurrences in a repeated measures observational design framework.

Figure 9.5   Graph illustrations of select teacher behavior chain representations across experimental teacher-training conditions and across experimental and control participants

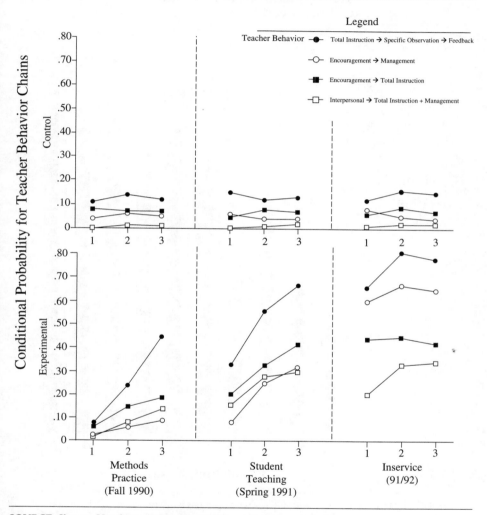

SOURCE: Sharpe, Hawkins, and Ray (1995). Reprinted by permission

Another, more specific alternative form of plotting sequential data is also available through the use of a more sophisticated version of a traditional bar graph. A representative illustration of this, from the same line of education research activity by Hawkins, Sharpe, and Ray (1994), is provided in Figure 9.6.

Figure 9.6   A bar graph illustration depicting a discrete percentage of
observational time measure of one target behavior (Student
Success) in the context of conditional probability measures of
sequentially related behaviors (Teacher Proximate and
Individual Teacher Focus)

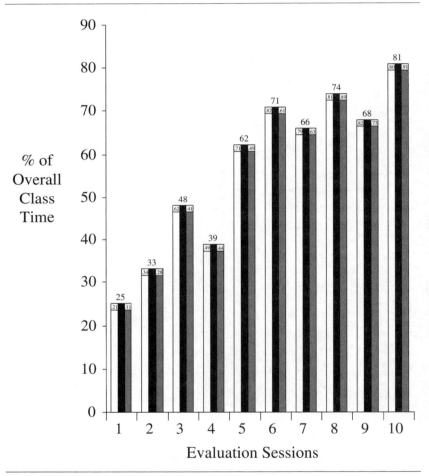

SOURCE: Hawkins, Sharpe, and Ray (1994). Reprinted by permission

In the graph representation in Figure 9.6, research interest was on
visually representing the conditional probabilities of select teacher
behaviors that tended to occur in time-based proximity with a particular student target behavior of interest. Specifically, Hawkins and
colleagues were interested in the types of teacher behaviors that might

be functionally related in a time-based manner with student success (i.e., effective engagement in skill appropriate activity). To this end, Figure 9.6 first represents the general percentage of class time that students tended to engage in successful skill appropriate activity (i.e., Student Success, or STS, as represented in Figure 9.6 and its corresponding legend) across 10 different observation sessions. This traditional discrete measure is represented by the vertical opaque bar contained in the center of each observation session bar graph. Next, the conditional probabilities of Teacher Proximate (i.e., TP, the teacher is in close proximity to a particular student) and Individual Teacher Focus (i.e., ITF, the teacher is attending to a particular student's needs rather than that of a large student group) that occurred in time-based proximity to STS are represented by respective clear and lined bars with the specific conditional probabilities reported at the top of those bars. In this type of graph format, both discrete measures of particular target behaviors and sequential data related to the time-based behavior sequences that surround and include the discrete measures may be reported across multiple observation episodes and experimental phases. When interpreting the data contained in Figure 9.6, for example, it can be seen through visual inspection that a substantial increasing trend in the percentage of STS was evident across observation sessions and that the same trend increases in the conditional probabilities of TP and ITF occurred in correspondence with the increases seen in STS. From this type of graphic juxtaposition of discrete and sequential data, important additional information regarding the form and character of behavior-event interactions over the course of an experiment may be uncovered—information that may never have been discovered without the addition of a sequential observation lens.

AN ENDNOTE ON SEQUENTIAL DATA

As is evident from our discussion of sequential data analysis, as well as from the corresponding information in Chapter 3 and related mathematical elaboration in Appendix A, there are a variety of visual representation forms for sequential data. These forms vary in the sophistication of the type of data characteristics they represent and in how they are used within or across observation sessions and corresponding data records.

In addition, although sequential data are typically reported in terms of (a) number of occurrences of specific behavior and event sequences, (b) rate of sequential occurrence when observational time frames are not consistent from one observation to the next, and (c) in some cases when the individual or average durations of those sequential events; a more complex and alternative language for describing sequential data records is often needed beyond these representation forms. As we articulated in Chapter 7's Measurement Options section, the use of terms such as *rhythm, complexity, coherence,* and *velocity* is oftentimes necessary to a more accurate and representative written description of the form and character of behavior-event sequences of interest.

From our discussion of possible sequential data representations, as listed in this chapter, it should be clear that although a very structured set of rules and procedures exists for the representation and analysis of traditional discrete measures of behavior, a comparable set of procedures does not exist for the representation of sequential data. Although there are a variety of visual and statistical analysis formats for sequential data, the appropriate matching among the particular character of a sequential data set and the many visual representation techniques available is a challenging task. In addition, new visual representation formats are continually the focus of experimentation.

The statistical modeling of conditional probabilities when representing sequential data in quantitative ways is also the subject of current methodological debate. The methodological contributions of Gottman and Roy (1990) provide an important illustration of this, as they detail a variety of alternative sequential analysis formulae to be implemented as a function of the varying character of behavior-event data sets that have been collected for particular purposes, the use of particular types of observation systems, and the implementation of particular measurement types for particular behavior-event topologies. For those interested in a more advanced understanding of the appropriate mathematical modeling of sequential behavior-event relationships, we recommend thoroughly reading their materials.

Perhaps the most important measurement tool that a sequential analysis provides is the use of a probability statistic to document the character of a time-based behavior-event relationship. When it is only event based, this statistic provides a ratio of the amount of a particular event (e.g., frequency or duration of occurrence) in relationship to the total amount of event activity in an observed setting. When this statistic is time based, probability acts in much the same way; however, the focus is on how certain behaviors or events tend to show up in the same general time frame as certain other behaviors or events. In this latter case, using a conditional probability measure provides important interbehavioral or transactional information about how certain behaviors and events might be functionally related to or have an effect on one another. This is an important component because it adds information to the prediction and control efforts of direct observation and behavior analysis activities in a variety of education, psychology, and social science settings.

Bakeman and Gottman (1986) provide an important illustration of this type of transactional or conditional probability that summarizes this measure's importance:

> A conditional probability . . . is the probability with which a particular "target" event occurred, relative to another "given" event. Thus if it rained 76 days last year, and if on 20 of those 76 days there were thunderstorms, then we would say that the probability of a thunderstorm occurring, given that it was a rainy day, was .263 (or 20 divided by 76). If "T" stands for thunderstorms and "R" for a rainy day, then the simple probability for thunderstorms is usually written $p(T)$, whereas the conditional probability for thunderstorm, given a rainy day, is usually written $p(T/R)$; in words, this is "the probability of [the occurrence of] T, given [the time-based presence of] R. (p. 123)

With regard to sequential data, then, it is important for the researcher to consider providing a time-based coding mechanism for recording data and then amenable representations of that data record to get specifically at its sequential character.

Finally, a variety of methodological and statistical cautions remain when analysis focus is on the sequential character of a data record. Issues such as committing a type I error and interpreting a particular behavior-event sequence as significant when it is not are perhaps the most pervasive challenge in analyzing behavior-event records sequentially. The issues that prevail as the methodology develops include establishing base rates of behavior and event occurrences, how well a particular data record coheres in terms of the number of sequences necessary to completely describe the data set, and whether data sets that do not conform to mutual exclusivity across behaviors and events in the category system designed to collect the data can be legitimately analyzed sequentially. In addition, the analysis of longer behavior-event sequences necessarily requires geometrically expanding the size of the observational data set to interpret the finding of particular behavior-event sequences as significant with any degree of confidence. Also, most behavior-event data records are considered stochastically dependent, meaning that serial dependency among behaviors and events that occur in close time-based proximity to one another most often exists; however, as these same behaviors and events become more distantly occurring in time, such dependency decreases. Determining when an acceptable dependency trade-off in terms of time sequence occurs is challenging, and it may depend on the form and character of the behaviors and events themselves as well as on the larger setting circumstances in which the behaviors or events occur.

Despite these challenges, and the fact that we are in the early stages of methodological development with respect to quantitative sequential analyses of time-based behavior-event data records designed to overcome these challenges, we feel, as do others, that the appeal of a sequential lens when performing direct observational activities far outweighs the potential cautions. Therefore, we hope that through these materials we have provided an appealing introduction to such sequential analyses. We also hope that by illustrating in Chapter 10 some appealing future directions that research and evaluation activities may take using static and sequential analyses of behavior, we will succeed in growing the contributions that researchers armed with these methods may make to their respective professional fields.

Part IV

Application Illustrations and a Window to the Future

10

Measurably Superior Instruction and Therapy

Measurably superior instruction [and therapy] means close, continual contact with the relevant outcome data. Revolutionary!

— Bushell and Baer (1994, p. 3)

After reading this chapter, you should be able to define the following terms and provide the information requested in the study guide.

TERMS

Deduction

Induction

Interactive simulation

Rule governed

Contingency managed

STUDY GUIDE

1. List and discuss four important areas of knowledge production in relation to direct observation data collection and analysis methods.
2. Provide an argument in favor of, or against, a "return to the counting of things" as a viable data collection and analysis method.
3. List and discuss the seven steps in the multidimensional game model presented by Timothy Leary.
4. Discuss the three appealing characteristics of data collection and analysis activity that the scientific methods contained in this book provide.

5. Discuss some potentially appealing educational, evaluative, and laboratory applications that are made available by the data collection and analysis methods contained in this book.
6. Explain the scientific methodology choice tenet as articulated by Landrum.

The first nine chapters of this book concerned themselves primarily with an introduction to the principles and practice of direct observation methods in relation to behavior and sequential behavior analysis activity. What we covered ranged from the presentation of the scientific history and conceptual evolution of the methodology, to the importance of field systems and sequential theory, to procedural detail from category system construction, to reliability issues, to a variety of data collection, measurement, representation, and analysis strategies. We hope that we have provided most of the information necessary to begin direct observation activity with a behavior analysis focus. As members of a scientific community, we believe that our efforts should be vigilant in striving for new and more effective ways for measuring the quality and effectiveness of professional practice. It is our hope that the materials contained in this book serve this purpose.

According to Bushell and Baer (1994), there are four important areas of knowledge production that, as applied scientists, researchers should hold important. First, effective professional practices must be developed and systematically documented so that we know just what we mean when we stipulate that effective practice has occurred. Second, we must figure out a best approach for the quantitative scientific measurement of relatively effective, or ineffective, professional practices. Third, we must develop and document effective approaches for teaching the most effective professional practices to others. And last, we must develop marketing and advertising strategies to ensure that larger professional and lay communities grow in their perception of the appeal of and receptivity toward both the documented effective professional practices discovered and the methods for instructing others in the appropriate use of those professional practices. The second of the four important scientific activities outlined above (Bushell & Baer, 1994) is the subject of this text; that is, measuring the relative effectiveness of a particular set of professional practices, be they designed for the therapeutic value of a particular client or set of clientele or for teaching others how to implement the professional practices themselves.

A RETURN TO THE COUNTING OF THINGS?

We, of course, feel strongly that the applied analysis of behavior as a research and evaluation methodology designed for study of a wide variety of education, psychology, and social science concerns has an appealing capacity for increasing our ability to document and measure in very concrete ways the relative effectiveness of a wide range of procedures in these professional areas. Most practicing behavior analysts make use of Parsonson and Baer's (1978, 1986) guiding methodological principle, which states that

> the behavior of the subject(s) controls the pace and procedures of the [treatment] program through the data, which are continually available to the experimenter when graphed after each session. Judgments, decisions, and changes can be made as the [treatment] program proceeds. (1978, p. 109)

In other words, close, continual contact with relevant quantitative process and outcome data is foundational to applied behavior analysis methods, thus a return to the counting of things that occur in experimental or evaluation settings is foundational to the documenting of the relative effectiveness of certain behavior-event relationships and to learning more of the applied professional world around us. We feel, as do Bushell and Baer (1994), that close, continual contact with relevant outcome data is necessary to any education, psychology, or social science enterprise in which the central focus is to provide something of therapeutic value to a particular client or group of clients. In this regard, the counting of things becomes a necessary and integral part of the documentation, representation, and analysis process designed to learn more about the relative effectiveness of a particular procedure. Most researchers and evaluators working in applied education, psychology, or social science settings focus their efforts on producing data that are designed to support the continued use of a particular procedure, due to some documented results of its effectiveness on some behavior change dimension, or to change or abandon that procedure due to its lack of effectiveness. Direct observers and behavior analysts using the principles and procedures described in this text collect numerical data on certain behaviors and events of interest, represent them visually in a variety of graphic ways, and make determinations of how to continue with a particular procedure based on just what is occurring from interpreting the data from observational episode to observational episode. Such determinations are essentially based on the counting of occurrences of behaviors and events. The more inclusive the counting of behaviors and events that are operating within a particular observational setting, and the more varied the counting measures across a variety of discrete and sequential options, the more complete and accurate the data-based representation becomes. We hope to encourage, through our presentation and discussion of an appealing set of procedures for counting things, an increase in the receptivity to the set of procedures discussed in this text to the point where large numbers of professionals are making productive use in a variety of applied professional settings.

Timothy Leary, a pioneering psychoanalyst at Princeton University and elsewhere during the 1960s, and a contemporary of B. F. Skinner's (though to many cultural and political leaders of his day he was recognized as either a pariah or a visionary depending on which pole of the cultural spectrum one held to at the time), perhaps summed best the importance of the counting-oriented methods described in this text. One of the early subscribers to field theory, Leary rejected most psychological terminology of the cognitive and constructivist academic camps as prescientific and vague in its attempt to operationalize psychological events:

> "We've got a contract among ourselves," [Leary] said, "that we're going to talk sense, and that means specifying where the bodies are in space-time and what sort of signals they're exchanging." This was the basic methodological position of post-Einstein physics. What was happening in interpersonal interactions, described objectively and relativistically, was various parties or coalitions interacting in neuro-muscular space. (Wilson, 1986, p. 38)

Leary's arch-rival at Harvard, B. F. Skinner, had been a pioneer of the behaviorist approach, which rejected the intuitive and poetic psychologies of Freudians and Jungians as unscientific. Although Leary agreed with this, he felt that Skinner himself had taken an equally wrong turn in using as a model the push-pull [action-reaction] mechanisms of Newtonian physics. "'Psychology doesn't become scientific by copying the physics of past centuries,' Leary said to me. 'We've got to learn to use the best models in the physics of this century'" (Wilson, 1986, p. 38). Such models, he felt, would be relativistic, describing differing reality coordinates experienced by different bodies as they exchanged signals in space-time.

Leary had developed a seven-dimensional game model and insisted on analyzing all behavior in terms of the

1. roles being played

2. rules tacitly accepted by all players

3. strategies for winning

4. goals of the game and purpose served

5. language of the game and the semantic worldview implied

6. characteristic space-time locations

7. characteristic movements in space-time

"'If you can't describe in some quantitative way those seven dimensions of an individual's or group's behavior, then you cannot expect to scientifically document and understand the game,' Leary insisted" (Wilson, 1986, p. 38).

In Leary's view, group processes are defined as "games." For Leary, the important scientific questions become, "What are the players doing in space-time? Who's at bat? Who's pitching? What are the behavioral rules of the game? How many strikes before you're out? Who makes the rules? Who can change the rules?" (Wilson, 1986, p. 38)

In these regards, we hope that we have provided a case for a counting-of-things method of scientific and evaluative inquiry. In addition, we hope that we have argued successfully for, and provided an appealing procedural introduction to, the implementation of a field systems and sequential component to direct observation and behavior analysis activity. What remains, in closing, is for us to provide a glimpse into a potential research and development future with respect to the thoroughgoing application of the methods introduced in this text in applied education, psychological, and social science settings.

RESEARCH AND DEVELOPMENT OPPORTUNITIES

A computer-based approach to the direct observation, visual representation, and resultant analysis of behavior and event occurrences provides many research and development possibilities not previously attainable without the aid of these methods and the advent of computer-based tools to support thoroughgoing implementation of the methods. This is particularly true for applied behavior analysis capabilities in light of how rapidly computer technologies are advancing and how quickly the capabilities of these technologies improve in levels of sophistication. Use of the various procedures discussed in this text and the computer-based tools to accomplish the kind of observational analysis described provides quite a range of appealing research and development directions. From reading these materials and becoming familiar with the software tools that are described in the back of this text, it should be clear that the direct observational methods in this book may enable researchers and evaluators in the education, psychology, and social sciences to better understand, predict, and control very complex behavior-behavior and behavior-event interactions across a variety of highly interactive applied settings. Although it is changing, it remains in large part today as Bronfenbrenner (1979) described over 20 years ago that education and social science literatures lack a strong database on the structure, distribution, and impact of behavior and setting event variables across various applied settings. In this regard, the more complex forms of behavior and the various settings in which they reside need to be more completely described and understood. It should also be apparent from the potential addition of sequential analyses that an understanding of how behaviors and events interact with one another over time may be necessary to a more inclusive description of interactive settings, and may be necessary to an enhanced understanding of the meaning and nature of behavior-event relationships in particular situations. More capable and more sophisticated data collection and analysis tools such as those provided by various computer applications allow us to accomplish these tasks, tasks that we could not accomplish without such tools. Questions involving complex interactive and multidirectional time-based stimulus←→response relationships, behavior-event latencies and related variable functional connections, complex time-based behavior-event treatment packages designed for challenging therapeutic settings, and potential functional interaction effects across fine discriminations of multiple potential stimulus and response classes, are all ripe for future experimentation as a function of our rapidly increasing methodological capability. A more inclusive behavior-event field systems orientation, real time data collection capability, and sophisticated time-based sequential analysis procedures should all contribute in substantial ways to increased methodological capability and related scientific discovery.

In teacher education, for example, Greenwood, Carta, Arreaga-Mayer, and Rager (1991) recommend the type of observational approach we provide and briefly discuss its implications as follows:

> The utility of a search and validate approach to the evaluation of effective instructional practices has only just begun to be undertaken. Because of its . . . analysis of classroom behavior, and temporally related situational features of classroom instruction, it is an approach consistent with current school improvement goals. It is also an approach that focuses on the contributions classroom teachers can bring to the development of effective instructional technology. Clearly, demonstrations of the approach are warranted. (pp. 188-189)

In a larger social science sense, many questions heretofore unanswered may now be investigated using a more capable observational lens. As Berliner (1992) states, this is particularly important in that a data-based, data-driven, and unabashedly quantitative approach to the analysis of fine discriminations of behavior is being provided that runs counter to the current qualitative/interpretive zeitgeist that surrounds social science research in general. Although the relative merits of differing methodological approaches remain arguable, what is important is that alternatives and counterpoints to each method are provided, enabling researchers to choose among a panoply of approaches what they feel best suits a particular set of observational questions. In this light, questions pertaining to the functional behavior-event differences across a variety of settings and across the varying characteristics of the clientele served may be more accurately and inclusively answered. In addition, scientific tools are provided through the behavior analysis methods discussed in this text to describe and analyze the salient differences in the same participant's behavior as a function of changing situations. What is now available is a way to make these differences clear in an inclusive, objective, and quantifiable way.

The methods we have discussed also provide the flexibility to describe and document various behavior-event relationships that are unique to particular situations, using the specific terminology that best captures a particular situation. For example, the instructional behaviors and events taking place in a public school mathematics classroom may be very different from the instructional behaviors and events that occur in a physical education classroom. Flexibility in term construction when developing a category system for observational purposes, multiple measurement use when tracking the events in applied settings, and the use of a variety of alternative data representation and analysis forms when interpreting data results are all important features designed to ensure that researchers have the full capacity to describe and analyze in quantitative behavioral ways just what they intend. It is also possible and desirable for the researcher to focus on a range of low-inference measures of behavior in context to high-inference measures of setting climate and atmosphere (e.g., humorous, warm, businesslike, etc.), with discovery of low-inference behavior changes as a function of high-inference contexts potentially providing valuable scientific insight. Allowing the collection of a greater volume and variety of quantitative data, contextualizing this data in qualitative ways, and providing greater economy and flexibility of data representation should indeed provide valuable information on most interactive settings in the social sciences. A return to Locke's (1992) illustrative education example, from his reading of a behavior graph of the form contained in Figure 9.4, provides important insight as follows:

> As I watched the individual teaching behaviors appear from beneath the moving ruler [on the sequential graphic], my attention was drawn to some unexpected juxtapositions. The teacher was modeling a skill and giving verbal instruction at the same time. This is not uncommon; teachers often recite critical verbal cues while they demonstrate—particularly when they do so in slow motion. The graphic also revealed that while she was modeling she was also observing an individual student and giving performance-specific feedback (apparently interspersed with verbal cues). Such a disparate combination of behaviors is not common at all (or so I thought), and my first response was to be incredulous. That is exactly what [this observational method] has an almost unique power to do—confront us with what is happening even when it differs sharply from our expectations. . . . I had never been conscious of this teaching move. . . . On the very next day, however, one of the videotapes used in the UMass undergraduate training program revealed several clear instances that would have matched the graphic perfectly. Had that been under my nose all the time? If so, why did it not make an impression on me?

Those questions show exactly what [this observational method] can do that other methods of inquiry are far less likely to accomplish. (pp. 86-87)

Clearly, much of what we discover about the world around us comes from having progressively more capable tools for observing it. Electron microscopes provide one clear example of this in that this tool helped researchers in the biological sciences to see things that they formerly could not. This phenomenon is the case in the education, psychology, and social sciences as well, in that more capable and inclusive observational recording instruments, and observation tools that allow us to analyze behaviors and events of interest in different ways, should help us see and understand behavior and event relationships that we formerly could not. The scientific tools contained in this book provide, as Siedentop (1992) states, two appealing additions to education and social science research arsenals. First, the capability of inductively deriving category systems designed for particular settings and contexts provides an appealing combination of qualitative and quantitative methodologies. Second, the ability that computer technology provides to record observations in real time eliminates traditional concerns of the relative validities of counting or timing the duration of behaviors and events. Third, as stated by Ray (1992), the methods provided in this text facilitate using alternative ways to observe behaviors and events quantitatively in addition to what has traditionally been available. These include, but are not limited to, regularities in behavior-event patterns (sequences of change), coherence and variability in those patterns (predictability and simplicity of sequence of change), and various velocity measures (rates of change or patterns in the rate of change).

These observational approaches also infer a particular perspective on the research process. Most traditional education and social science work has a long history of deductively driven investigations based on predisposed theory. Pavlov's studies of classical conditioning discussed in Chapter 1 provide a nice example of this approach, in which most of a researcher's efforts were spent on theory construction and the experimental documenting of the veracity of that theory. This *deductive* approach is in direct contrast to many of the observational recommendations in this text. On the other hand, an *inductive* approach, in which category systems are built on the behaviors and events that actually occur in particular situations, is designed to add to what we know about that situation and to add to what we know about other similar situations. In other words, the perspective we recommend is to conduct descriptive-analytic observation efforts, from those observations to build an integrated knowledge-base, and from that slowly building knowledge-base to direct further research efforts designed to uncover what we come to realize we know little about (i.e., induction). In this regard, Kantor's (1970) theoretical framework, on which we base much of our text materials, remains as true today as it was when he conceptualized it:

> Of extreme importance for the appreciation of behavior fields is their uniqueness and individuality. There is no fixed or universal type. Implied in the field construct is the principle that each class of behavior events must be analyzed according to its intrinsic [and unique] factors . . . it is imperative to be alive to the greater complexity of non-reflex behavior, especially the interpersonal aspects of human performance. (p. 105)

INSTRUCTION AND EVALUATION

Clearly, as education, applied psychology, and social scientists, we are continually endeavoring to understand more about effective and not-so-effective behavior-event practices in various cultural, professional, and research and training situations. The information gained from these types of applied research and development activities should serve in large part to drive and to enhance our instruction and evaluation efforts in those same professional settings. Whether new information lies in additional knowledge about new or existing behaviors and events or in the new and unique ways in which we describe and document those behaviors and events, in the ideal, these efforts should be designed to improve professional practice and should be designed to change the various practices of our selected clientele in therapeutic ways. In these regards, the observational approaches we have described in this text have great appeal for those involved in education and evaluation efforts.

Although application in the broad professional area of instruction and evaluation may serve a variety of professional activities, the teacher education profession serves as an ideal illustration of the potential benefits of a quantitative direct observational approach might provide to education and evaluation concerns. Historically, the predominant evaluation methods when observing teachers teaching in their environments have included tactics such as anecdotal records, narrative accounts, and Likert scale-type questionnaire assessments. The challenges inherent in all these methods have been their subjective character and potential inclusion of user bias. Thus users of these traditional assessment types have been challenged by the potential for differing evaluation outcomes within and across observers, even when observing very similar teaching situations. This has led to what Sharpe, Hawkins, and Ray (1995) refer to as an oftentimes vague and nonspecific educational process in which the important scientific components of (a) quantitative metrics of improvement discriminations over time for the same teacher-trainee and (b) a consistent metric across different teacher-trainees have been elusive.

Consider, on the other hand, the possibility that quantitative direct observation of behavior-event relationships may offer in terms of the ability to discriminate and articulate those teacher activities most influential in guiding the specified as desirable and undesirable student practices in a given subject matter or situation. This is particularly important in relation to contemporary education reform's return to the notion of performance- and competency-based education—subject-matter competencies now regularly recommended to be measured in some quantitative way. Although each instructional situation observed may contain a very different set of behavior-event interactions, each situation may be described and analyzed using a large and inclusive set of terms or definitions, or the same category system. If this is the case, then the observational practices discussed in this text provide a means to relatively inclusive and thoroughly quantitative and objective description of teaching practice in the context of student practice.

In addition, and because teaching practices are interactive on several levels, describing and documenting fine discriminations of verbal and nonverbal behaviors and the setting events in which they are manifest may also be included in an observational data record. Oftentimes, many more subtle but still potentially objectively described events may be recorded using a multilevel coding system, given that they are atypical of a particular category system code or are more difficult to capture in traditional coded descriptions. Some examples of these events include verbal intonations and inflections, word usage based on connotative rather than denotative meanings, and the social and physical distances that may exist between a teacher and student. Within such a quantitative data record to be used for evaluation purposes, all coded descriptions are provided in a quantitative measurable form of behavior and event occurrences, thereby retaining an element of objectivity and consistency in the evaluation process. Observational data, such as that provided through the use of enhanced software applications like the one described in the back of this text, that are coded live in the setting to be evaluated, serve as a powerfully effective immediate feedback and goal-setting tool for teachers-in-training (see Sharpe, 1997a, 1997b, Sharpe, Hawkins, & Ray, 1995, Sharpe & Lounsbery, 1998, for a detailed procedural discussion). Such an approach also clearly holds appeal for the education and training of a host of professionals and various clientele in a variety of professional settings beyond teacher education within which particular behavior-event changes are recommended to ensure effective professional practice.

Siedentop and Eldar's (1989) point is well taken, that one means to attain effective professional practice is to develop specific behavioral processes that are fundamental to those practices. In this context, it is important not only to provide professional trainees with one, two, or even a limited package of interactive behavioral responses but also to provide insight into the interconnected, contextual nature of the larger behavior-environment fields in which they may operate. Otherwise, behavioral implementation may become misleading and even frustrating. The frustration may be due, for instance, to the inappropriate use of certain behavioral responses in the context of the unique professional setting in which the trainee may be operating. These inappropriate responses may flow from a lack of understanding of the larger context of a complete field system, including the many so-called extraneous variables of a traditional experimental model that are virtually always present in applied settings. The advantage of a field model such as that advocated in this text lies in its ability to enable professionals to more adequately conceptualize their activities in their interdependent, interconnective framework and, accordingly, to operate more effectively within their particular situations. Most expert professionals seem to be contingency managed, implementing a complex behavioral strategy appropriately and within the immediate unique setting characteristics. This reinforces the need to move away from an isolated element approach to research and evaluation and toward enabling professionals to understand their settings systemically, albeit in specific quantitative and behavioral ways.

LABORATORY APPLICATIONS

The direct observation and behavior analysis methods that we have presented also hold great appeal for a wide variety of laboratory-type instructional experiences in which educators are interested in improving the behavior and interactions of various professionals and clientele toward more effective and therapeutic ends. This is particularly the case in the context of rapidly advancing computer hardware and software developments. Setting up a prescribed set of guided observations from videotape examples using the software-based data collection and analysis tools such as that described in the back of this text enables a first level of such applications. Using this type of guided observation technique allows educators to help various professionals-to-be to (a) learn a common observational language with which to talk over in meaningful ways the important characteristics of effective and not-so-effective professional practices across a host of situations, (b) learn how to be accurate self- and external monitors of professional practices felt to be effective and desirable in certain situations, and (c) learn how to discriminate among effective and not-so-effective practices with a view toward the continuous improvement of their own professional practice outside of the primary instructional training environment. This level of applications also allows the flexibility of moving from a very simple set of only a few behaviors or events in a similar context, and using only one measurement type; to gradually increasing in complexity the number of behaviors and events, measurement types, and variable situations in which those behaviors and events are observed. The possibilities of this type of education experience are many, based on the collecting and archiving of a videotape library of various situations representing various types of interactions chosen for illustration. Given the emphasis on residency-based or purposeful practice experiences of most professional endeavors—the education, medical, and legal professions, for example, all offer prominent illustrations of this—and the related emphasis upon holding professionals-in-training explicitly accountable for learning specific behavioral skills, this type of application of the direct quantitative observation of behavior-event occurrences as they unfold in particular professional practice situations is rife with laboratory-based instructional opportunities.

   At a second level, and pending further developments in recently available computer technologies, another variation involves computer-operated *interactive simulation* of various behavior-behavior and behavior-event interactions in specifically defined situations using professional-trainee viewer keyboard inputs to guide future video illustrations. At this level of instructional laboratory applications, operating in similar fashion to children's novels that provide alternative story lines depending on readers' choice functions and turning to alternative pages, videotape viewers could first watch relatively ineffective behavior practice examples until they recognized the types of professional challenges being demonstrated. Then, through a CD-ROM-based videotape library connected with matched behavior-event sequential data records and related conditional probabilities, viewers could choose alternative videotape illustrations by choosing particular behaviors and events once the videotape illustration was stopped at a certain point in time. In other words, after viewing a particular situation, professionals-in-training or target clientele would be given a behavioral choice (e.g., What would you do next in this situation?) that by pressing a key on a keyboard would specify their chosen action and in turn drive the selection of the next videotape illustration to show the probable outcome of that choice given the behaviors and events that occurred up to that point. Using this approach, teacher educators, for example, could teach teacher-trainees relatively more effective practices in challenging situations without the potential contraindicated effects of placing them in actual classrooms before they were ready for that level of live professional practice with actual student clientele. As the professional competencies of various groups being educated through this approach become relatively more important in terms of the potential negative impact on their clientele (e.g., a surgeon-to-be practicing particular lifesaving techniques versus a teacher-in-training practicing in an elementary physical education classroom) an interactive laboratory-based approach to professional instruction clearly gains in appeal. The practical education of clinical psychologists, the procedural education of medical specialists, and the pedagogical education of special educators dealing with severe and profound and violent clientele are just a few of the many professional training areas that could benefit from such simulated professional practice experiences and also alleviate the potential for negative impact by professionals who may make interactive mistakes when operating in applied training experiences (see Hawkins et al., 1994, Ray, 1992, and Ray & Delprato, 1989, for a more thorough discussion of laboratory simulation applications).

ENDNOTE

Only a few general areas have been discussed here regarding how the direct quantitative observation of behavior-event occurrences that we recommend may be applied in uniquely appealing ways, providing more capable recording and analysis tools that in turn provide an expanded set of possibilities when designing and implementing a wide range of research, evaluation, and related educational experiences. Whether observational focus is on discovering more of the functional relationships among behaviors and events in a particular situation, conveying information to groups of learners to hold them accountable for particular professional or therapeutic practices, or providing information to be used in an evaluation capacity, we hope that the data collection and relatively immediate analysis provided by the direct observation procedures we have introduced and discussed will facilitate a host of impacting research, education, and evaluation experiences of benefit to various professionals-in-training and the various clientele with whom they work.

Many contemporary tools offered through the research and development community are dependent on existing computer-based technologies to allow their thoroughgoing development and productive application. In addition, effective implementation of these tools to the point of data-based information dissemination and use by a variety of practicing professionals is dependent in large part on a vital culture of research faculty←→professional practitioner collaboration. Using the education literature as an example, it is apparent that education researchers have found it to be an ongoing challenge to find instruments that accurately and comprehensively describe, measure, and analyze the complex, rapidly occurring array of behaviors and events that tend to characterize live instruction and complex human interaction (Dawe, 1984; Eisner, 1983; Rubin, 1985). Hrycaiko and Martin (1996) point in a disheartening manner to the fact that in education literature very little data-based information is published using collaboratively driven behavior analysis methods—even though these methods are now readily available and even though many teachers and coaches use just these types of data gathering methods in more informal ways in their educational settings without the benefit of any formal scientific training. Taking a larger view, many scientists whose main area of expertise lies in behavior analysis, and related systematic observation methodologies in the social sciences, have wrestled with just how to quantitatively describe and analyze the vast complexity of human interaction in context (see, e.g., Ray & Delprato, 1989), and this challenge remains in many respects.

In spite of these current challenges, we are committed to and cautiously optimistic about the appeal of quantitative direct observation methods of data collection and analysis, and we find recent advancements in data collection and analysis tools of great appeal in moving direct observation methodologies from a rule-governed approach in which particular behaviors are targeted for change, and clients demonstrate that change in terms of a static measure, to a contingency managed approach in which clients are taught what behaviors might be best to use in certain circumstances and a sequential analysis is used to determine whether those clients have chosen appropriately when those circumstances present themselves (Morris, 1992; Sharpe, 1997a).

A couple of closing messages about behavioral research and development are clear to us. First, the scientific community is far from realizing all of the possible methods of description and analysis that might be used to learn more about the world around us. Second, advancements in computer-based applications may provide one of many means to providing important alternative methods of data collection and analysis in the applied sciences.

Clearly, as computer application development evolves in concert with a desire for greater scientific insight into what comprises effective (and not-so-effective) human interaction in general, we have within our grasp the potential to discover much more of what comprises interaction designed to ensure productive ends. We also have the potential to design and implement some appealing professional educational experiences, experiences that may be far more effective and that, until now, we have been incapable of delivering. What remains is thoroughgoing development and application of computer-based and other toolbuilding technologies according to the rigors of scientific methodology and the relevant input of practicing professionals who can contribute a knowledge of the contemporary challenges of particular professional situations. This will require a willingness on the part of the scientific and professional preparation communities to be cautiously receptive to alternative experimental lenses and to the use of the data gathering and analysis methodologies that are compatible with those alternative lenses and with what professional practitioners hold important.

We believe that to argue, in some technocratic or generalized way, that there is only one right data gathering and analysis method or instructional material that is somehow superior in effectiveness to all the others, or even to argue that a clear hierarchy of relative effectiveness exists among sets of professional procedures, is contraindicated in this context. Landrum (1997) elegantly states the methodological tenet that we subscribe to:

> Practitioners must fully understand the principles of [a variety of] effective practices, not so they can choose from among different strategies so much as adapt specific strategies to meet the individual, contextual demands they will face. . . . Data should matter a great deal, in at least two important ways. First, we must prepare [professionals] by training them in the use of the array of validated methods that our own rich scientific efforts have offered. Second, we must prepare them to be knowledgeable and critical consumers of research. (p. 128)

We applaud Landrum's position in that we believe that only through collaboratively designed and implemented data collection and analysis practices; and only through objective, comprehensive, relevant, and readily understandable data-supported descriptions of effective practice, will social science professions such as the education profession be thought of as conducting legitimate and thoroughgoing science.

With regard to the need for thoroughgoing science in order to continue to increase our knowledge of effective professional practice, over a decade ago Sulzer-Azaroff (1986) summarized well the positive impact of applied behavior analysis to that point in her presidential address to the American Psychological Association's Division 25 as follows:

> Since the late fifties, when behavioral principles began to be applied toward the solution of educational [and social science] problems . . . progress has continued to accelerate. By the mid-eighties, behavioral studies have demonstrated that essentially all clientele, regardless of preparedness, deprivations, or disability, are capable of simple and complex learning. Principles of behavior have been applied effectively to remove barriers to learning, to help a variety of clientele to learn rapidly, precisely, durably and

cost effectively; and to express what they have learned in new situations. (p. 55)

We also feel, as Johnston and Pennypacker (1980) stated over 20 years ago, that "our task, then, is to hasten the development of a scientific understanding of human behavior and the resulting evolution of a beneficent technology [in facilitation]" (p. 19). If Heward and Cooper (1992) are on the mark by stating that change in the social science professions occurs by revolution rather than evolution and that major revolution occurs about every 20 years, then the time may be ripe for an awakening of collaboratively driven behavioral research and development to the point of receptive dissemination by research faculty←→professional practitioner teams and to the point of productive use by a variety of research and clinical professionals. The science of applied behavior analysis is clearly evolving from simple rule-governed and limited analyses to very sophisticated and comprehensive analyses of complex interactive settings. If this evolution occurs as Heward and Cooper (1992) state, then "[professional] practice will be based on the need to know rather than the need to believe" (p. 361).

We find that many of us who professionally call ourselves scientists, and are engaged in what we would like to think of as scientific labor, find that most of the ideas and theories we use to guide our daily operations are not "new" but are more accurately characterized as "borrowed." Typically, our ideas are borrowed from significant others whom we have encountered in our professional lives, and they are packaged with some appeal for a previously unfamiliar audience. In this sense, we have attempted to provide an alternative to the subjective and qualitative forms of data gathering and analyses that currently predominate the education, psychological, and social sciences. Although our materials are designed to be compatible and collaborative with more qualitative methods, we hope that we will succeed in helping those who are interested in a more thoroughgoing quantitative method of describing and analyzing interactive settings of interest and also in helping with the descriptive, predictive, and controlling (or arranging) stages of the scientific enterprise.

We felt that it would be most appropriate to close this text by quoting Bakeman and Gottman, as we have founded a large portion of our sequential analysis thinking on their important foregrounding work, and as the sequential analyses we have introduced are based on the mathematical algorithms that they pioneered. As Bakeman and

Gottman (1986) so elegantly put the perspective we have attempted to bring across, and as we follow in their footsteps in our research in education pursuits, we would like to end with the following quote as acknowledgement:

> Observing and discovering pattern is what [we are] about. We do this kind of thing for a living, and we have chosen to do it because it is what we think science is about. Obviously we think it is not really that hard to do. But we are lonely. We want company in this enterprise. Only about 8 percent of all psychological research is based on any kind of observation. A fraction of that is programmatic research. And, a fraction of that is sequential in its thinking. This will not do. Those of us who are applying these new methods of observational research are having great success. (pp. 200-201)

We, as applied behavior analysts and direct observers of behavior-event phenomena, have experienced productive results from using these methods across a variety of research, evaluation, and education applications in the education and social sciences. We have also learned a lot from those who pioneered this type of work and from those who we have encouraged down this research pathway. It is now our hope that the compilation of direct observation materials we provide through this text, and our accompanying software tools described in the back of this book, provide help to those with a potential interest in the methods and procedures that we have used productively.

Appendix A

Sequential
Analysis Formulae

As this text has illustrated, the types of data recording and data analysis methods advocated by direct quantitative observation of multiple behaviors and events, and their multiple characteristics as they interact with one another in time, are activities that are not only facilitated but in many cases made feasible by the use of computer-based recording and analysis tools. This is particularly the case with the sequential analysis of behavior-event data. This appendix provides a summary of terms often used when describing a mathematical equation construction and related sequential analysis process, as well as an introduction to the type of equations recommended for use in such an analysis. These equations are based on the important sequential analysis methodological work of Bakeman and Gottman (1986, 1997) and thus we only summarize them here. For a detailed discussion of the theoretical constructs on which mathematical modeling of sequential data are founded, and for a representative set of illustrations of the variety of equations that should be implemented in particular analysis activities, consult Bakeman and Gottman's (1986, 1997) foundational *Observing Interaction: An Introduction to Sequential Analysis* texts or Gottman and Roy's (1990) more advanced textbook materials on the subject. For a user-friendly and sophisticated computer-based sequential analysis tool, we recommend that the reader request a demonstration copy of the BEST software tools advertised in the flyer that accompanies this text and also available through Scolari/Sage Publications at www. scolari. com or (805) 499-1325 for dedicated customer service.

The reader may find it useful if we first define some terms that are specific to how we characterize a data record in relation to how we characterize events when analyzing how they tend to follow one another in time. Quantitative behavior-event *data* generated and analyzed by using the methods recommended throughout this text are defined as a set of observable *events* that have quantifiable start and stop times of occurrence. In other words, each behavior or event contained within a particular data record is typically represented by an alphanumeric *type number*[1] and *time stamp*[2] indicator for start and stop time parameters for particular behavior or event occurrences. Therefore, while separate behaviors or events may have the same type numbers, their time stamps are always different.[3] A data record that is collected with a view toward analyzing behavior and event occurrences sequentially must necessarily include an ascending order of start time stamps for all recorded behaviors and events that when taken together form a *chronological sequence*.

Any two behaviors or events that immediately follow one another in start time chronological sequence are considered to be *linked*. It is also important to note here that although two behaviors or events may be linked, the second behavior or event may begin prior to the first event's ending time stamp, allowing for an overlapping behavior-event occurrence record. The first of two linked behaviors or events is termed the *predecessor* and the second the *successor*. Linked behaviors and events are termed *consecutive* if no third data event's start time occurs chronologically between the start times of the linked events. Therefore, any behavior or event may be linked with many successors or predecessors but is consecutive with only *one* predecessor and *one* successor. Behaviors and events that are not immediately linked are termed *proximate* to any other event that follows each behavior or event and has a time stamp that isn't beyond a predefined *lag time*. Again, any behavior or event is immediately linked to at most one other event but may be proximately linked to many within a specified lag time preceding or following the start time of that particular behavior or event.

The consecutive type numbers of a sequence of linked behaviors and events form a *chain* or *sequence*. As only type numbers and not time stamps are considered in the description of a particular chain or sequence, a chain may occur any number of times within a data set. The number of occurrences of a chain is termed the *frequency* of that chain. A set or list of different chains with some common behaviors and events forms a *chain pattern*. *Probabilities* of a particular chain occurring are defined as relative, or *conditional*, to a chain pattern within which it may be contained. In other words, a probability number is based on the ratio of the frequency of a particular chain of interest to the combined frequency of all of the chains within a given pattern.[4]

When analyzing chain patterns, frequencies of chains of exactly two behaviors or events may also be searched to represent a *matrix* of succeeding and preceding events for all of the behaviors and events contained within a particular data set. If this procedure is implemented, the *row index* of the alphanumeric indicator within a matrix is the type number of the predecessor in the corresponding chain and the *column index* is the type number of the successor. The respective probability (and statistical) indices are then relative, or conditional, to the chain pattern consisting of all two-event chains.

The sequential analysis applications described in this text, and contained in the software program described at the end of this text, are based on the specific mathematical equations in Bakeman and Gottman (1986) and on the theoretical summary information contained in portions of Gottman and Roy (1990). As this type of analysis is fairly complex in theoretical and methodological structure, we provide only a simplistic overview in this appendix of what we feel to be the most important points in relation to mathematical modeling of the sequential character of a behavior-event data set. We hope that the summary contained here will prove helpful to those incorporating this type of analysis into their direct observational activities, and that the source materials that we have referenced will provide an additional link to more complete mathematical discussion.

To begin, complex mathematical modeling of just how each behavior in an observation system interacts with others in sequence comprises a complete sequential analysis. In a sense, a sequential analysis focuses first on the characteristics of particular behaviors within a data set but, most important, on the characteristics of the interactions or transactions among those behaviors as they present themselves over time. In the complete mathematical equations used to represent these behavior-event interactions, such representations are not limited to the effects of other immediately preceding and succeeding behaviors and events but, instead, may be analyzed as more complex patterns of interactive activity—patterns that a computer-based sequential analysis is well capable of uncovering and that many research literatures have begun hypothesizing as potential characteristics of optimally effective human interaction.

As a mathematical model, sequential analysis focuses on the problem of identifying and quantifying immediate and more distant interactional relationships of particular behaviors and events in sequence. It provides a means for determining in a situation-specific manner the probable effects one behavior may have on another based on their repeatedly close appearances together in time. When implementing this type of analytic model, a first step is to compute the unconditional probability of occurrence of each of the behaviors and events in a particular data set by dividing the frequency of occurrence of a particular behavior or event by the total number of occurrences of all other behaviors and events in that data set. Next, the conditional probability of each possible behavior and event (including itself) is calculated as a function of the successive lags (or steps) of each event from each possible event with which it could have possibly occurred before. This is akin to counting the number of times each behavior or event follows each of the other events occurring within a data file. Included in this count are the number of times a behavior or event immediately follows another (termed *lag-1*), the number of times an event occurs one event away (termed *lag-2*), and so forth up to the largest sequential step of interest. The lag probabilities are computed by dividing the frequency of occurrence of each event at lag-n by the number of times the interactive event under analysis occurred.

Sequential chains of interest in a sequentially ordered behavior-event data record are defined in terms of suffixes and prefixes (i.e., succeeding and preceding events). The *suffix* of a chain is defined as the last behavioral event appearing in it, and the *prefix* of the chain is the subchain obtained by omitting the suffix. Referring to our education example in Chapter 3, the behaviors of "instruction-engagement" may be a prefix and the behaviors of "feedback" a suffix in the behavior sequence instruction-engagement-feedback. A statistical Z-score transformation is then computed to determine the *meaningfulness* (or *significance*; *meaningfulness* is a term coined by Bakeman & Gottman, 1986) of a particular chain within a larger sequential data record.

The meaningfulness of a particular behavior-event chain in a particular sequential data record is calculated by analyzing the conditional probabilities of all prefixes and suffixes permitted by the universe of chains in the data set. In other words, a particular behavior chain of interest is determined meaningful as a function of the larger sequential structure of a particular data file and as a function of of the number of total event occurrences within that data record.

For those interested in an overview of mathematical modeling with respect to a sequential analysis of behavior-event chain prefixes and suffixes, the following summary may be helpful. Again, the *suffix* of a chain is defined as the last event number appearing in it, and the *prefix* of an event chain is the subchain obtained by omitting this suffix. For instance, events designated by 9-6 characterize a prefix and event 5 the suffix of the chain 9-6-5. The Z-score and related meaningfulness of this chain are calculated with respect to all prefixes and suffixes permitted by the universe of chains in the larger data file from which 9-6-5 originates. Consider, for example, a matrix "M" having rows indexed by the distinct prefixes permitted by the behaviors and events in a data record, and columns by the distinct suffixes contained in that same data record. Let $M(i, j)$ be the frequency of the chain having prefix i and suffix j.

Therefore,

$M(i, -) = M(i, 1) + M(i, 2) + \ldots$ is the row sum of the matrix

$M(-, j) = M(1, j) + M(2, j) + \ldots$ is the column sum of the matrix

$M(-, -) = M(1, -) + M(2, -) + \ldots = M(-,1) + M(-,2) + \ldots$ is the matrix sum

The probability of an event chain having prefix i and suffix j is then calculated using

$$M(i, j) \, / \, M(-, -)$$

Analogously,

$$p(-, j) = M(-, j) \, / \, M(-, -)$$

The Z-score of the chain having prefix i and suffix j is calculated using

$$\frac{M(i, j) - M(i, -)p(-, j)}{M(i, -)p(-, j)[1 - p(-, j)]}$$

and its corresponding meaningfulness is computed as

$$M(i, -)p(-, j)[1 - p(-, j)]$$

If a behavior or event chain consists of a single event, it has no prefix and the formulas stated become undefined. When this is the case, f is the frequency of the given event, x is the number of the one-event chains that occur in the data file, n is the combined frequency of these chains, and

$$p = 1/x.$$

The probability of the given chain then is then:

$$f/n$$

and its corresponding Z-score is:

$$\frac{f - np}{np(1 - p)}$$

Its meaningfulness is then:

$$np(1 - p)$$

Analyzing behavior and event occurrences in interactive settings as a function of their relationships among one another in time provides for a wealth of additional information with respect to the study of interaction in the education, social, and psychological sciences. For example, preceding or succeeding matrices of dual chains may be built giving frequency, conditional probability, and statistical significance data cell by cell. Rates of responding across multiple stimulus events may thus be discerned. Using computer-based data analysis tools, the level of complexity of a sequential analysis is only limited by investigative interest and the original alphanumeric coding scheme used to collect the data file. When data collection is synchronized to a video-tape record, multiple data collection files may be merged and arranged temporally in constructing a very complex overlapping event record, furthering the fine interactive discrimination capabilities such as that offered by the BEST software advertised in the flyer accompanying this text. Given that a sequential analysis application is based on the start times of behaviors and events that are recorded by a particular data collection program platform, and given the time sensitivity of the data collection mechanism that is made available by computer-based recording methods, sequential analyses of rapid and multiple occurrences of multiple overlapping events can be readily undertaken within a host of complex interactive situations.

NOTES

1.   When using amenable computer tools such as BEST software, the type number is typically an integer between 1 and 36. Each type number indicates a particular behavior or event. On a computer keyboard that is used for data collection, the keys 1 to 9 represent themselves, 0 represents the number 10, A represents the number 11, B represents 12, and so forth, with Z representing 36. As most source code programming only recognizes numerical notations, while you may record letters with the computer keyboard, the actual data set and related sequential analysis representations use numbers to represent the letters used for recording.

2.   Each time stamp is typically represented by a positive integer measuring the time of the event from a particular onset or start time to a particular termination or end time in a specified time unit (e.g., seconds, etc.). Time measurement in a particular data record begins at time zero with the start-up of the data recording apparatus and continues in *ticks* (i.e., time units) in which in most computer-based programs approximately 51.2 ticks equals 1 second, and a time conversion application must also be included in the software program application.

3.   Although in principle the recording of two or more behaviors or events may be simultaneous with regard to start times, in practice each start time stamp is necessarily recorded as distinct, due to a computer-based data recorder's inability to register more than one event during the exact same time tick.

4.   This is typically termed a *conditional probability* (see Bakeman & Gottman, 1986, 1997, and Gottman & Roy, 1990, for a detailed discussion of this issue). To ascertain the unconditional probability of a given chain, a wider chain search that encompasses all possible patterns of a particular behavior-event length is typically implemented.

Appendix B

Behavior Evaluation Strategy and Taxonomy (BEST) Software

Data Collection and Analysis Application

Over the past decade, advances in computer technology development have facilitated the design and implementation of a variety of software-based applications for behavioral research. The Implications of Computer Technology section in Chapter 3 makes clear that computer hardware and software advances have provided a variety of appealing tools for the collection and analysis of real-time observational data. According to Kahng and Iwata (1998), using computer-based software tools is appealing due to their ability to significantly enhance the reliability and accuracy of recording in relation to the more traditional paper-and-pencil and stopwatch recording methods. Additional activities, such as data graphing, training staff according to a data collection criterion, and more sophisticated statistical and mathematical modeling of behavioral data, are also made feasible through computer-based tool use.

As we have established throughout many of the chapters in this book, as computer-based tools continue to develop the capacity for more inclusive and varied alternatives, direct observation activities continues to improve and/or become available. It remains, however, as

Kahng and Iwata stipulated 5 years ago, that computer-based tools for direct observation are not widely known to the professional communities that would benefit most from using them, and that they are difficult to access due to limited marketing and information sharing among professionals. This appendix, therefore, summarizes one commercially marketed computer-based data collection and analysis tool, Behavior Evaluation Strategy and Taxonomy (BEST) software, which was developed by the authors of this textbook. Although there are other, similar tools on the market and in the literature, the BEST tool summarized here (and advertised in the flyer included with this text) provides a representative example of one of the few tools that is marketed commercially and made available in a packaged and user-friendly format to professional and scientific communities. In addition, the BEST tool described in this appendix is representative of the majority of systems in that it is based on compatibility with IBM Windows operating platforms, and it includes a variety of features (e.g., interrater reliability, data file merging, data graphing, and sequential analysis applications) that may not be provided by other computer-based tools.

BEST SOFTWARE CAPABILITY SUMMARY

The BEST software platforms are divided into two separate and distinct data collection and data analysis applications. Both are completely compatible with Windows 95, 98, 200, NT, and XP, and they operate identically in terms of menu structure, with similar user-friendly features. Data collection applications facilitate the construction of observation systems by defining alphanumeric keys on a computer keyboard. Up to 36 different behaviors and events may be recorded during a session, and each key may also be notated numerically and narratively for additional behavior and event subcategorization. A variety of recording methods are made available within the application and multiple occurrences of simultaneous or overlapping events may be recorded using this application. By generating a time-based data record with quantitatively measured start and stop times of each recorded event, response frequency, duration, intervals (variable duration), average duration and standard deviations, rate, latency, interresponse time, percentage of observational time; and time-based measures (such as first, last, span, longest, shortest, etc.) may be extracted using the data analysis program. Due to the time-based nature of the data file generated, a sophisticated sequential analysis application is also made readily available. A numerical and text notation feature also allows the recording of notes for unique or atypical event occurrences in the time-based sequence in which they occurred. In addition, pause and other data management features are available that permit the interruption and restarting of observational sessions as the need arises, and entry errors made while recording may be immediately edited.

The data analysis program provides a variety of user-friendly options including the calculating of response frequency (total number and rate), duration, latency, interresponse time, percentage of observation time and related subintervals, percentage of trials, and conditional probabilities of sequentially based behavior and event relationships. The analysis application also allows the compartmentalizing of subgroups of behaviors and events to analyze as a logically grouped data file. Options also include the calculation of mean and median data, variability in relation to range and frequency distributions, and statistical significance data in relation to sequential analyses. Reliability programs with simple frequency, point-by-point, and Cohen's kappa options are also included to facilitate staff training and interrater reliability check procedures. Graphic analyses include tables, pie charts, temporal records, sequential analysis tables, and traditional time-series graphs. Statistical applications such as mean, standard deviation, and line of best fit are included to complement the standard graphic applications. All of BEST software's graphing applications are exportable to most commercial graphics programs, such as Windows Paint, Powerpoint, and Delta Graph.

The BEST programs require an IBM-compatible desktop or laptop computer with a minimum 386 processor running a Windows operating platform. The applications have minimal RAM and hard disk requirements. Data collection applications for handheld PCs are available, as are digital video synchronization applications for the data collection platform and remote data collection apparatus for those who desire direct hookup to laboratory applications (e.g., bar press, lights, temperature switches, pellet containers, etc.) that obviate the constant presence of a human data collector. Fully functional demonstration copies are available on request (see the Scolari/Sage Publications flyer that accompanies this text or contact the developers at www.skware. com). Included in the CD-ROM contained in the software package are example observation systems, example data files, a complete and illustrated users guide in PDF format, and a PDF format summary version of the materials contained this textbook. A complete software tutorial in movie and sound format is also included to provide an initial overview of the software programs' many capabilities and applications. The latter materials require an Adobe Acrobat reader and a QuickTime movie player (but for those without these applications an Internet connect is provided on the CD-ROM to locate and download the appropriate free software for viewing these materials).

Appealing advantages of BEST software include

1. behavioral, quantitative, and qualitative data collection with a push of a button

2. a wide range of sophisticated analyses, including descriptive and predictive statistics, qualitative memo-noting, and a variety of graphic and sequential analysis representations

3. complete compatibility with a wide variety of statistical and graphics packages

4. user customizability to specific data collection and analysis needs

5. immediate data-based feedback capability in field settings or as an ongoing evaluation tool

6. built-in reliability application for staff training and inter-observer comparisons

7. data file merging and sorting functions for compiling purposes

Its general features include

1. allowing the you, the user, to create your own category system to meet your specific observational needs

2. storing multiple observation systems storage for particular applications

3. recording the start and stop times of multiple events as they naturally occur, providing a variety of descriptive statistics

4. recording narrative fieldnotes in concert with behavioral and quantitative data

5. recording information live or synchronized with videotape at almost any location

6. qualitatively, quantitatively, and sequentially representing and analyzing observational data

7. providing staff training and ensure reliability of data collection

8. interfacing with other software programs for multitasking and remote site use

9. being compatible with a range of hardware, including Windows CE hand-held computers for data collection in the field

The specific data collection capabilities of BEST software incude

1. recording and categorizing data using complex multiple event observation systems

2. using numerical and narrative notations to further delineate event types

3. recording multiple events simultaneously as they actually occur in time

4. taking advantage of a user-friendly screen representation when collecting data

5. facilitating the data collection process with multiple means of recording, including press and hold keys, toggle keys for turning on and off, and remote key access

6. pause feature for entering and exiting the same data collection episode at time of exit

7. editing data collection efforts on the fly and viewing data records as they are collected

8. automatic recording of response frequency, rates, percentage of total experimental time, shortest and longest event occurrences, event occurrence spans, duration, intervals, time samples, latency, inter-response time, and discrete trials

9. multitasking when collecting data by assigning keys to perform additional functions, such as starting another software application

10. taking advantage of MicroSoft CE hand-held compatibility when collecting data in particular field settings

Its specific data analysis applications include

1. identifying frequency, total and mean duration, standard deviations, rate, and experimental time percentages of each category system event in tabular and graphic formats

2. identifying time-based information for each category system event, including first and last event occurrence, time-spans between events, longest and shortest event occurrences, and related means and standard deviations

3. searching for keywords and memos in narrative notations and represent narrative data within and across data files

4. processing and comparing multiple data files across one another, and across multiple recorded events and measurement types

5. conducting a variety of reliability analysis functions among data files including simple frequency, point-by-point, and Cohen's kappa

6. conducting sequential analyses of the time-based connections among events documented in terms of frequency, conditional probability, and statistical significance (Z-score transformations)

7. merging and time-sorting multiple data files enabling comprehensive observational description from videotape

8. performing event subgrouping routines to allow a separate analysis of subgroups of events within all program applications

9. representing data with a host of sophisticated graphing applications for individual data files and for multiple data files across event and measurement type

10. graphically analyzing mean, standard deviation, and regression across multiple data files and multiple events and measures

11. printing, saving, and clipboard/pasting data representations into other statistical analysis and graphics editing software packages

References

Aeschleman, S. R. (1991). Single subject designs: Some misconceptions. *Rehabilitation Psychology, 36,* 43-49.

Allport, G. W. (1961). *Pattern and growth in personality.* New York: Holt, Rinehart & Winston.

Altmann, S. A. (1965). Sociobiology of rhesus monkeys: II. Stochastics of social communication. *Journal of Theoretical Biology, 8,* 490-522.

Astley, C. A., Smith, O. A., Ray, R. D., Golanov, E. V., Chesney, M. A., Chalyan, V. G., Taylor, D. J., & Bowden, D. M. (1991). Integrating behavior and cardiovascular responses: The code. *American Journal of Physiology, 261,* 172-181.

Bailey, J. S., & Burch, M. R. (2002). *Research methods in applied behavior analysis.* Thousand Oaks, CA: Sage.

Bakeman, R. (1978). Untangling streams of behavior: Sequential analyses of observation data. In G. P. Sackett (Ed.), *Observing behavior: Data collection and analysis methods* (Vol. 2, pp. 63-78). Baltimore, MD: University Park Press.

Bakeman, R., & Gottman, J. M. (1986). *Observing interaction: An introduction to sequential analysis.* New York: Cambridge University Press.

Bakeman, R., & Gottman, J. M. (1997). *Observing interaction: An introduction to sequential analysis* (2nd ed.). New York: Cambridge University Press.

Barlow, D. H. (1980). Behavior therapy: The next decade. *Behavior Therapy, 11,* 315-328.

Barlow, D. H., & Hersen, M. (1984). *Single case experimental designs: Strategies for studying behavior change* (2nd ed.). Elmsford, NY: Pergamon.

Bakker, G., & Clark, L. (1988). *Explanation: An introduction to the philosophy of science.* Mountain View, CA: Mayfield.

Barone, T. (2001). Science, art, and the predispositions of educational researchers. *Educational Researcher, 30*(7), 24-28.

Bergin, A. E., & Strupp, H. H. (1972). *Changing frontiers in the science of psychotherapy.* Chicago, IL: Aldine-Atherton.

Berliner, D. C. (1986). In pursuit of the expert pedagogue. *Educational Researcher, 15*(7), 5-13.

Berliner, D. C. (1992). Some perspectives on field systems research for the study of teaching expertise [Monograph]. *Journal of Teaching in Physical Education, 12,* 96-103.

Bijou, S. W., Umbreit, J., Ghezzi, P. M., & Chao, C. (1986). Manual of instruction for identifying and analyzing referential linguistic interactions. *Psychological Record, 36,* 491-518.

Binder, C. (1994). Measurably superior instructional methods: Do we need sales and marketing? In R. Gardner, D. M. Sainato, J. O. Cooper, T. E. Heron, W. L. Heward, J. Eshleman, & T. A. Grossi (Eds.), *Behavior analysis in education: Focus on measurably superior instruction* (pp. 21-31). Pacific Grove, CA: Brooks/Cole.

Bliss, J., Monk, M., & Ogborn, J. (1983). *Qualitative data analysis for educational research*. London: Croom Helm.

Bohme, G., Van Den Daele, W., & Krohn, W. (1978). The "scientification" of technology. In W. Krohn, E. T. Layton, & P. Weingart (Eds.), *The dynamics of science and technology* (pp 219-250). Dordrecht, The Netherlands: D. Reidel.

Bronfenbrenner, U. (1979). Contexts of child rearing: Problems and prospects. *American Psychologist, 34*, 84-89.

Brown, J. F., & Hendy, S. (2001). A step towards ending the isolation of behavior analysis: A common language with evolutionary science. *The Behavior Analyst, 24*, 163-171.

Brown, S. R. (1980). *Political subjectivity: Applications of Q methodology in political science*. New Haven, CT: Yale University Press.

Buchler, J. (Ed.). (1955). *Philosophical writings of Peirce*. New York: Dover.

Bushell, D., Jr., & Baer, D. M. (1994). Measurably superior instruction means close, continual contact with the relevant outcome data. Revolutionary! In R. Gardner, D. M. Sainato, J. O. Cooper, T. E. Heron, W. L. Heward, J. Eshleman, & T. A. Grossi (Eds.), *Behavior analysis in education: Focus on measurably superior instruction* (pp. 3-10). Pacific Grove, CA: Brooks/Cole.

Campbell, D. T., & Stanley, J. C. (1963). *Experimental and quasi-experimental designs for research*. Chicago: Rand McNally.

Carnine, D. W., & Fink, W. T. (1978). Increasing the rate of presentation and use of signals in elementary classroom teachers. *Journal of Applied Behavior Analysis, 11*, 35-46.

Carroll, L. (1946). *Alice's adventures in wonderland*. New York: Random House.

Chance, P. (1998). *First course in applied behavior analysis*. Pacific Grove, CA: Brooks/Cole.

Chatfield, C., & Lemon, R. E. (1970). Analyzing sequences of behavioural events. *Journal of Theoretical Biology, 29*, 427-445.

Cohen, J. (1960). A coefficient of agreement for nominal scales. *Educational and Psychological Measurement, 20*, 37-46.

Cohen, J. (1965). Some statistical issues in psychological research. In B. B. Wolman (Ed.), *Handbook of clinical psychology*. New York: McGraw-Hill.

Cook, T. D., & Campbell, D. T. (1979). *Quasi-experimentation: Design and analysis issues for field settings*. Boston, MA: Houghton Mifflin.

Cooper, J. O., Heron, T. E., & Heward, W. L. (1987). *Applied behavior analysis*. Toronto: Merrill.

Cooper, M. L., Thomson, C. L., & Baer, D. M. (1970). The experimental modification of teacher attending behavior. *Journal of Applied Behavior Analysis, 3*, 153-157.

Cossairt, A., Hall, R. V., & Hopkins, B. L. (1973). The effects of experimenter's instructions, feedback, and praise on teacher praise and student attending behavior. *Journal of Applied Behavior Analysis, 6*, 89-100.

Croll, P. (1986). *Systematic classroom observation.* Philadelphia: Falmer.

Crosbie, J. (1993). Interrupted time-series analysis with brief single-subject data. *Journal of Consulting and Clinical Psychology, 61,* 966-974.

Darst, P. W., Zakrajsek, D. B., & Mancini, V. H. (Eds.). (1989). *Analyzing physical education and sport instruction.* Champaign, IL: Human Kinetics.

Davison, M., & McCarthy, D. (1988). *The matching law: A research review.* Hillsdale, NJ: Lawrence Erlbaum.

Dawe, H. A. (1984). Teaching: Social science or performing art? *Harvard Educational Review, 54,* 111-114.

Day, W. F. (1983). On the difference between radical and methodological behaviorism. *Behaviorism, 11,* 89-102.

Delprato, D. J. (1992). Behavior field systems analysis: History and scientific relatives [Monograph]. *Journal of Teaching in Physical Education, 12,* 3-8.

Delprato, D. J. (1999, May). *Informal communication.* Discussion conducted during a poster session display at the International Meeting of Applied Behavior Analysis, Chicago.

DeProspero, A., & Cohen, S. (1979). Inconsistent visual analysis of intrasubject data. *Journal of Applied Behavior Analysis, 12,* 573-579.

Doyle, W. (1990). Themes in teacher education research. In W. R. Houston, M. Haberman, & J. Sikula (Eds.), *Handbook of research on teacher education* (pp. 3-24). New York: Macmillan.

Dunkin, M. J., & Biddle, B. J. (1974). *The study of teaching.* New York: Holt, Rinehart & Winston.

Dwyer, D. (1996). We're in this together. *Educational Leadership, 54*(3), 24-26.

Einstein, A., & Infeld, L. (1938). *The evolution of physics.* New York: Simon & Schuster.

Eisner, E. W. (1983). The art and craft of teaching. *Educational Leadership, 40,* 4-13.

Ekman, P. W., & Friesen, W. (1978). *Manual for the facial action coding system.* Palo Alto, CA: Consulting Psychologist.

Eliot, T. S. (1971). *The complete poems and plays.* New York: Harcourt, Brace & World.

Ellul, J. (1964). *The technological society.* New York: Knopf.

Erickson, F. (1982). The analysis of audiovisual records as a primary data source. In A. Grimshaw (Ed.), Sound-image records in social interaction research [Special Issue]. *Journal of Sociological Methods and Research, 11*(12), 213-232.

Espinosa, J. M. (1992). Probability and radical behaviorism. *The Behavior Analyst, 15,* 51-60.

Faraone, S. V. (1983). The behavior as language analogy: A critical examination and application of conversational interaction. *Behaviorism, 11,* 27-43.

Finn, C. E. (1988). What ails education research. *Educational Researcher, 17*(1), 5-8.

Firestone, W. A. (1987). Meaning in method: The rhetoric of quantitative and qualitative research. *Educational Researcher, 16*(7), 16-21.

Flanders, N. A. (1970). *Analyzing teacher behavior.* Reading, MA: Addison-Wesley.

Friman, P. C., Wilson, K. G., & Hayes, S. C. (1998). Behavior analysis of private events is possible, progressive, and nondualistic: A response to Lamal. *Journal of Applied Behavior Analysis, 31,* 707-708.

Fuchs, L. S., & Fuchs, D. (1986). Effects of systematic formative evaluation: A meta-analysis. *Exceptional Children, 53,* 199-208.

Gardner, R., Sainato, D. M., Cooper, J. O., Heron, T. E., Heward, W. L., Eshleman, J., & Grossi, T. A. (Eds.). (1994). *Behavior analysis in education: Focus on measurably superior instruction.* Pacific Grove, CA: Brooks/Cole.

Garrison, J. W. (1986). Some principles of a postpositivistic philosophy of science. *Educational Researcher, 15*(9), 12-18.

Glaser, B., & Strauss, A. L. (1967). *The discovery of grounded theory: Strategies for qualitative research.* Chicago: Aldine.

Good, T. L. (1979). Teacher effectiveness in the elementary school. *Journal of Teacher Education, 30,* 52-64.

Gottman, J. M. (1979a). Detecting cyclicity in social interactions. *Psychological Bulletin, 86,* 338-348.

Gottman, J. M. (1979b). *Marital interaction: Experimental investigations.* New York: Academic Press.

Gottman, J. M., & Roy, A. K. (1990). *Sequential analysis: A guide for behavioral researchers.* New York: Cambridge University Press.

Greenwood, C. R., Carta, J. J., Arreaga-Mayer, C., & Rager, A. (1991). The behavior analyst consulting model: Identifying and validating naturally effective instructional methods. *Journal of Behavioral Education, 1,* 165-191.

Greenwood, C. R., Carta, J. J., & Atwater, J. (1991). Ecobehavioral analysis in the classroom: Review and implications. *Journal of Behavioral Education, 1,* 59-77.

Greenwood, C. R., Delquadri, J. C., Stanley, S. O., Terry, B., & Hall, R. V. (1985). Assessment of eco-behavioral interaction in school settings. *Behavioral Assessment, 7,* 331-347.

Greer, R. D. (1985). *Handbook for professional change agents at the Margaret Chapman School.* Hawthorne, NY: The Margaret Chapman School.

Gresham, F. M., Gansle, K. A., & Noell, G. H. (1993). Treatment integrity in applied behavior analysis with children. *Journal of Applied Behavior Analysis, 26,* 257-264.

Hake, D. F., & Olvera, D. (1978). Cooperation, competition, and related social phenomena. In A. C. Catania & T. A. Brigham (Eds.), *Handbook of applied behavior analysis: Social and instructional processes* (pp. 208-245). New York: Irvington.

Hall, R. V., Panyon, M., Rabon, D., & Broden, M. (1968). Instructing beginning teachers in reinforcement procedures which improve classroom control. *Journal of Applied Behavior Analysis, 1,* 315-322.

Hartmann, D. P., Gottman, J. M., Jones, R. R., Gardner, W., Kazdin, A. E., & Vaught, R. (1980). Interrupted time-series analysis and its application to behavioral data. *Journal of Applied Behavior Analysis, 13,* 543-559.

Hawkins, A. (1992) Preface: A personal introduction [Monograph]. *Journal of Teaching in Physical Education, 12,* 1-2.

Hawkins, A., & Sharpe, T. L. (Eds.). (1992). Field systems analysis: An alternative for the study of teaching expertise [Monograph]. *Journal of Teaching in Physical Education, 12,* 1-131.

Hawkins, A., Sharpe, T. L., & Ray, R. (1994). Toward instructional process measurability: An interbehavioral field systems perspective. In R. Gardner, D. M. Sainato, J. O. Cooper, T. E. Heron, W. L. Heward, J. Eshleman, & T. A. Grossi (Eds.), *Behavior analysis in education: Focus on measurably superior instruction* (pp. 241-255). Pacific Grove, CA: Brooks/Cole.

Hawkins, A., Wiegand, R. L., & Landin, D. K. (1985). Cataloguing the collective wisdom of teacher educators. *Journal of Teaching in Physical Education, 4,* 241-255.

Hawkins, R. P. (1982). Developing a behavior code. In D. P. Hartmann (Ed.), *Using observers to study behavior: New directions for methodology of social and behavior science* (pp. 21-35). San Francisco: Jossey-Bass.

Hawkins, R. P., & Dobes, R. W. (1977). Behavioral definitions in applied behavior analysis: Explicit or implicit. In B. C. Etzel, J. M. LeBlanc, & D. M. Baer (Eds.), *New developments in behavioral research: Theory, methods, and applications. In honor of Sidney W. Bijou.* Hillsdale, NJ: Lawrence Erlbaum.

Hendel, C. W. (1963). *Studies in the philosophy of David Hume.* Indianapolis, IN: Bobbs-Merrill.

Henry, J. (1886). The improvement of the mechanical arts. In *Scientific writing of Joseph Henry* (Vol. 1, pp. 306-324). Washington, DC: Smithsonian Institution.

Henton, W. W., & Iverson, I. H. (1978). *Classical conditioning and operant conditioning: A response pattern analysis.* New York: Springer.

Heward, W. L., & Cooper, J. O. (1992). Radical behaviorism: A productive and needed philosophy for education. *Journal of Behavioral Education, 24,* 345-365.

The Holmes Group. (1990). *Tomorrow's schools: Principles for the design of professional development schools.* East Lansing, MI: Author.

Howe, K. R. (1988). Against the quantitative-qualitative incompatibility thesis or dogmas die hard. *Educational Researcher, 17*(8), 10-16.

Hrycaiko, D., & Martin, G. L. (1996). Applied research studies with single-subject designs: Why so few? *Journal of Applied Sport Psychology, 8,* 183-199.

Huitema, B. E. (1986). Statistical analysis and single-subject designs: Some misunderstandings. In A. Poling & R. Fuqua (Eds.), *Research methods in applied behavior analysis: Issues and advances* (pp. 209-232). New York: Plenum.

Hunt, P., Alwell, M., Farron-Davis, F., & Goetz, L. (1996). Creating socially supportive environments for fully included students who experience multiple disabilities. *Journal of the Association for Persons With Severe Handicaps, 21,* 53-71.

Ingham, P., & Greer, R. D. (1992). Changes in student and teacher responses in observed and generalized settings as a function of supervisor observations. *Journal of Applied Behavior Analysis, 25,* 153-164.

Issues in Interobserver Reliability. (1977). *Journal of Applied Behavior Analysis, 10*(2).

Jacob, E. (1982). Combining ethnographic and quantitative approaches: Suggestions and examples from a study on Puerto Rico. In P. Gilmore &

A. Glatthorn (Eds.), *Children in and out of school: Ethnography and education* (pp. 124-147). Washington, DC: Center for Applied Linguistics.

Jacob, E. (1988). Clarifying qualitative research: A focus on traditions. *Educational Researcher, 17*(1), 16-24.

Jacobson, N. S., & Anderson, E. A. (1982). Interpersonal skill and depression in college students: An analysis of the timing of self-disclosures. *Behavior Therapy, 13,* 271-282.

Johnson, H., Blackhurst, A. E., Maley, K., Bomba, C., Cox-Cruey, T., & Dell, A. (1995). Development of a computer-based system for the unobtrusive collection of direct observational data. *Journal of Special Education Technology, 12,* 291-300.

Johnson, L. M., & Morris, E. K. (1987). When speaking of probability in behavior analysis. *Behaviorism, 15,* 107-129.

Johnson, S. M., & Bolstad, O. D. (1973). Methodological issues in naturalistic observation: Some problems and solutions for field research. In L. A. Hamerlynck, L. C. Handy, & E. J. Mash (Eds.), *Behavior change: Methodology, concepts, and practice* (pp. 7-67). Champaign, IL: Research Press.

Johnston, J. M., & Pennypacker, H. S. (1980). *Strategies and tactics of human behavioral research.* Hillsdale, NJ: Lawrence Erlbaum.

Jones, R. R., Vaught, R. S., & Weinrott, M. (1977). Time series analysis in operant research. *Journal of Applied Behavior Analysis, 10,* 151-166.

Kahng, S. W., & Iwata, B. A. (1998). Computerized systems for collecting real-time observational data. *Journal of Applied Behavior Analysis, 31,* 253-261.

Kamps, D. M., Leonard, B. R., Dugan, E. P., Boland, B., & Greenwood, C. R. (1991). The use of ecobehavioral assessment to identify naturally occurring effective procedures in classrooms serving students with autism and other developmental disabilities. *Journal of Behavioral Education, 1,* 367-397.

Kantor, J. R. (1922). Can the psychophysical experiment reconcile introspectionists and objectivists. *American Journal of Psychology, 32,* 481-510.

Kantor, J. R. (1953). *The logic of modern science.* Chicago: Principia.

Kantor, J. R. (1959). *Interbehavioral psychology.* Granville, OH: Principia.

Kantor, J. R. (1969). *The scientific evolution of psychology* (Vol. 2). Chicago: Principia.

Kantor, J. R. (1970). An analysis of the experimental analysis of behavior (TEAB). *Journal of the Experimental Analysis of Behavior, 13,* 101-105.

Kantor, J. R. (1977). *Psychological linguistics.* Chicago: Principia.

Kantor, J. R. (1979). Psychology: Science or nonscience? *The Psychological Record, 29,* 155-163.

Kauffman, J. M. (1996). Research to practice issues. *Behavioral Disorders, 22,* 55-60.

Kazdin, A. E. (1982). *Single case research designs.* New York: Oxford University Press.

Keppel, G. (1982). *Design and analysis: A researcher's handbook* (2nd ed.). Englewood Cliffs, NJ: Prentice Hall.

Kerlinger, F. N. (1986). *Foundations of behavioral research* (3rd ed.). New York: Holt, Rinehart & Winston.

Landin, D. K., Hawkins, A. H., & Wiegand, R. L. (1986). Validating the collective wisdom of teacher educators. *Journal of Teaching in Physical Education, 5*, 252-271.

Landrum, T. J. (1997). Why data don't matter. *Journal of Behavioral Education, 7*, 123-129.

Lawson, H. A. (1985). Knowledge for work in the physical education profession. *Sociology of Sport Journal, 2*, 9-24.

Lawson, H. A. (1990). Sport pedagogy research: From information gathering to useful knowledge. *Journal of Teaching in Physical Education, 10*, 1-20.

LeCompte, M. D., & Preissle, J. (1993). *Ethnography and qualitative design in educational research* (2nd ed.). San Diego, CA: Academic Press.

Levin, J. R., & O'Donnell, A. (1999). What to do about educational research's credibility gaps? *Issues in Education, 5*, 177-229.

Lichtenstein, P. E. (1983). The interbehavioral approach to psychological theory. In N. W. Smith, P. T. Mountjoy, & D. H. Ruben (Eds.), *Reassessment in psychology: The interbehavioral alternative* (pp. 3-20). Washington, DC: University Press of America.

Light, J., Collier, B., & Parnes, P. (1985a). Communicative interaction between young nonspeaking physically disabled children and their primary caregivers: I. Discourse patterns. *Augmentative and Alternative Communication, 1*, 74-83.

Light, J., Collier, B., & Parnes, P. (1985b). Communicative interaction between young nonspeaking physically disabled children and their primary caregivers: II. Communicative functions. *Augmentative and Alternative Communication, 1*, 98-107.

Light, J., Collier, B., & Parnes, P. (1985c). Communicative interaction between young nonspeaking physically disabled children and their primary caregivers: III. Modes of communication. *Augmentative and Alternative Communication, 1*, 125-133.

Lindsley, O. R. (1981, December). *Current issues facing standard celeration charts.* Paper presented at the Winter Precision Teaching Conference, Orlando, FL.

Lloyd, J. W. (1992). How do we know? *Journal of Behavioral Education, 2*, 333-335.

Locke, L. F. (1989). Qualitative research as a form of scientific inquiry in sport and physical education. *Research Quarterly for Exercise and Sport, 60*, 1-20.

Locke, L. F. (1992). Field systems research: Sport pedagogy perspectives [Monograph]. *Journal of Teaching in Physical Education, 12*, 85-89.

Lutz, F., & Ramsey, M. (1974). The use of anthropological field methods in education. *Educational Researcher, 3*(10), 5-9.

Magoon, A. J. (1977). Constructivist approaches in educational research. *Review of Educational Research, 47*, 651-693.

Mahoney, M. J. (1974). *Cognition and behavior modification.* Cambridge, MA: Ballinger.

Malott, R. W., & Whaley, D. L. (1983). *Psychology.* Holmes Beach, FL: Learning Publications.

Martens, B. K., & Witt, J. C. (1988a). Ecological behavioral analysis. In M. Hersen, R. M. Eisler, & P. M. Miller (Eds.), *Progress in behavior modification* (Vol. 27, pp. 115-140). Beverly Hills, CA: Sage.

Martens, B. K., & Witt, J. C. (1988b). Expanding the scope of behavioral consultation: A systems approach to classroom change. *Professional School Psychology, 3,* 271-281.

Marx, M. H., & Hillex, W. A. (1963). *Systems and theories in psychology.* New York: McGraw-Hill.

Mayer, R. E. (2000). What is the place of science in educational research? *Educational Researcher, 29*(6), 38-39.

Mayer, R. E. (2001). Resisting the assault on science: The case for evidence-based reasoning in educational research. *Educational Researcher, 30*(7), 29-30.

McDowell, C., & Keenan, M. (2001). Developing fluency and endurance in a child diagnosed with attention deficit hyperactivity disorder. *Journal of Applied Behavior Analysis, 34,* 345-348.

McSweeney, F. K., Farmer, V. A., Dougan, J. D., & Whipple, J. E. (1986). The generalized matching law as a description of multiple-schedule responding. *Journal of the Experimental Analysis of Behavior, 45,* 83-101.

Metzler, M. (1989). A review of research on time in sport pedagogy. *Journal of Teaching in Physical Education, 8,* 87-103.

Michael, J. (1991). Historical antecedents of behavior analysis. *The Applied Behavior Analysis Newsletter, 14*(2), 7-12.

Miles, M. B., & Huberman, A. M. (1984). *Qualitative data analysis: A sourcebook of new methods.* Newbury Park, CA: Sage.

Miller, S. P., Harris, C., & Watanabe, A. (1991). Professional coaching: A method for increasing effective and decreasing ineffective teacher behaviours. *Teacher Education and Special Education, 14,* 183-191.

Mjrberg, A. A. (1972). Ethology of the bicolor damselfish, Eupomaclatsus partitus (Pisces Pomacentridae): A comparative analysis of laboratory and field behaviour. *Animal Behavior Monographs, 5.*

Morris, E. K. (1984). Public information, dissemination, and behavior analysis. *The Behavior Analyst, 8,* 95-110.

Morris, E. K. (Ed.). (1989). *The Interbehaviorist, 17*(1), 2.

Morris, E. K. (1991). Deconstructing "technological to a fault." *Journal of Applied Behavior Analysis, 24,* 411-416.

Morris, E. K. (1992). The aim, progress, and evolution of behavior analysis. *The Behavior Analyst, 15,* 3-29.

Morris, E. K., Baer, D. M., Favell, J. E., Glenn, S. S., Hineline, P. N., Malott, M. E., & Michael, J. (2001). Some reflections on 25 years of the Association for Behavior Analysis: Past, present, and future. *The Behavior Analyst, 24,* 125-146.

Morris, E. K., Higgins, S. T., & Bickel, W. K. (1983). Contributions of J. R. Kantor to contemporary behaviorism. In N. W. Smith, P. T. Mountjoy, & D. H. Ruben (Eds.), *Reassessment in psychology: The interbehavioral alternative* (pp. 51-89). Washington, DC: University Press of America.

Mosteller, F. (1981). Innovation and evaluation. *Science, 211*(4485), 881-886.

Moxley, R. A. (1989). Some historical relationships between science and technology with implications for behavior analysis. *The Behavior Analyst, 12*(1), 45-57.

Myerson, J., & Hale, S. (1988). Choice in transition: A comparison of melioration and the kinetic model. *Journal of the Experimental Analysis of Behavior, 49,* 291-302.

Neale, J. M., & Liebert, R. M. (1973). *Science and behavior: An introduction to methods of research.* Englewood Cliffs, NJ: Prentice Hall.

Newman, B. (1992). *The reluctant alliance: Behaviorism and humanism.* Buffalo, NY: Prometheus.

Nietzsche, F. W. (1978). *Thus spake Zarathustra* (W. Kaufmann, Trans.). New York: Penguin. (Original work published 1892)

Odom, S. L., & Haring, T. G. (1994). Contextualism and applied behavior analysis: Implications for early childhood education for children with disabilities. In R. Gardner, D. M. Sainato, J. O. Cooper, T. E. Heron, W. L. Heward, J. Eshleman, & T. A. Grossi (Eds.), *Behavior analysis in education: Focus on measurably superior instruction* (pp. 87-99). Pacific Grove, CA: Brooks/Cole.

Okyere, B. A., Heron, T. E., & Goddard, Y. (1997). Effects of self-correction on the acquisition, maintenance, and generalization of the written spelling of elementary school children. *Journal of Behavioral Education, 7,* 51-69.

O'Reilly, M. F., & Renzaglia, A. (1994). A systematic approach to curriculum selection and supervision strategies: A preservice practicum supervision model. *Teacher Education and Special Education, 17,* 170-180.

Page, T. J., Iwata, B. A., & Reid, D. H. (1982). Pyramidal training: A large scale application with institutional staff. *Journal of Applied Behavior Analysis, 15,* 355-352.

Parker, M., & Sharpe, T. L. (1995). Peer tutoring—An effective coaching tool. *Journal of Physical Education, Recreation and Dance, 66*(8), 50-55.

Parsonson, B. S., & Baer, D. M. (1978). The analysis and presentation of graphic data. In T. R. Kratochwill (Ed.), *Single-subject research: Strategies for evaluating change* (pp. 101-165). New York: Academic Press.

Parsonson, B. S., & Baer, D. M. (1986). The graphic analysis of data. In A. Poling & R. W. Fuqua (Eds.), *Research methods in applied behavior analysis* (pp. 157-186). New York: Plenum.

Penman, R. (1980). *Communication processes and relationships.* London: Academic Press.

Peterson, L., Homer, A., & Wonderlich, S. (1982). The integrity of independent variables in behavior analysis. *Journal of Applied Behavior Analysis, 15,* 477-492.

Pett, M. A., Vaughan-Cole, B., Egger, M., & Dorsey, P. (1988). Wrestling meaning from interactional data: An empirically-based strategy for deriving multiple molar constructs in parent-child interaction. *Behavioral Assessment, 10,* 299-318.

Pronko, N. H. (1980). *Psychology from the standpoint of an interbehaviorist.* Monterey, CA: Brooks/Cole.

Ray, R. D. (1983). Interbehavioral systems, temporal settings and organismic health. In N. W. Smith, P. T. Mountjoy, & D. H. Ruben (Eds.), *Reassessment in psychology: The interbehavioral alternative* (pp. 361-380). Washington, DC: University Press of America.

Ray, R. D. (1992). Interbehavioral methodology: Lessons from simulation [Monograph]. *Journal of Teaching in Physical Education, 12,* 105-114.

Ray, R. D., & Delprato, D. J. (1989). Behavioral systems analysis: Methodological strategies and tactics. *Behavioral Science, 34,* 81-127.

Ray, R. D., Upson, J. D., & Henderson, B. J. (1977). A systems approach to behavior: III. Organismic pace and complexity in time-space fields. *Psychological Record, 27,* 649-682.

Rechsly, D. J., & Wilson, M. S. (1996). Assessment in school psychology training and practice. *School Psychology Review, 25,* 9-23.

Richardson, V. (1990). Significant and worthwhile change in teaching practice. *Educational Researcher, 19*(7), 10-18.

Rist, R. (1977). On the relations among educational research paradigms: From disdain to detente. *Anthropology and Education Quarterly, 8,* 42-49.

Rodger, R. S., & Rosebrugh, R. D. (1979). Computing a grammar for sequences of behavioral acts. *Animal Behavior, 27,* 737-749.

Rosenshine, B. V., & Furst, N. (1973). The use of direct observation to study teaching. In R. M. W. Travers (Ed.), *Second handbook of research on teaching* (pp. 122-183). Chicago: Rand McNally.

Ruben, D. H., & Delprato, D. J. (Eds.). (1987). *New ideas in therapy.* Westport, CT: Greenwood.

Rubin, L. J. (1985). *Artistry in teaching.* New York: Random House.

Russell, B. (1929). *Mysticism and logic.* New York: W. W. Norton.

Russell, B. (1948). *Human knowledge: Its scope and limits.* New York: Simon and Schuster.

Sackett, G. P. (1979). The lag sequential analysis of contingency and cyclicity in behavioral interaction research. In J. D. Osofsky (Ed.), *Handbook of infant development* (pp. 623-649). New York: John Wiley.

Sackett, G. P. (1980). Lag sequential analysis as a data reduction technique in social interaction research. In D. B. Sawin, R. C. Hawkins II, L. O. Walker, & J. H. Penticuff (Eds.), *Exceptional infant* (Vol. 4, pp. 300-340). New York: Brunner/Mazel.

Sage, G. H. (1989). A commentary on qualitative research as a form of scientific inquiry in sport and physical education. *Research Quarterly for Exercise and Sport, 60*(1), 25-29.

Scheflen, A. E. (1982). Comments on the significance of interaction rhythms. In M. Davis (Ed.), *Interaction rhythms* (pp. 13-22). New York: Human Sciences Press.

Schmidt, R. A. (1988). *Motor control and learning: A behavioral emphasis* (2nd ed.). Champaign, IL: Human Kinetics.

Schutz, R. W. (1989). Qualitative research: Comments and controversies. *Research Quarterly for Exercise and Sport, 60*(1), 30-35.

Sharpe, T. L. (1997a). An introduction to sequential behavior analysis and what it offers physical education teacher education researchers. *Journal of Teaching in Physical Education, 16,* 368-375.

Sharpe, T. L. (1997b). Using technology in preservice teacher supervision. *The Physical Educator, 54,* 11-19.

Sharpe, T. L. (2001). Research paradigm and technology in physical education: Recommendations from a behavioral technologist. In J. Yoo (Ed.), *Emergent trends in sport-based research and training* (pp. 1-27). Seoul, Korea: The Research Institute for Sport Science, Chung-Ang University Press.

Sharpe, T. L., Brown, M., & Crider, K. (1995). The effects of a sportsmanship curriculum intervention on generalized positive social behavior of urban elementary school students [Special Section]. *Journal of Applied Behavior Analysis, 28,* 401-416.

Sharpe, T. L., Brown, M., & Foulk, L. (1999). Description and effects of positive social instruction using a recreational team sport environment. *Proven Practice: Prevention and Remediation Solutions for Schools, 1,* 68-72.

Sharpe, T. L., Crider, K., Vyhlidal, T., & Brown, M. (1996). Description and effects of prosocial instruction in an elementary physical education setting. *Education and Treatment of Children, 19,* 435-457.

Sharpe, T. L., Harper, W., & Brown, S. (1998). In response: Further reflections on technology, science, and culture. *Quest, 50,* 332-343.

Sharpe, T. L., & Hawkins, A. (1992a). Field systems analysis: Prioritizing patterns in time and context among observable variables. *Quest, 44,* 15-34.

Sharpe, T. L., & Hawkins, A. (1992b). The implications of field systems for teacher education[Monograph]. *Journal of Teaching in Physical Education, 12,* 76-84.

Sharpe, T. L., & Hawkins, A. (1992c). Expert and novice elementary specialists: A comparative analysis [Monograph]. *Journal of Teaching in Physical Education, 12,* 55-75.

Sharpe, T. L., & Hawkins, A. (1998). Technology and the information age: A cautionary tale for higher education. *Quest, 50,* 19-32.

Sharpe, T. L., Hawkins, A., & Lounsbery, M. (1998). Using technology to study and evaluate human interaction: Practice and implications of a sequential behavior approach. *Quest, 50,* 389-401.

Sharpe, T. L., Hawkins, A., & Ray, R. (1995). Interbehavioral field systems assessment: Examining its utility in preservice teacher education. *Journal of Behavioral Education, 5,* 259-280.

Sharpe, T. L., & Koperwas, J. (2000). *Software assist for education and social science settings: Behavior evaluation strategies and taxonomies (BEST) and accompanying qualitative applications.* Thousand Oaks, CA: Sage-Scolari.

Sharpe, T. L., & Lounsbery, M. (1998). The effects of a sequential behavior analysis protocol on the teaching practices of undergraduate trainees. *School Psychology Quarterly, 12,* 327-343.

Sharpe, T. L., Lounsbery, M., & Bahls, V. (1997). Description and effects of sequential behavior practice in teacher education. *Research Quarterly for Exercise and Sport, 68,* 222-232.

Sharpe, T. L., Lounsbery, M., Golden, C., & Deibler, C. (1999). Analysis of one ongoing district-wide collaborative approach to teacher education. *Journal of Teaching in Physical Education, 19,* 79-96.

Sharpe, T. L., Lounsbery, M., & Templin, T. (1997). "Cooperation, collegiality, and collaboration": Reinforcing the PETE scholar-practitioner model. *Quest, 49,* 214-228.

Sharpe, T. L., Spies, R., Newman, R., & Spickelmier-Vallin, D. (1996). Assessing and improving the accuracy of inservice teachers' perceptions of daily practice. *Journal of Teaching in Physical Education, 15,* 297-318.

Shavelson, R. J., & Berliner, D. C. (1988). Erosion of the education research infrastructure: A reply to Finn. *Educational Researcher, 17*(1), 9-14.

Shriver, M. D., & Kramer, J. J. (1997). Application of the generalized matching law for description of student behavior in the classroom. *Journal of Behavioral Education, 7,* 131-149.

Shulman, L. (1987). Knowledge and teaching: Foundations of the new reform. *Harvard Educational Review, 51,* 1-22.

Siedentop, D. (1992). New folks in the neighborhood: A sport pedagogy perspective [Monograph]. *Journal of Teaching in Physical Education, 12,* 90-95.

Siedentop, D., & Eldar, E. (1989). Expertise, experience, and effectiveness. *Journal of Teaching in Physical Education, 8,* 254-260.

Silverman, S. (1996). How and why we do research. In S. J. Silverman and C. D. Ennis (Eds.), *Student learning in physical education: Applying research to enhance instruction* (pp. 35-51). Champaign, IL: Human Kinetics.

Silverman, S., & Solmon, M. (1998). The unit of analysis in field research: Issues and approaches to design and data analysis. *Journal of Teaching in Physical Education, 17,* 270-284.

Skinner, B. F. (1938) *The behavior of organisms.* New York: Appleton-Century-Crofts.

Skinner, B. F. (1944). A review of Hull's Principles of behavior. *The American Journal of Psychology, 57,* 276-281.

Skinner, B. F. (1945). The operational analysis of psychological terms. *Psychological Review, 52,* 270-277.

Skinner, B. F. (1948). *Walden Two.* New York: Macmillan.

Skinner, B. F. (1953). *Science and human behavior.* New York: Macmillan.

Skinner, B. F. (1956). A case history in scientific methods. *American Psychologist, 11,* 221-233.

Skinner, B. F. (1957). The experimental analysis of behavior. *American Scientist, 45,* 343-371.

Skinner, B. F. (1968). *The technology of teaching.* New York: Appleton-Century-Crofts.

Skinner, B. F. (1983). *Notebooks.* Englewood Cliffs, NJ: Prentice Hall.

Skinner, B. F. (1984). Selection by consequences. *The Behavioral and Brain Sciences, 7,* 477-481.

Skinner, B. F. (1989). *Recent issues in the analysis of behavior.* Toronto: Merrill.

Smith, J. K. (1983). Quantitative versus qualitative research: An attempt to clarify the issue. *Educational Researcher, 12*(3), 6-13.

Smith, M. C., & Lytle, S. L. (1990). Research on teaching and teacher research: Issues that divide. *Educational Researcher, 19*(2), 2-11.

Smith, M. L. (1987). Publishing qualitative research. *American Educational Research Journal, 24,* 173-183.

Sprague, J. R., & Horner, R. H. (1992). Covariation within functional response classes: Implications for treatment of severe problem behavior. *Journal of Applied Behavior Analysis, 25,* 735-745.

Sprague, J. R., & Horner, R. H. (1994). Covariation within functional response classes: Implications for treatment of severe problem behavior. In T. Thompson & D. B. Gray (Eds.), *Destructive behavior in developmental disabilities: Diagnosis and treatment.* Sage focus editions, vol. 170 (pp. 213-242). Thousand Oaks, CA: Sage.

Stallings, J., Needels, M., & Sparks, G. M. (1987). Observation for the improvement of classroom learning. In D. Berliner & B. Rosenshine (Eds.), *Talks to teachers* (pp. 129-158). New York: Random House.

Stokes, T. F., & Baer, D. M. (1977). An implicit technology of generalization. *Journal of Applied Behavior Analysis, 19,* 349-367.

Sulzer-Azaroff, B. (1986). Behavior analysis and education: Crowning achievements and crying needs. *Division 25 Recorder, 21,* 55-65.

Sulzer-Azaroff, B., & Mayer, G. R. (1991). *Behavior analysis for lasting change.* New York: Harcourt Brace Jovanovich College Publishers.

Suppes, P. (1970). *A probabilistic theory of causality.* Amsterdam: North Holland Press.

Thibaut, J. W., & Kelley, H. H. (1959). *The social psychology of groups.* New York: John Wiley.

Thomas, J. R., & Nelson, J. K. (1996). *Research methods in physical activity* (3rd ed.). Champaign, IL: Human Kinetics.

Thoreau, H. D. (1962). *Walden and other writings.* New York: Bantam.

Titus, H. H., Smith, M. S., & Nolan, R. T. (1986). *Living issues in philosophy* (8th ed.). Belmont, CA: Wadsworth.

Touchette, P. E., MacDonald, R. F., & Langer, S. N. (1985). A scatter plot for identifying stimulus control of problem behavior. *Journal of Applied Behavior Analysis, 18,* 343-351.

Toulmin, S. E. (1961). *Foresight and understanding: An inquiry into the aims of science.* Bloomington: Indiana University Press.

Unks, G. (1986). Product oriented teaching: A reappraisal. *Education and Urban Society, 18,* 242-254.

Utley, B. L., Zigmond, N., & Strain, P. S. (1987). How various forms of data affect teacher analysis of student performance. *Exceptional Children, 53,* 411-422.

van der Mars, H. (1989). Systematic observation: An introduction. In P. W. Darst, D. B. Zakrajsek, & V. H. Mancini (Eds.), *Analyzing physical education and sport instruction* (pp. 3-17). Champaign, IL: Human Kinetics.

von Mises, R. (1964). *Mathematical theory of probability and statistics.* New York: Academic Press.

Wahler, R. G., & Hann, D. H. (1987). An interbehavioral approach to clinical child psychology: Toward understanding troubled families. In D. H. Ruben & D. J. Delprato (Eds.), *New ideas in therapy* (pp. 53-78). Westport, CT: Greenwood.

Wampold, B. E. (1986). State of the art in sequential analysis: Comment on Lichtenberg and Heck. *Journal of Counseling Psychology, 33,* 182-185.

Wampold, B. E. (1992). The intensive examination of social interactions. In T. R. Kratochwill & J. R. Levin (Eds.), *Single-case research design and analysis: New directions for psychology and education* (pp. 93-131). Hillsdale, NJ: Lawrence Erlbaum.

Warger, C. L., & Aldinger, L. E. (1984). Improving teacher supervision: The preservice consultation model. *Teacher Education and Special Education, 7,* 155-163.

Watkins, M. W., & Pacheco, M. (2000). Interobserver agreement in behavioral research: Importance and calculation. *Journal of Behavioral Education, 10,* 205-212.

Watson, J. B. (1970). *Behaviorism.* New York: W. W. Norton.

White, O. R. (1971). *The "split middle" or "quickie" method of trend estimation.* Eugene: University of Oregon Press.

White, O. R. (1972). *A manual for the calculation and use of the median slope—A technique of progress estimation and prediction in the single case.* Eugene: University of Oregon Press.

Willems, E., & Raush, H. (Eds.). (1980). *Naturalistic viewpoints on psychological research.* New York: Holt, Rinehart & Winspton.

Wilson, R. A. (1986). *Cosmic trigger: The final secret of the illuminati.* Phoenix, AZ: Falcon.

Wilson, S. (1977). The use of ethnographic techniques in educational research. *Review of Educational Research, 47,* 245-265.

Witt, J. C., Noell, G. H., Lafleur, L. H., & Mortenson, B. P. (1997). Teacher use of interventions in general education settings: Measurement and analysis of the independent variable. *Journal of Applied Behavior Analysis, 30,* 693-696.

Author Index

Subject Index

About the Authors

Tom Sharpe is an Associate Professor and Program Coordinator in the Department of Educational Leadership in the College of Education at the University of Nevada–Las Vegas. He draws from a wealth of varied professional experiences and activities in public and private school, coaching, and university teaching settings and from a long education and social science research career in a variety of graduate programs at different universities. Trained by many of the leading applied and experimental behavior analysts in the profession at West Virginia University, Tom has pursued academic work largely in the education and social science application of observational methodologies and in related computer-based tool development. He has authored over 100 refereed articles and book chapters and is a regular contributor to the principles and practice of applied behavior analysis through conference and workshop presentations and a variety of consulting activities.

John Koperwas has been a practicing software developer for the past 20 years. After developing a variety of direct observation software and hardware systems, he went into a research and development collaboration with Tom Sharpe through Educational Consulting, Inc. John currently serves clients worldwide ranging from teacher education programs to medical rehabilitation clinics to public school districts and special education and activity-based outreach centers—all interested in the continuing development and use of the direct observation computer tools and related information offered through Educational Consulting. You may visit the company website at www.skware.com for more information on the authors' background, experience, and current software development efforts.